Screens of Blood

A Critical Approach to Film and Television Violence

GREGORY DESILET

McFarland & Company, Inc., Publishers

Jefferson, North Carolina

LIBRARY OF CONGRESS CATALOGUING-IN-PUBLICATION DATA

Desilet, Gregory E.
  Screens of blood : a critical approach to film and television
violence / Gregory Desilet.
      p.   cm.
  Includes bibliographical references and index.

  ISBN 978-0-7864-7791-3 (softcover : acid free paper) ∞
  ISBN 978-1-4766-1337-6 (ebook)

  1. Violence in motion pictures.   2. Violence on television.
  I. Title.
  PN1995.9.V5D473 2014
  791.43'6552—dc23   2013048314

BRITISH LIBRARY CATALOGUING DATA ARE AVAILABLE

On the cover: TV series *The Walking Dead*, Season 1, 2010
(Photofest)

Manufactured in the United States of America

McFarland & Company, Inc., Publishers
  Box 611, Jefferson, North Carolina 28640
  www.mcfarlandpub.com

To my wife, Christine,
for her enthusiasm and patience

Acknowledgments

I give foremost thanks to the members of the "Villanova group," whose support and comments over the past several years have contributed significantly to my ongoing exploration of "poetic categories" and dramatic conflict. I salute you all, in order of seniority: Herbert W. Simons, Edward C. Appel, John Hatch, Camille K. Lewis, and Les Bruder. Thank you for your inspiration and insight. (I should add that readers must not assume the members of this group are necessarily in agreement with the ideas and judgments expressed herein.)

Also, I thank my friends in Colorado and around the country who have, from time to time, engaged me in conversation about film and offered their insights for my benefit. I am especially grateful to Michael Riberdy, David Pearlman, and Stephen Walker for their long term friendship and contributions to my thinking about conflict and storytelling in many conversations over the years.

Among out-of-state friends, Adam Pogioli must also be thanked for numerous comments on film and television and for providing feedback on early drafts of several chapters along with supplying a provocative quotation from Marshall McLuhan. (Readers should also not assume Adam agrees with all the views expressed herein about screen criticism or particular films.)

Also, I thank good friend and fellow writer Mark Shaw for supplying astute comments on several draft chapters.

Lastly, my wife, Christine, deserves thanks for many hours spent together watching and analyzing films and television dramas during which she has made noteworthy contributions to my thinking along with having raised red flags on occasions when I appear to be taking a wrong turn. But do not blame her if you conclude after reading this book she did not raise the red flag often enough!

Table of Contents

Table of Contents

Preface

Much has been written about entertainment violence in recent decades. Due to the variety of contrasting perspectives offered, the most urgent requirement at the outset of another work ought to be acknowledgment of the general approach generating its observations. Because potential misunderstanding may so quickly arise when broaching entertainment and violence, I hastily note first the paths *not* taken along with prominent examples of these approaches.

This book *is not* motivated by …

- theological or religious convictions (*Media Violence and Christian Ethics* [2007])
- the assumption that screen violence is generally harmful (*Stop Teaching Our Kids to Kill: A Call to Action Against TV, Movie, and Video Game Violence* [1999])
- the assumption that screen violence is generally harmless (*Preposterous Violence* [1989])
- the desire to clean up a decadent Hollywood culture (*Hollywood Mission (Im)possible: Piercing the Darkness of a Decadent Industry* [2011])
- the desire to save youth from exposure to violence (*Media Violence and Children: A Complete Guide for Parents and Professionals* [2003]; *Children, Adolescents, and Media Violence: A Critical Look at the Research* [2006])
- the desire to save youth from lack of exposure to violence (*Killing Monsters: Why Children Need Fantasy, Super Heroes, and Make-Believe Violence* [2002])
- concerns with censorship or ratings issues (*Sex and Violence: The Hollywood Censorship Wars* [2009])
- concerns about violent media productions in a runaway

consumer capitalist economy (*Mythologies of Violence in Postmodern Media* [1999])

This book *is* motivated by …

• the desire to provide a clearer basis for discerning what many consumers already intuitively understand and emotionally sense: (1) that there are better and worse portrayals of violence in screen dramas regarding the potential for promotion of aggression, violence, and related effects; and (2) that none of these portrayals are without significant social and cultural consequences.

What is needed, and what is still largely lacking in literature, is a coherent set of reasons for explaining and justifying intuitions. This book provides those reasons, illustrates them through key examples, and concludes with a broad assessment of the current cultural condition. In light of current culture, it also presents recommendations for how best to respond (in what limited ways are available in a free society) to improve the odds for making a cultural difference regarding concerns about specific kinds of violent screen entertainment.

My previous work on screen violence, *Our Faith in Evil: Melodrama and the Effects of Entertainment Violence*, sought to break new ground on the subject in two ways. It exposed the cultural and philosophical basis on which a high percentage of violent drama—namely melodrama—rests and linked melodrama directly to high potential for promoting aggressive, dysfunctional, and often destructive modes of conflict resolution. It also contrasted melodramatic structure with an alternative dramatic structure of conflict—tragic drama—and illustrated how violent tragic drama presents and exposes the pathology of violence through a multi-sided depiction of the core conflict. This current work elaborates on these themes, provides a detailed schematic for understanding the relevant dramatic structures, adds refinements of theory, and illustrates these refinements by examining a selected collection of films and television dramas.

Introduction

The Growing Power of Media Influence

> Thirty seconds worth of glorification of a soap bar sells soap.
> Twenty-five minutes of glorification of violence sells violence.
> —Paul Simon, former senator from Illinois

Senator Simon spoke these words in 1993 to a gathering of the Communitarian Network, an organization self-described as engaged in the task of shoring up the "social, moral, and political environment." His observation strikes with stunning simplicity. Obviously, millions of advertising dollars flow every day toward persuading consumers to buy products. Advertising would not be the robust industry it is if communication media in general did not exert a financially rewarding influence on audiences. The question for advertisers has never been whether influence exits. It has always been: how can it be improved? Part of a general answer to this question requires knowing something about what consumers want. The other part requires knowing something about what consumers *will* want but don't yet know they want. The former reflects the influence of the consumer on the advertiser. The latter reflects the influence of the advertiser on the consumer. This same cycle of mutual influence operates within the entertainment arts of film and television. Expressed in familiar maxims, art imitates life and life imitates art. This opening section addresses the nature and range of media influence as it may relate to the question of the potential effects of screen violence. The second section examines varieties of dramatic structure and the third section discusses dramatic structure as it relates to violent content. Not all violent screen productions sell violence but, as will be explained, the ones that do, sell to a culture receptive to that message because it sent the message. Although advertisements often precede and interrupt screen dra-

3

mas, these dramas are now usefully understood as advertisements themselves. But they count as advertisements for reasons beyond the prominent placement of branded products in carefully choreographed scenes. They count as advertisements because screen productions sell a product—a vision of the world—to consumers. And much like pharmaceutical manufacturers, producers of screen entertainment may not explicitly know or understand all the potential side effects of the products they sell. But unlike pharmaceutical companies, entertainment conglomerates need not worry about being held accountable for hazardous side effects. This analogy is instructive for consumers. All media content has effects. And, currently, responsibility rests with consumers in assessing what violent content in media may have substantial negative effects. Appreciating the significance of this responsibility requires broad awareness of all the doors through which effects reach consumers.

Turning from screen to print technology, the *New York Times* claims it prints "all the news fit to print." Printing "all the news" would be like drawing a map the same scale as the terrain mapped. Editors must decide what is "fit to print." The necessity for editing makes available, by default as well as by design, only a portion of the news. News content holds potential for influence through what is left out as much as what is included. In this regard, print and screen technology share the same constraints by and through which influence may be achieved. Another source of influence, generally underappreciated, originates in the technology or the medium itself. Media theorist and pop-culture guru of the 1960s Marshall McLuhan famously proclaimed, "The medium is the message" (1964). This slogan calls attention to the process whereby the medium through which any particular message arrives also, itself, transmits a broader and deeper message. To draw further attention to the wide and hidden influence of this process, McLuhan further proclaimed, "The medium is the *massage*" (1967). Here the word "massage" refers to the kneading of the sensory faculties engaged in the use of any given medium. He offered as primary examples the contrast between print and electronic media, between the book and the screen (1962; 1968). Passing over all the nuances and controversy of his analyses, it suffices to say that McLuhan sought to demonstrate that print and screen media exert influence in profoundly different ways—ways that shape how content is received and experienced.

4

A story in print exerts influence and registers differently from the same story told on film or television. A book leads its reader with an orderly stream of visually perceived signs along a timeline, stimulating the imagination with its information. The imagination may add visual and auditory qualities to the unfolding content. The reader actively participates by filling in the content, perhaps even imaginatively digressing along many detours only suggested by the content. A book, therefore, "massages" readers' sensory perceptions in a controlled, linear way while also stimulating participation through construction of virtual experience in the imagination. This sense of participation is so strong the reader may feel almost like another character in the drama.

Screen media, on the other hand, massage the viewer's senses simultaneously with a more complex array of stimuli, now including full-color, high-definition moving pictures and enveloping high-fidelity soundscapes. McLuhan theorized a difference between the screen media of television and film, calling the former a *cool* medium and the latter a *hot* medium (1964). A cool medium requires more active participation in achieving its sensory effects. Television was cool in McLuhan's view because it presented an image composed of small dots needing to be filled in, much like a mosaic image. Film was hot because its image contained more information for the eye, appearing less as mosaic representation and more like an actual window to the world.

With the development of high-definition, wide-screen fiber-optic cable television the difference between cinema and television, between the movie theater and the home theater, decreases to the extent that McLuhan's 1960s distinction between television and film collapses substantially. In fact, digital-imaging systems have now largely replaced film as the medium through which cinematic creations are made. And these digital systems are at such high resolution the mosaic effect is effectively eliminated as it was with high-resolution celluloid technology.

Screen media have for some time replaced print media as the dominant technology through which people acquire information and engage in entertainment. According to a 2011 survey conducted by head of research Christina Clark of the National Literacy Trust (a British charity), one third of the children between ages 11 and 16 do not own a book. This is a dramatic increase over the figure of one in ten recorded in 2005. An estimated 12 percent in the 2011 survey said they had never been to a bookstore (Clark, 2012). It may be safely surmised that these numbers are the same (if not worse) in the United States. Though many children and adults may read on the Internet, this activity is not like reading a book. Internet texts tend to be short features accompanied by strong visual stimulation, often with embedded video clips, as in the case of Facebook. And, with the increasing popularity of video sites like YouTube, Hulu, and Netflix, experience on the Internet creeps ever more in the direction of video as the source of information and entertainment.

Technologically developed countries have moved from print to screen media dominance and from strong participatory imaginative experience to a more passive quality of experience. Readers of stories fill in the text with imagination and uniquely construct the experience for themselves. But when experiencing a story told through high-definition moving images, viewers are more written upon than participants in the writing. As part of a more fully textured virtual experience, viewers of contemporary screen productions are themselves transformed into a medium onto which a packaged experience is etched and thereby more fully allowed to record its influence. Film turns viewers into passive observers standing on the outside looking in as events pass. Viewers are positioned like gods with privileged, intimate access to the lives of characters. Like lived experience, the color, motion, sound, and now even depth—through 3D technology—of screen imagery assaults the senses with a broad simultaneity of effects greatly exceeding the self-paced, narrow, linear stream of information flowing from the printed page. Contemporary visual media are hot in McLuhan's sense—high in sensory information—and should not be underestimated in their ability to bypass controlled, rational processing. Similarly, these media should not be underestimated in the influence they exert and the impressions they make on everyone, especially during the formative teenage years.

The power of screen media to produce *imitative* effects is also stronger than that of print media. This is not to argue that what viewers may bring to screen media in the way of past experience, education, attitudes, motivations, and general mental awareness plays no significant role in how the content of screen media may get processed, understood, and acted on. Rather, what must be acknowledged is the more persuasive "massaging" potential of screen media and its content. Moreover, repetition of the same visual content has become ridiculously easy with digital visual technology. McLuhan emphasized the way in which particular media stretch, expand, and heighten the dominance of a corresponding sensory faculty and its way of processing stimuli. In the contemporary information age it now becomes necessary to emphasize the way in which the combination of visual and auditory stimuli in video media dominate the other senses and exert influence through the potential for endless repetition. The time and effort required for such repetition is much less than that required for reading a book. Such repetition need not be viewed as entirely numbing, however, since repetition can exert influence in many positive and beneficial directions. But the expanded and still expanding power of screen media over and above print media poses dangers of persuasive, even hypnotic, potential influence not encountered in previous generations.

These dangers are not merely limited to the potential for screen media to induce *imitative behaviors*, though that is a factor not to be discounted and one that will be discussed below. The more significant danger lies in the potential for screen media to induce imitative ways of structuring and perceiving the world and other people. In other words, it is not merely potential for inducing imitative behaviors that may be of concern but, more important, the broader and deeper potential for inducing imitative *attitudes*—particular ways of assessing others and structuring relations with them. Imitations of these attitudes and structures may not have immediate and direct effects following a viewing. But they may have long-term effects on how people conduct themselves and how they perceive their role in the world.

Dramatic Structures and Attitudes Toward Conflict

In drama and storytelling, fresh information content resides in the informing particulars of plot and character. But particulars of plot and character come together in patterns transcending information. For example, it is not news that a drama becomes dramatic because the characters engage in some manner of conflict. But interactions between characters draw attention and become interesting to the extent that these interactions involve conflict. Conflict functions like the hub of a wheel around which all interaction turns and returns.

Though conflict may be the defining element of drama, it is not inevitably part of every form of human interaction. But as imitations of life, dramatic productions present imitations of the primary varieties of conflict found in real life. Major categories of drama, then, offer a taxonomy of the primary ways of structuring conflict. These primary ways of structuring conflict correspond to attitudes having motivated structuring one way rather than another. Because of the reciprocal relation between art and life, the potential for life to imitate art underwrites the potential for drama to sell and up-sell attitudes toward conflict. And all attitudes toward conflict are not equal with respect to how they promote management and resolution of conflict. Only particular kinds of drama structure conflict in ways facilitating, necessitating, and rewarding the use of violence. In response to different structuring of conflict and corresponding attitudes toward conflict, the remainder of this section proposes a basis for refining distinctions between violent screen dramas and assessing which types may or may not exert significant influence toward increasing potential for aggression and violence in viewers.

The chapters in this book present films and television shows selected for their noteworthiness as key examples illustrating a variety of dramatic conflict structures and corresponding character traits of protagonists relevant to the presentation of violence. These chapters are divided into two sections. The first section examines popular films and the second section examines popular serialized television dramas.

The first section opens with three chapters, each presenting violent films serving as slightly different examples of what *not* to do in portraying violence. These films exemplify correspondingly different structures of conflict with great potential for "selling" attitudes toward violence as rewarding or redeeming. The next five chapters examine a series of films of different genres exemplifying what can be done and ought to be done when portraying violence. These films situate violence in ways subverting its potential appeal while illuminating sobering entanglements of motive, character, and circumstance inherent in real-life conflict.

The second section begins with an extended examination of the television series *The Sopranos*. This series is noted for violent content and appears to qualify as a negative example of television violence. However, a closer examination reveals why this series is experienced as a decisive and extraordinary statement not only against racketeering but also against the life of violence behind organized crime. After this extensive look at a positive example, the next six chapters explore a variety of counter-examples of violent television dramas. The last three chapters return again to recent examples of what may constitute part of a growing positive trend in television dramas as producers and audiences increasingly demand higher quality of programming involving violence.

Seeing screen violence and its potential influence on audiences as divided according to positive and negative types aligns with a tradition of violent media analysis beginning with the work of George Gerbner (1988, 1994, 2002). Gerbner distinguishes between what he calls *happy violence* and more sobering forms of violence. He focused attention on the critique of happy violence and its predominance in television and film culture. Gerbner explains happy violence and its effects as follows:

> Violence on television is just one of the areas that causes a distorted concept of reality. Most of the violence we have on television is what I call happy violence. It's swift, it's thrilling, it's cool, it's effective, it's painless, and it always leads to a happy ending because you have to deliver the audience to the next commercial in a receptive mood. Our studies have shown that growing up from infancy with this unprecedented diet of violence has ... consequences, which, in combination, I call the "mean world syndrome." What this means is that if you are growing up in a home where there is more than say three hours of television per day, for all practical purposes you live in a meaner world—and act accordingly—than your next-door neighbor who lives in the same world but watches less television. The programming reinforces the worst fears and apprehensions and paranoia of people [1994].

Sissela Bok (1998) is another analyst of violent media in the Gerbner tradition of distinguishing between good and bad presentations of violence. She distinguishes between the bulk of entertainment violence on the one hand and productions qualifying as tragic drama on the other and their corresponding differences in cathartic effects—little or none in the former and significant measures in the latter.

However, analysts in this tradition have not offered a thorough discussion of particular dramatic conflict structures and how these structures promote or "sell" *attitudes toward conflict* which, in turn, influence viewer behavior in conflict situations. These attitudes comprise a predisposition toward conflict supporting default recourse to violence as a matter of calculated and reasonable judgment rather than merely an outburst of rage. Orientations of this nature, as will be argued more extensively in the next section, form the basis of a *culture of violence*— a collectively popular attitude toward conflict and violent response, pervasive to one degree or another in many cultures, but especially in American culture.

Historian and professor of American studies Richard Slotkin (1973, 1985, 1992) presents the most extensive investigation of how American stories and narratives fuel a mythology-promoting violence. These stories and narratives exhibit belief in violence as the means of choice for protecting against threats along the borders of shifting "frontiers." Slotkin's celebrated trilogy of American history includes these informative titles: *Regeneration Through Violence: The Mythology of the American Frontier, 1600–1860*; *The Fatal Environment: The Myth of the Frontier in the Age of Industrialization, 1800–1890*; and *Gunfighter Nation: The Myth of the Frontier in Twentieth-Century America*. This history of American mythology meshes well with Gerbner's understanding of American film and television violence as powerful technology shaping American culture through repetitive violent program messages. Although statistics on violence are important and sources for this kind of information are provided at the end of this introduction, statistics alone do not adequately reflect a culture's potential for qualifying as a culture of violence. Dominant perceptions of violence and the value ascribed to it in conflict resolution determine whether a culture is a culture of violence. The degree to which a culture's popular stories support a culture of violence can be read from the ways in which conflict is predominantly structured in these stories. Explaining this claim requires identifying basic distinctions in dramatic structure and how these different structures relate to conflict and violence.

The following table with its set of terms provides a glimpse of major distinctions used in explaining dramatic structural *context* in relation to violent *content*. The table identifies the categories used in the chapter discussions of relationships between types of dramatic conflict and potential effects of corresponding portrayals of violence on audiences. This table derives primary inspiration from the work of language theorist and literary critic Kenneth Burke (1984). However, it departs from his categorization scheme with inclusion of the category of melodrama and use of the terms *antagonal* and *synagonal*. An explanation of all the terms follows below the table.

Dramatic Taxonomy by Conflict Structure

	External Conflict		Internal Conflict	
	Antagonal	Synagonal	Antagonal	Synagonal
Comedy	*Satire*	*High comedy*	*Satirical Psychodrama*	*Comedic psychodrama*
Classic Examples	*Tartuffe; Gulliver's Travels*	*Don Quixote; An Ideal Husband*	*Doctor Faustus; Candide*	*Faust; The Magus*
Tragedy	*Tragic drama*	*High tragedy*	*Tragic psychodrama*	*Tragic psychodrama*
Classic Examples	*The Hunchback of Notre-Dame; Othello*	*Oresteia; Antigone; Women in Love*	*Hamlet; Heart of Darkness*	*Oedipus Tyrannus; Death in Venice*
Melodrama	*Classic Melodrama*	*Reflexive Melodrama*	*Psycho-melodrama*	*Reflexive Psycho-melodrama*
Classic Examples	*The Count of Monte Cristo*	*Les Misérables; Moby Dick*	*The Confessions of St. Augustine*	*Crime and Punishment*

The table above contains examples of iconic stories all of which can be found in screen versions. Rather than attempt to provide a brief synopsis of each of these classic stories and an explanation for how it fits into the chosen category, it will be more efficient to proceed to an explanation of the categories. This approach is preferable because not all the selections fit the chosen category to an unchallengeable degree; it also exceeds the scope of this book to justify all these acts of naming. Although such discussions may be interesting and useful, they are best left for another occasion. For now, suffice it to say these stories are intended as representative examples drawn from classic works and are, at this point, intended to be only suggestive in an illustrative capacity. As listed in the far left column, the three primary dramatic categories are comedy, tragedy, and melodrama.

Comedy consists of plots in which protagonists engage in varieties of competitive, non-deadly conflict accompanied by soul-expanding denouements. The stakes of conflict generally involve potential loss of pride, status, heart, soul (as in the case of *Faust*), purpose, or similar tokens of the human spirit. But in the end, events usually turn out favorably for the main protagonists.

Tragedy involves darker plots wherein the conflict generally turns on a matter of life and death. Similar to comedy, tragic protagonists gain insight through conflict, even though the insight may come too late. They may survive violence in the end but appear not to deserve the measure of hardship or ruin befalling them.

Melodrama also involves extreme conflict but here the conflict always begins or centers on morally weighted poles—factions of relative good and evil. Also, the fates of the protagonists seem proportional to their character and actions whereby, unlike tragic drama, the featured protagonist generally triumphs in the end (except in some varieties of melodrama explained below).

The terms *external* and *internal* indicate the setting for the primary conflict—external for conflict between individuals and internal for psychological conflict within the main protagonist or protagonists.

The terms *antagonal* and *synagonal* are derived from the Greek root *agon* as contest or struggle (Karagiannis and Wagner, 2005). All conflict is polarized or agonal in the sense that it embodies a tension of contrasting or competitive differences. In conflict viewed antagonally, each side appears alien and unnecessary to the other and, therefore, functions as an illegitimate and threatening intrusion. This conflict reflects a tension of differences approaching all or nothing, life or death, the mutually exclusive outcome of a zero-sum game model.

Synagonal conflict, conversely, draws out mutually dependent (*syn*-agonal) rather than mutually exclusive (*ant*-agonal) differences. Synagonal indicates agon or struggle but with the added sense (implicit or explicit) that the sides involved are at some level necessary to each other and struggle *with* and *through* each other rather than thoroughly *against* each other. The conflicting sides are shown to be essentially co-involved and mutually implicated even if essentially different. Each side manifests a measure of legitimacy but often also a point of view initially blind or resistant to this legitimacy. Synagonal drama constructs proportional conflict whereby audience loyalties are torn and direct factional commitment to one side or another becomes difficult. In synagonal tragedy, therefore, audiences see merit early in the plot on both sides of the conflict. This divided commiseration is often achieved, as Aristotle notes in his *Poetics*, by portraying conflict between family members or between close friends and colleagues.

In synagonal melodrama, however, a pronounced shift occurs in audience perception of the conflict. Throughout much of the drama sentiments align with the chief protagonist. But as the drama progresses, this alignment appears increasingly inadequate and, as it draws to a conclusion, a measure of empathy spreads to include both sides of the conflict. The adjustment in audience perceptions then serves to undermine the legitimacy of the attitude of strong factional polarity with which the drama began. This significant shift in emotional alignment accounts for why this form of drama is also referred to as *reflexive* melodrama. It turns the traditional melodramatic antagonal good/evil conflict back on itself in a way sufficient to reveal the inadequacy of that orientation for structuring and labeling the given conflict.

At the conclusion of synagonal melodrama, audiences experience proportional sentiment with regard to the factions in the conflict. This relative balanced alignment parallels a superficial appearance of justice and proportion in outcomes for the characters. But the residual sense of justice in outcomes gives way at the conclusion of synagonal melodrama as the cost in the suffering and violence brought about through the conflict clouds the clarity of justice at the end. The superficial sense of proportion attached to outcomes yields to a broader and deeper sense of cosmic injustice in the suffering and/or ruin incurred on both sides. Consequently, synagonal melodrama resembles synagonal tragic drama in this important respect.

It may be helpful at this point to move from the abstract to the concrete and briefly examine and compare the two examples of synagonal melodrama listed in the table. *Les Misérables* and *Moby-Dick* both present tales of antagonal alignments which shift toward the end to synagonal insight. In the former, Inspector Javert persecutes Jean Valjean and, in the latter, Captain Ahab persecutes the white whale Moby Dick. But in addition to Valjean being human and Moby Dick being an animal, the two stories differ in that the chief protagonist in *Les Misérables*, Valjean, is the persecuted whereas in *Moby-Dick* the chief protagonist, Captain Ahab, is the persecutor. In *Moby-Dick*, Ahab's excessive fanaticism toward the whale gradually comes into view as persecution, whereas in *Les Misérables* Inspector Javert's fanatical persecution becomes apparent near the outset. The broader vision into Javert's humanity comes into focus only near the end of the drama through Valjean's eyes and his compassion toward Javert. Despite the differences in featured protagonists, however, both narratives qualify as synagonal, reflexive melodramas. At the conclusion, both works lead to full appreciation of the destructive consequences of obsessive devotion to the task of sweeping away imagined evils in the mistaken belief that such obsessive efforts advance the cause of the general good.

Examining the table of dramatic categories, it may occur to some readers that an important category of drama has been left out, a category often associated with the art of the screenplay and cinematic plot structures. For example, what category corresponds to Joseph Campbell's mythic drama—the journey of the hero with a thousand faces? The answer lies in the use of the word *hero* and the significance traditionally associated with the hero as a person inviting identification and modeling successful negotiation of life's challenges. Here is Campbell's description of the structure of the hero's journey:

> A hero ventures forth from the world of common day into a region of supernatural wonder: fabulous forces are there encountered and a decisive victory is won: the hero comes back from this mysterious adventure with the power to bestow boons on his fellow man [1973: 30].

Since these heroic journeys are as much journeys of self-discovery and self-overcoming as journeys of worldly exploration and adventure, the dramatic structure of these stories may be usefully read as depicting either internal or external conflict, or both. And since the hero wins a "decisive victory," these stories do not conform well to the general model of tragic drama. Therefore, when these mythic stories consist of violent, deadly encounters—victorious slayings of monstrous adversaries, for example—they fall into the category of antagonal melodrama, which also aligns with chivalrous and romantic traditions of storytelling. But when these journeys consist of nonviolent outwitting and overcoming of adversarial forces, they belong, as Campbell rightly suggests, in the trajectory of antagonal or synagonal *comedic* conflicts. An extensive development of the category of comedy would include nonviolent myths and fairy tales. But since comedy is not part of the focus of this study, these storylines are only mentioned to provide a glimpse of ways in which the table of dramatic categories may be filled out, not with additional categories but with further variations and examples.

Also, video games will be mostly excluded from the discussion.

Even though video games may have strong narrative, dramatic, and conflict components, the element of active consumer participation in video games introduces a sufficiently different variable to make video games worthy of an entirely separate analysis. Having said this, it remains the case that points made about dramatic structure in relation to violence may, nevertheless, be highly relevant to the narrative elements of video games.

Journey to the Heart of a Culture of Violence

Eliciting identification with heroic figures is a good part of the intent of dramatists. And, as will be discussed more thoroughly in the chapters to come, any character featured as a main protagonist in a drama exerts strong influence toward identification. This is a point not always appreciated by those who create screen dramas with intense violence. Anything looked at significantly becomes significant.

In response to an interview by a film critic after the release of his film *Natural Born Killers* (1994), Oliver Stone absolved himself from blame for any consequences of violence arising from the film by claiming he was only the messenger and that his film merely reflected the bankrupt mode of current violent society (Caputi, 1999: 155). This argument is analogous in many ways to complaints made by celebrity athletes when criticized for bad behavior. They claim they have a right to be who they are and behave however they want, without regard for potential influence they may have on fans. If the media sensationalizes their bad behavior, then the media and media culture are to blame. But as already suggested in the discussion of McLuhan's views and contrary to these deflections, media and messengers are *always* more than mere conveyances. Sports celebrities always function as messages as well as messengers. The choices they make actively impart messages through platforms of access they establish in the media culture. Whoever aims the spotlight and whoever stands in the spotlight are both, like it or not, far from innocent regarding the question of influence. Consequently, sports celebrities, journalists, filmmakers, and all others with media platforms have a responsibility to understand the influence their behaviors and productions exercise among fans and consumers. What they do and what they create will likely lead to varieties of imitation. In the case of filmmakers especially, this point refers not so much to personal behavior but rather to the products, the films—since these carry much greater potential influence than publicized personal behavior.

Similarly, any character given star status in a violent drama becomes, to one degree or another, whether intended or not, a product being sold. Not everyone is a true buyer but many are buyers in ways they may not suspect. A percentage of viewers pay their money and run with a product that may count for them as a dangerous drug. Screen drama copycat crimes are prime examples of this kind of transaction. But not just any kind of violent film becomes noteworthy regarding copycat crime.

Following, in chronological order, is a partial list of screen dramas associated with copycat crimes. This list includes those notorious for generating the most egregious as well as the highest number of copycat crimes: *The Collector* (1965), *Bonnie and Clyde* (1967), *A Clockwork Orange* (1971), *Taxi Driver* (1976), *Nightmare on Elm Street* (1984), *Child's Play* (1988, with the infamous "Chucky" doll character), *Natural Born Killers* (1994), *Scream* (1996), *The Queen of the Damned* (2002), *Saw* (2004), *American Psycho* (2004), *Dexter* (2006–), *The Dark Knight* (2007). This inventory derives from several sources listed in the bibliographic section at the end of the book. These sources also contain more extensive information on the nature of copycat crime which this book does not provide since such analysis lies beyond the scope of this work. These sources also supply information on the number of crimes, the perpetrators' names, the circumstances of the crimes, and the dates. The names and crime details are also not directly presented herein consistent with the policy of the less publicity provided for these perpetrators, the better. (For copycat crime details, see Coleman, 2004; Ramsland, 2005; Ramsland, 2013; Stephens, 2012; see also CJDG, 2012; Brainz.org, 2013.)

The dramas in this list all have something noteworthy in common. The extremism of their dramatic structure leans toward or falls off the edge of the categories in the table presented previously. They all feature dark, troubled, unstable or psychopathic characters who commit extraordinary acts of violence. These characters are made to stand out in ways traditionally reserved for more balanced characters. They also stand relatively alone and are not confronted by a contrapuntal character or characters adequate to probe beneath crude surface motivations.

Horror films such as *Nightmare on Elm Street, Child's Play, Scream, Saw,* and others of the horror and slasher genres follow a slightly different pattern. The predominantly evil character may not dominate screen time but, nevertheless, dominates and controls the action. Although similar to classic melodrama in that evil may not triumph in the end, this is not a defining consequence in these genres because evil triumphs throughout the film. And, in many cases, the evil character is resurrected in a sequel, demonstrating that evil was not really defeated. The "good guys" in some horror and slasher films are often only a string of lackluster and dispensable victims. In some cases, such as *Saw,* the victims appear sufficiently unlikable to seem to warrant their fate. Consequently, evil characters may project an uncanny glow of heroic powers which, in some cases, even tend toward the supernatural. For emotionally vulnerable members of the audience who may regard themselves as victims, such portrayals of shrewd and powerful villains having their destructive way with the world may generate intense identification.

By contrast, the other works from the list above, such as *The Collector, Bonnie and Clyde, A Clockwork Orange, Taxi Driver, Natural Born Killers, The Queen of the Damned, American Psycho, The Dark Knight,* and *Dexter,* all feature pathological protagonists front and center. Consequently, these productions generated significant controversy when they were released and fueled controversy with ensuing copycat crimes. These types of dramas present high potential for audience identification with their featured protagonists through the glorification accomplished by positioning them as stars of a motion picture. When sufficiently intense, this identification leads, as experience has shown, to potential instances of copycat crime. Having said this, it must be noted that only a small percentage of those who see these films commit copycat crimes. But, of course, prospects for copycat crime are only one part of the range of significant potential effects.

All of the types of works initially listed fall outside the dramatic taxonomy proposed above because they lack genuine conflict and substitute violence and the tension of violence in its place. Portrayals of inscrutable or inadequately contextualized violence perpetrated by narrowly drawn characters fall short of achieving conflict sufficient for drama and are, therefore, excluded from the table above. But for purposes of providing a reference point in relation to the proposed taxonomy, this category of entertainment will be called *reverse* antagonal melodrama. This reversal is primarily a reversal of focus. A troubled, anti-heroic character and this character's actions receive featured attention throughout the film without, conveniently, significant conflict or confrontation with the source of the trouble. Side-stepping the source of the trouble in the troubled anti-hero is convenient because productions of this type seek to highlight action in violence rather than conduct psychotherapy. Any show of analysis serves only to provide a measure of plausibility for the implausible acts of violence scripted for the star perpetrator as conceived by screenwriters seeking shock-value atrocities. Many starring perpetrators in the slasher genre lie at the extreme end of this form of entertainment.

The broader category from which the notion of reverse antagonal melodrama derives includes the greater portion of violent screen dramas. Films of this type—antagonal melodrama—include primarily those in the violent action-thriller genres. These genres include chains of films such as the Spaghetti Western series, the Martial Arts series, and series featuring comic-book heroes, which have been the dominant action-thrillers in theaters during the first decade of the 21st century. This list also includes the James Bond, Death Wish, Dirty Harry, Terminator, Rambo, RoboCop, Lethal Weapon, and Die Hard series and a host of similar franchises and one-offs. Certain films of this type have also gained notoriety for spawning copycat crimes. Examples include *Magnum Force* (1973), *The Matrix* (1999), and *The Dark Knight*—although this last film straddles the line between reverse antagonal and antagonal melodrama and will be discussed in detail in Chapter Three. But copycat crime, while a significant concern, is not the primary concern in relation to this category of film. Fully appreciating this broader concern requires returning to the differences between antagonal melodrama and the synagonal versions of tragedy and melodrama.

As previously mentioned, tragic drama in general leaves audiences with a sense of injustice through the disproportion of the tragic outcomes for all the protagonists. Classic or antagonal melodrama, on the other hand, imparts a sense of justice through the disproportion of factionally appropriate allotments of rewards and punishments. And where synagonal tragedy and melodrama elicit proportional emotional alignments toward protagonists, antagonal melodrama elicits disproportional alignments toward the differently weighted factions. Consequently, antagonal melodrama upholds division whereas synagonal tragedy and melodrama weaken division between factions.

Classic melodrama, thereby, also seals the marriage of violence and justice. It does so within the context of retribution for assigned responsibility in wrongdoing. As a result, in the context of retribution, deadly violence in the service of justice becomes something to cheer and celebrate. But any drama promoting direct links between violence, justice, and celebration courts substantial risks and problematic disconnection from reality in its reduction of conflict to simple extremes.

Violent antagonal melodramas fail to convey the reality that violence, whether authored by heroes or villains, is always tragic. *All violence is tragic.* Even when violence is necessary to stop violence it is never something to be celebrated. Moreover, *there can be no justice in violence.* Regardless of the justifications giving rise to violence, violence always ends in loss, not justice. Perfect villains exist in drama but are hard to find in real life. This is not to suggest those in real life who commit violent crimes merit a flood of sympathy and no punishment. But highly antagonal dramas fail to adequately expose the tragic dimension of villains. In doing so, such dramas fail to portray the tragedy of the violence which, in some circumstances, must be used to stop them. Instead, antagonal melodramas only succeed in glorifying violence by deliberately liberating audiences from feelings of hesitation and guilt concerning the use of deadly force. Dramatic designs joining justice and celebration to violence detach violence from tragic emotions and fuel dysfunctional attitudes toward the complexity of conflicts and people in the real world.

Nonetheless, it will be argued by many that knee-jerk bloodlust is an inevitable, if unadmirable, part of human nature and, therefore, should, and will, get fed. Gratuitous screen violence, like its sexual counterpart, is a popular confection and, like junk food and tobacco habits, hard to curb on a societal level. But there are healthier ways to feed an appetite. Screen dramatists' determination to show extreme violence carries with it an obligation to show adequate background for the violence in the complexities and details of character and circumstance through which the violence arises. The desire for justice—the raw element of bloodlust—is more profoundly satisfied through portrayals that, instead, do justice to the conflict. Doing justice to the conflict requires including the pieces of context and genealogy relevant to the trail of actions and events involved. It also requires a protagonist who not only understands the importance of getting beneath the mask of an adversary but who also knows how to do that effectively.

Films and television shows exposing the synagonal and tragic nature of violence do so by providing a context through which audiences become exposed to complexities of characterization. This type of drama effectively feeds the appetite for adventure and provocative entertainment while subverting the arousal of simplistic knee-jerk bloodlust. Portraying the complexities of intense conflict constitutes the substantial difference in the content of synagonal drama. Chapters four through nine and several chapters in the television section are devoted to illustrating the variety of creative ways in which dramatists achieve the effects of violent synagonal drama. This kind of violent drama has not been adequately identified and discussed in literature on screen violence and consequently deserves more extensive treatment. Some of the films and television shows selected for favorable analysis herein may be surprising because they superficially appear to be antagonal dramas with considerable splashes of graphic violence. But even these dramas, as will be illustrated, succeed through their structure in portraying conflict and violence in ways significantly undermining the potential for contributing to real acts of violence and cycles of victimization.

Before concluding, an important methodological question ought to be addressed. Readers may grant the preceding logic is all well and good, but where is the evidence? Where is the proof of negative social consequences? Where is the proof that Americans live in a pervasive culture of violence? Surprisingly, answering such questions need not require appealing to crime statistics. The ubiquitous presence and consistent popularity of antagonal screen violence confections in the entertainment marketplace confirm a broad obsession and fascination, not just with violence in general, but with violence of the kind associated with justice and celebration. The broad appeal of this kind of entertainment, with its increasing extremes of shocking intensity, offers compelling proof in itself of a culture of violence precisely because of the success of this entertainment in the marketplace. When producers of violent entertainment respond to complaints with the refrain that they are only giving audiences what they want, they speak the truth—but only part of the truth. Audiences can have intense and engaging drama, including violent content, and with far less risk to communities. The purpose of this book is to show how this can be done and why it must be approached as a collective cultural project. America needs to re-evaluate its cultural mythology about the role of violence in conflict in particular and life in general. The cultural breadth of the issue of violence is addressed again with further explanation and discussion in the first section of Chapter Nine on *The Sopranos*.

For those who would like to become better acquainted with the empirical evidence and research concerning the thesis of a culture of violence in the United States, two books offer noteworthy and comprehensive discussion of the issue with differing perspectives on the evidence.

A widely cited, comprehensive, and compelling study—mentioned in the preface—appeared in 1999 in: *Stop Teaching Our Kids to Kill: A Call to Action Against TV, Movie and Video Game Violence*. This work shows that in the second half of the 20th century United States violent crime rates increased across the board, with aggravated assaults up by 600 percent. The murder rate increased by 170 percent and would have been much higher if not for the mitigating factor of improved medical technology and emergency treatment response measures. The authors of this book also note that the statistics on assault are acknowledged by police to be notoriously under-reported. This work also provides sources to the empirical research studies conducted on the relationship between viewing screen violence and aggressive behavior and discusses the evidence in support of a significant link.

In 2008, however, a book appeared which called for a more cautious approach to the conclusions of *Stop Teaching Our Kids to Kill*, drawing attention to the problematic nature of the empirical research. This intelligent and measured study, titled *Grand Theft Childhood: The Surprising Truth About Violent Video Games and What Parents Should Know*, contains detailed discussion of empirical studies and the design difficulties and outright flaws in much of this research. While this work features video games, it also includes considerable information relevant to violence in film and television. Although the authors present a good case for vigilance in interpreting the results of evidence provided by media violence research, they also concur that the evidence supports concerns and that screen violence, especially in the form of video games and extreme screen violence, requires exercising judgment and cautionary actions on the part of parents and society. *Grand Theft Childhood*, therefore, acknowledges the need for judgment in choices relating to viewing violent screen entertainment due to the risk potential. The concluding section offers precautionary advice and commentary on possible public action.

Turning now to discussion of specific films and television shows, the commentaries describe, evaluate, and persuade in the manner of serious argument while also seeking to inform, surprise, provoke, amuse, and entertain. In the current culture of screen technology nothing gets done, even in the print world, without some measure of entertainment value. The late cultural critic and media analyst Neil Postman (1985) famously proclaimed that Americans are amusing themselves to death with screen media consumptions. If such is the case, the only way out may be for Americans to improve screen entertainment to the point of amusing themselves back to life. But since the book now goes the way of the horse and buggy, I gladly solicit Hollywood for offers on the screen rights to this book.

PART I

Violence in Popular Film—Doing It Wrong and Doing It Right

1

Django Unchained

How Not *to Do Screen Violence*

"Extreme violence in film is the best way to control the emotions of audiences." Like a bullet, this point punctuated Quentin Tarantino's speech to an audience of the British Academy of Film and Television in January of 2010. With this claim, director Tarantino continued the typically candid expression of his views about violence and why he makes violence central to the plots of his stories. Unlike many filmmakers, Tarantino not only defends the use of violence in his films but positively advocates violence as the key to driving an engaging narrative. In the same interview he went on to say that violence is good because it is the most enjoyable form of entertainment. Putting it even more bluntly, what he wants to see in film is someone "bleeding like a stuck pig" (Warren, 2010).

For Tarantino, the audience is an orchestra and violence is the baton. "I feel like a conductor and the audience's feelings are my instruments. I will be like, 'Laugh, laugh, now be horrified.' When someone does that to me I've had a good time at the movies" (Warren, 2010). With these words Tarantino discloses his fundamental ambition and the driving force behind his artistry. He desires to produce intense effects on audiences, to orchestrate a roller-coaster ride of extravagant emotional responses. It would not be unlike him to say, "I want to shock you, turn and twist you, first one direction and then another. I want you leaving the theater jacked like a fruit cocktail—stirred, shaken, and whipped to froth."

The first time I experienced something like the chain of emotional whiplashings of a Tarantino film I was an undergraduate at the University of California at Santa Barbara. This was back in the early 1970s, long before Tarantino's film career began. A playwright by the name of Megan

Jamie Foxx as Django (*Django Unchained*, Weinstein Company, 2012).

Terry created a series of three one-act plays using a handful of actors and minimal stage settings and props. Since it was impossible to tell from the setting the nature of the situation dramatized, audience members were left to extrapolate from the dialogue alone. Initially, the dialogue led the audience to interpret the context as, say, humorous and this would produce appropriate laughter. But as the dialogue proceeded, it became obvious the context was not humorous. Laughter stuck in the throat as those watching suddenly felt the scene turn on a dime and reveal itself to be tearfully tragic.

As soon as the audience settled into feeling stunned sadness, the continuing dialogue revealed new information showing the situation as again humorous. Using dialogue alone, these sudden alterations of context were cleverly done and forced audience members to continually adjust perceptions of what was happening and, thereby, quickly shift between opposing emotional responses.

I recall leaving the theater that night with the impression I had witnessed a series of vignettes adding up to little in the way of substance. More than this, though, I left with a strong feeling of having been used and manipulated for no purpose other than verifying the playwright's virtuosity in arousing emotion for the sake of arousal. I admit to having the same response to many of Tarantino's films. I feel emotionally controlled and used without having gone to a place in my imagination which makes those aroused emotions seem attached to anything authentic and admirable at their source. This emotional hijacking resembles that of someone in an old western swept along in a crowd, riled and ready for a lynching, only to discover the passionate outburst exceeds judgments worthy of the emotion. Scenes in *Django Unchained*, to one degree or another, repeatedly engineer this embarrassment for viewers.

But considering the popularity of Tarantino's films, many viewers apparently do not have the experience of being emotionally manipulated for questionable ends. (In fact, I can imagine a few Tarantino fans reading to this point and saying to themselves: "You know what? Tarantino enjoys making his films, I enjoy watching them, and I don't care to know why I shouldn't like them. I don't think there can be anything wrong with liking them, so take your fancy analysis and shove it. End of story." I recognize there are Tarantino fans who may feel no need to examine judgments and question tastes. But I recommend fans keep reading because parts of what follows may prove persuasive.) Nevertheless, this chapter is not primarily directed at Tarantino fans—or even Tarantino detractors. The targeted audience consists of students of film, film aficionados, film critics, reviewers, festival panels, and members of award societies. It can be asserted with a high degree of confidence that Tarantino's work is neither great cinema nor great art. So it is one thing for Tarantino's films to be popular among his fans but it is altogether something else for his work to be praised by critics and receive nominations and awards for exceptional quality and value. For example, *Django Unchained* was given the Best Screenplay and Best Supporting Actor Awards for the Golden Globe, the Academy of Motion Picture Arts and Sciences, and the British Academy of Film and Television.

Praise has also come from high places in review circles—the resident film critics of America's most widely read and influential news publications. One form of praise in particular regarding *Django Unchained* has been especially puzzling: its treatment of slavery. In the case of some reviewers, the praise also given for its extreme use of violence only adds to the puzzlement.

Consider, for example, this sampling of critical acclaim from prominent reviewers:

Tarantino doesn't shrink from the inhumane realities of life for enslaved people in 19th century America: One of the first shots of the film captures the horrifically scarred backs of several men as they're force-marched through the Texas countryside on a chain gang…. For viewers who already share Tarantino's love of genre, *Django Unchained* is … enormously satisfying [Ann Hornaday, *Washington Post* (2012)].

This is a brilliant entertainment, in which Tarantino takes on the subject of slavery as he did the Holocaust in his previous film, *Inglourious Basterds*…. When QT begins a movie, I believe, his destination is to aim over the top. The top itself will not do…. What Tarantino has is an appreciation for gut-level exploitation film appeal, combined with an artist's desire to transform that gut element with something higher, better, more daring. His films challenge taboos in our society in the most direct possible way, and at the same time add an element of parody or satire…. [T]he audience expects to see violence but doesn't expect to get it at such an extreme; he's rubbing it in…. But it's not what a film does but how it does it, and in one sense the violence here reflects Tarantino's desire to break through audience's comfort level for exploitation films and insist, yes, this was a society and culture that was inhuman [Roger Ebert, *Chicago Sun* (2013)].

The film doesn't play it safe, so neither will I. Instead, I'll say that it finds Mr. Tarantino perched improbably but securely on the top of a production that's wildly extravagant, ferociously violent, ludicrously lurid and outrageously entertaining, yet also, remarkably, very much about the pernicious lunacy of racism and, yes, slavery's singular horrors [Joe Morgenstern, *Wall Street Journal* (2012)].

Django Unchained is outrageous in the best sense of the word, a diabolical action-comedy about cleansing the stain on the American soul [Joe Williams, *St. Louis Post-Dispatch* (2012)].

Perhaps the best thing to be said for *Django Unchained* is that it shows that *Inglourious Basterds* was no anomaly. Tarantino leaped forward in that film— in his ability, skill, meaning and purpose—and he gives nothing back with *Django*. He has found that elusive spot that all artists strive for, complete spontaneity and absolute control. By itself, that would be only mildly interesting, but in context it's illuminating. Tarantino is showing that the world slaves inhabited was nothing like conventional drama, nothing like the consoling movies we've all seen before. It was more like an amoral, violent nightmare, with little recourse and no justice…. The violence is outsize, epic, enormous, bloody— but not disturbing, and not dehumanizing. There's a place for violence onscreen, and this is the place, a Quentin Tarantino movie that's rated R. Just as there was nothing dispiriting about watching Hitler get his in *Inglourious Basterds*—

it was about time—the same could be said for the events in *Django Unchained*. And if next time around, Tarantino wants to give it to the Spanish Inquisition, he deserves our full support [Mick LaSalle, *San Francisco Chronicle* (2012)].

These reviews have been cited extensively because they are thoroughly jaw-dropping to read, especially comments such as: "enormously satisfying," "brilliant entertainment," "challenges taboos," "outrageously entertaining," "outrageous in the best sense of the word," with violence "epic, enormous, bloody—but not disturbing, and not dehumanizing." All of these claims, as will be demonstrated, are so extraordinarily wrong as to be delusional.

But criticizing a film such as *Django Unchained* is, in one sense, a dangerous task. The reason for this arises from whether the film is even a work that can be taken seriously. As some reviewers have commented, it presents itself on most every level as a cartoonish parody. If the work is not serious and the critic approaches it as if it were, then the commentary will itself look cartoonish. Due to its excesses in portrayal, its historical inaccuracies, and its moments of pure slapstick, *Django Unchained* likely qualifies as parody. But there are many ways to do parody and it is certainly possible to do it badly. And there are many ways to frame and present aspects of the era of slavery in the United States, and many of these choices are counterproductive. Slavery is a difficult subject to address in film or other media because of the persistent emotional charge around the issue of racism.

Based on Tarantino's public comments, he sees his film as something to be taken seriously for its potential to confront viewers with the depth of the ugliness, brutality, and injustices of slavery. Speaking in 2007 to John Hiscock of the *Telegraph* about future film projects, Tarantino commented on *Django Unchained* and his motivation for making a film of this type.

I want to explore something that really hasn't been done. I want to do movies that deal with America's horrible past with slavery and stuff but do them like spaghetti westerns, not like big issue movies. I want to do them like they're genre films, but they deal with everything that America has never dealt with because it's ashamed of it, and other countries don't really deal with because they don't feel they have the right to. But I can deal with it all right, and I'm the guy to do it [2007].

But is Tarantino really "the guy to do it"? If he understands that filmmakers from other countries may not feel they have the right to make films dealing with American slavery, how is it that he sees himself, an Italian-American Caucasian, as the right guy to make a film showing a black man rising against slavery—a film he claims also provides blacks a new heroic figure with which to identify?

Oddly enough, the slave owner Calvin Candie (Leonardo DiCaprio) in *Django Unchained* makes the case—in a scene designed to maximally exploit the issue of race—that blacks are genetically induced to be "obedient" and to follow rather than lead. Tarantino clearly includes this scene not because he believes any such thing but because he wants to mock what many whites of the period did believe while also inflaming audience contempt for the Candie character. But in drawing significant attention to the wrongful and perverse claim that blacks are docile, obedient followers and in need of white instruction and leadership, Tarantino sets himself up for viewers to connect the following series of dots: the white Calvin Candie speaks of blacks as obedient followers, the white Dr. Schultz (Christoph Waltz) leads Django (Jamie Foxx) out of slavery, and the white Tarantino creates a black hero. This is not to suggest that whites cannot take up the cause of black freedom, nor does it imply that whites cannot voice black characters or create black heroes. But a film which, in both content and production, features blacks being guided by white leaders would seem well advised to avoid making such a blatant point. By including and highlighting this message in the film, Tarantino effectively shoots himself in the foot.

But there are larger concerns troubling Tarantino's handling of slavery in the film. Placing scenes of the brutality of slavery in America at the center of a film styled as a spaghetti western—a style notorious for packaging and presenting violence in the manner of a symphony for consumer titillation—is at best a dubious artistic decision. This point was not lost on Spike Lee, who understood it without even needing to see the film. In a Twitter post about *Django Unchained*, Lee wrote: "American Slavery Was Not a Sergio Leone Spaghetti Western. It Was A Holocaust. My Ancestors Are Slaves. Stolen From Africa. I Will Honor Them" (Dillon, 2012). To suppose his ancestors could be honored in a film done in Tarantino's style—where violence is used for shock and awe entertainment value—is a notion Lee could not stomach for an instant.

As noted, many, including Tarantino, see *Django Unchained* as a major commentary on the exploitation of antebellum blacks, wrapped in a popular film genre. But the film emerges instead as only further *exploitation* of antebellum blacks. Black slaves serve Tarantino as the Jews did in *Inglourious Basterds*—as the perfect incendiary victims. They function crucially for his primary purpose, which is to use them as the ideal means to liberate audiences from all residual guilt for taking pleasure in a carnival of gratuitous, vengeful, Grand Guignol bloodletting. In this case, the blood is the blood of perfect villains—American slave owners and anyone allied with them. In *Inglourious Basterds*, Nazis and the Gestapo serve the same purpose.

This complaint about a dramatic requirement for perfect villains should not be confused with any manner of backhanded defense of slave owners or the Nazi regime. This complaint harbors nothing of the kind. Tarantino's films of extreme violence require conflicts of extreme polarization—all for the purpose of controlling and arousing extreme audience emotions. He seeks historical villains not for the purpose of astute commentary on social injustices but instead for the purpose he clearly expresses as cited in the first sentence of this chapter—to use extreme violence in order to "control the emotions of audiences." He seeks to create cheap thrills and audience titillation through the exploitation—not the exploration—of history.

But the film's gross failure as commentary on slavery is not the least of its problems. It also lacks a plot rising above the level of a comic book. Here is how to imagine the thought process that likely transpired in Tarantino's adolescent imagination:

> I want an action story—with lots of VIOLENCE—placed in the old South before the war. Okay, how about a bounty hunter because that'll get us an easy path to all the violence. I want Christoph in the film, so let's make the bounty hunter German. Plus, it'll be good he's German because American whites of the period have too much collusion in slavery to qualify for the role. We'll give him a conscience and hook him up somehow with a black slave called Django. Don't sweat the details. They'll have adventures shooting down unsuspecting bounty poster boys (what a hoot!), they'll make some cool cash for corpses, and then ride into the deep South for higher stakes. We'll give Django a wife who's in the clutches of Snidely Whiplash fiends on some old plantation. To juice things up to the right level, we'll make the plantation owner a colossal tyrant, racist, and sadist. We'll show how he forces slaves to fight each other to the death for his amusement, how he releases his attack dogs on uncooperative fighters, and then add a bit of spice to it all by giving him impeccable gentlemanly manners. Yah, that'll fire up

audiences for full enjoyment of the bloodbath finale where everybody who richly deserves it will get what's coming to them. Oh, and as an extra touch, just to show how cheeky and hip to the times I am, let's toss in a black Uncle Tom with the villains to show white viewers I don't fall prey to reverse racism when it comes to who all the bad guys are. That way everybody is happy at the end! What a hoot!

With this comic book nail-biter in hand, Tarantino thought he could do no wrong. Unfortunately, in addition to skimping on plot he also skimped on character development. The first part of the film amounts to no more than a series of vignettes designed to showcase Tarantino's obsession for slowly unfolding lethal confrontations in which bad guys are disposed of after foolish displays of arrogance. Tarantino begins the march through these vignettes with the opening sequence, after which Schultz and Django spend time together hunting criminals for bounty money. The bounty hunting continues through the Sheriff Bill Sharp, Brittle Brothers, Big Daddy, and Smitty Bacall executions. What little audiences learn about Schultz and Django in this first part of the film Tarantino squeezes into a campfire scene in which Schultz reveals his limited knowledge of German myth and Django discloses he has a wife named Broomhilda held somewhere on a plantation. After raking in profits on their killing expedition, the two badass gunslingers now have money to buy Broomhilda, so they journey south for the second part of the film. Any hombres getting in their way will wish they had not. What more does anyone need to know about Schultz and Django?

The substance of the plot, insofar as it makes sense to speak of substance, materializes in the second part of the film when Schultz and Django trace Broomhilda to Calvin Candie's Candyland Plantation spread. At this point it would be hoped Leonardo DiCaprio as Calvin Candie will deliver a performance justifying the price of admission. DiCaprio's adolescent features (he'll be forever young!) make him ideal for the role of an effete Southern gentleman. And to his credit, he delivers a performance as adequate as is possible given the cartoonish dialogue written for him. But DiCaprio's mere presence forces the disturbing question—what is an actor of his talent doing in this film?

At one point even DiCaprio's talent is not sufficient for the challenge of his sadistic cardboard character. The role requires him to exude gushing words of praise and animated gestures of glee as two Mandingo fight-

Django (Jamie Foxx, left) and Calvin Candie (Leonardo DiCaprio) get acquainted (*Django Unchained*, Weinstein Company, 2012).

ers engage in a brutally repulsive, grunting struggle to the death on the floor in front of him. DiCaprio's delivery and facial expressions fail him, appearing strained and contrived. Apparently sensing the same thing about DiCaprio's performance in the film, Audie Cornish of NPR asks Tarantino if he was concerned about the portrayal of the "white actors" being "over the top." He assures her, "No. I wasn't worried. Oh, I'm not going to let them be bad. They're going to be terrific. And I'm going to stop them from being over the top, unless that's appropriate" (2012). With the bizarre lines and actions given many of the characters, including blacks, it would be astonishing to learn what counts for Tarantino as "over the top."

Regarding over-the-top performances in the film, Samuel L. Jackson's role as the house slave Stephen comes first to mind. In his opening scene at the front of the Candyland mansion he confronts Master Candie and, while pointing to Django on horseback, impertinently asks, "Who's that nigger on that nag?" His tone of familiarity with Candie, his authoritative posturing as he moves freely among those gathered, and his continued questioning on the matter while Candie is speaking are all behaviors failing to register as a convincing portrayal of a house servant, no matter how entitled he might have been. And Candie's tolerance of his behavior is inconsistent with his lack of tolerance toward any hint of insubordination and uncooperativeness from his "property." This intolerance is made abundantly evident in a previous scene, already mentioned, in which he releases dogs on a black slave who refuses to continue Mandingo fighting.

By the way, most historians agree that Mandingo fighting—an event in which male slaves are forced to fight each other to the death for the amusement of white owners—was not practiced in the antebellum South. Tarantino borrows this idea from another film (*Mandingo*, 1975). He does so for the explicit purpose of constructing Candie as the worst kind of villain. This, in turn, makes him perfect for complete destruction. Tarantino's use of Mandingo fighting provides further proof he has no interest in portraying the real violence done against slaves. Instead, he seeks to exploit every means for amplifying emotions and creating appetite in audiences for even more extreme bloodletting.

The use of grandiose, non-period music throughout the film offers further evidence that, if viewed in the most generous light, *Django Unchained* must be counted as an attempt, at least, at a species of parody. The soundtrack makes it impossible to take the film seriously. The music plays havoc with the film's gruesome images of violence. The track for the opening credits falls far short of the cynical chic sounds of the spaghetti western heyday. Composed by Louis Bacalov (director of an orchestra from Tarantino's namesake town of Taranto, Italy) and sung by Rocky Roberts, the theme song is more reminiscent of trite western film themes from the 1950s. Roberts sounds like an enthusiastic Elvis impersonator, giving full throat to a ballad so corny in lyrics and pretentious fanfare it could be mistaken for a Las Vegas lounge act.

The soundtrack music at times feels so out of place and heavy handed the effect competes with fingernails scraping on a blackboard for sheer annoyance. In at least one case it seems this was Tarantino's intention. Near the end of the film a scene transpires in the drawing room following Candie's discovery of the true identities and intentions of Schultz, Django, and Broomhilda. A woman plays "Für Elise" on a harp in the corner as Candie signs documents. The music continues as Tarantino not-so-subtly inserts jump-cuts of scenes earlier in the film of a black slave being torn apart by dogs. These insertions are, of course, only for the eyes of the audience. Nevertheless, Schultz, still fuming after having his intentions exposed by Candie, can take no more of the beautiful music in this ugly situation and mercifully—for viewers as well as those in the scene—asks the harpist to stop playing. When she pays him no heed and continues, he springs from his seat, crosses the room, and grabs her hands to stop the music.

Tarantino's use of soundtrack accompaniment throughout the film is as heavy-handed as Candie's. The mood established by the music often grates inaptly against the visual images it accompanies. This disjointedness seems especially strong in the flashback scene in which Broomhilda is whipped as Django is forced to watch. The soundtrack plays the song "Freedom," sung by Elayna Boynton to a driving contemporary beat. Audiences do not need this kind of ham-fisted musical commentary in order to grasp the implications of the images. The pumping dance rhythm only succeeds in trivializing the gravity of the scene.

The soundtrack also oddly intrudes in the scene in which Schultz, Django, Calvin Candie, and his convoy journey to Candyland. As Django rides his horse, looking cool with sunglasses (inaccurate for the period of the film) and hat dipped low, Rick Ross raps to a funky drumbeat. Granted, Tarantino attempts here to evoke the connection between the angry power of Django and the driving power and anger of rap, but the effect works clumsily, breaks the spell of the film narrative, and intrudes more like an MTV music video intermission than a relevant sequence.

The track at the end credits creates the same kind of dissonance in relation to the entire film. After witnessing a festival of execution-style slayings throughout the film, viewers are treated to an end theme, borrowed from another spaghetti western parody, *They Call Me Trinity* (1971). With a swinging beat and jazzy horns, this track serenades viewers with lyrics relating how the "cool" abandon of the gunslinger leads to fame throughout the west as he makes a living with his "Colt 45." When this breezy encomium to gunplay runs its lengthy course, the end credits continue and a new track begins, this one written and performed by RZA (hip-hop Grammy winner Robert Diggs). As the track lays down a steady drumbeat, Diggs recounts the film's adventures while a female voiceover in the background repeats a worshipful refrain about Django's fearsome qualities, how he "enjoys killing," and how much she loves him. This glorification of violence is not only the signature of *Django Unchained* but, as Tarantino admits, the signature of all his work.

It is true, as is so often said by proponents of film violence such as Tarantino, that film is make-believe. But, as argued in the introduction, to suppose, as many apparently do, that make-believe has no significant influence on real-life behavior overlooks and underplays the force in the double-entendre meaning of "make-believe." Songs and lyrics in advertisements work to keep products in the collective mind of consumers. Is it likely that members of the audience who identify with Django and the song lionizing him—"He enjoys killing"—remain entirely immune to the cinematic and musical message—the enticement that they, too, might enjoy killing?

Turning from the music to direct focus on the violence, in *Django Unchained* much of the gun brutality is of a particularly disturbing kind. It is mostly conducted vigilante-style and in the form of executions. Unlike most confrontations in *Kill Bill* (2003, 2004), in which the violence occurs in martial-arts combat and each opponent is armed and aware of entering into combat, in *Django Unchained* the bounty hunters Schultz and Django catch several targets by surprise and dispatch them with gunshots before they even know what is happening. In the Old West this was called "bushwhacking," and those who did it were regarded with contempt. Schultz justifies his actions to others by showing them documents confirming the men killed were wanted by the law, "dead or alive." But his victims were given no option to surrender alive. Nor were they given any chance to confirm or deny their identities. Schultz and Django shoot down one of their victims as he shows his young son how to plow a field. This, apparently, is justified because this victim's portrait is on a Wanted poster for murder. But before killing a man it might be a good idea—even in the make-believe of a film—to confirm his identity, especially when the film solicits viewer identification with these "heroes."

One possible rationalization for the ambush gun violence in the first half of the film might be that those executed were white and accused of being murderers and participants in the slave trade. Given the lack of due process in the way slaves were treated, perhaps the film is suggesting the execution of criminal whites without due process is justifiable payback. Viewers are, then, invited to appreciate and enjoy this payback. But what kind of psychological architecture needs to be in place to find vigilante ambush executions enjoyable and worthy of approval? Even if these are make-believe executions, they are still executions. And even if similar events occurred in the Old West, that does not make execution-style killings something to emulate and model through characters portrayed as if they were true heroes. Even in the Old West, bounty hunters were a class of men well regarded by few. Admittedly, Tarantino has a penchant for reversals and surprises in characterization, but heroizing a bounty hunter as someone who makes a profitable sport of shooting down unwary targets is a challenge that even Tarantino's love of renegade violence cannot overcome.

Consider the question from a slightly different angle. In another NPR interview on *Django Unchained*, this time with Terry Gross, Tarantino says, "There's two types of violences [sic] in this film: There's the brutal reality of the violence that slaves lived under, under the slavery laws, 245 years. And then there's the violence of Django's retribution. And that's movie violence, and that's fun, and that's cool, and that's really enjoyable. It's kind of what you're waiting for" (2013). Tarantino wants his film to be taken as serious commentary on slavery and thereby wants the violence done to slaves to be understood as real violence. But he wants the retributive violence in the film to be treated as fantasy violence. So audiences are asked to feel the pain of real violence done to slaves but enjoy the unreal violence done to slavemasters. But this asks viewers of the film to be of two minds about violence. There are times to be repulsed by it and times to enjoy it. The difference depends on who the victim is.

Regardless of the extent to which violence may, on some occasions, be deserved and may need even to be carried out, the inclination to revel in any instance of violence, real or unreal, requires the kind of disposition brought into question above. The notion that the payback violence depicted is only fantasy overlooks the real emotions aroused by the violence and the attitudes of polarization and payback inflamed by the film's depictions of glorious vengeance. These emotions and attitudes do not disappear into thin air after viewing the film. They work consciously and unconsciously as templates for organizing orientations toward real-world conflicts. But real-world conflicts require much greater subtlety of perception, understanding, and response.

As stated in the introduction, a basic truth is all too often lost through enthusiastic portrayals of violence. *There is no justice nor can there ever be justice in violence.* There can be only tragedy at all levels. Sometimes violence must be done to protect life. But, at the same time, there is no need to be made to feel good about it. Films like Tarantino's do not only encourage feeling good about violence, they raise violence into glory, spectacle, and entertainment and thereby obscure its tragic dimension while promoting the notion that violence has something to do with justice. Understanding that violence and justice have nothing to do with each other completely dismantles the psychological architecture necessary for experiencing as pleasurable *any* kind of violence—onscreen or offscreen.

In Tarantino's way of thinking, however, violence and justice belong together when in the service of retributive payback. Films like *Kill Bill, Inglourious Basterds*, and *Django Unchained* are extended and intense revenge fantasies. Referring to potential audience reactions to his films, Tarantino explains, "[I]f you don't cheer at the end, I haven't done the job, I haven't pulled off the movie I was trying to pull off. I mean, it's very easy for me if I've failed or succeeded. If the audience cheers at the end, I've succeeded" (Gross, 2013).

When Tarantino says he wants audiences to cheer at the end, he leaves nothing of *Django Unchained* on the cutting-room floor which he thinks will guarantee that response. After pieces of Calvin Candie's plantation fill the entire screen in an exploding fireball of destruction, Django joins Broomhilde on horseback as the ruins burn in the background. Given the tone of the entire film, their knowing smiles and triumphant celebration are expected. But the "dance" Django has his horse perform gives the impression that it would be more appropriate as the conclusion of a Roy Rogers singing-cowboy picture show than the coda for a bloodbath of destruction. This dance places all the preceding violence in a context belonging more to a lighthearted romantic comedy. But, then, recollection of streams of blood flying from bullet holes in human flesh makes any impulse toward laughter and celebration stick in the throat. If audiences are supposed to cheer at the end, the film leaves little to cheer about.

By way of conclusion, of all the critics who have praised *Django Unchained*, Roger Ebert's praise is perhaps the most disappointing. Ebert was a fine critic who could often be relied on for perceptive analysis. On some occasions, however, Ebert could be surprisingly obtuse, especially in his assessments of Tarantino's work. Ebert rightly expressed many reservations about *Reservoir Dogs* but when *Pulp Fiction* appeared, he committed wholeheartedly, giving it high praise and including it in his *Great Movies* collection. Having lauded *Pulp Fiction*, which I think was a colossal mistake (see *Our Faith in Evil*, Chapter 24), he remained stuck in his appraisal of Tarantino's work, unable to reverse himself, scrambling to find genius in works of crass mediocrity. Ebert's review of *Django Unchained*, however, contains an unmistakable subtext indicating he struggled to find the film likable—and struggled especially with its depictions of violence. Nevertheless, he found ways to give Tarantino a pass not only on the film's treatment of violence but also on its lack of character development and its simplistic and ridiculous plot. This is disappointing because it seems even *he* knew better.

Highly regarded critics such as Ebert are well placed to have considerable cultural impact. If prominent critics were to put forth the kind of critical review this film so richly deserves, it would make a solid contribution toward giving consumers pause before partaking of Tarantino's violent confections. The American struggle with violence needs the voices of popular critics weighing in on the downside of glorifications of violence in film. Popular critics need to adequately understand and publicly criticize the structural weaknesses, negative effects, and societal risks of violent antagonal melodramatic entertainment and the ways in which this form and its makers contribute so blithely to America's culture of violence.

2

From *Taxi Driver* to
The Brave One
What Have We Learned?

There have been many cases of crimes linked directly to the imitation of characters portrayed in violent films, as the partial list in the introduction indicates. Naturally, cases of direct imitation prompt questioning the cultural role of violent film. But since, by all appearances, only a very small percentage of the viewing public engages in imitative violent crime, the relevant question becomes, "Why are some motivated to commit violent copycat acts when others are not?" Given the current limitations of human knowledge in brain science, psychology, and social and cultural influences, answers to this question are shaky and speculative. The difficulty of the question, though, need not force complete capitulation to the problem and the issues surrounding it. One case of copycat crime, however, is particularly instructive, prompting an additional line of questioning in relation to the topic of violent film and its potential effects on audiences. That line of questioning shifts from those who copy the actions of characters in violent films to those who make the films.

On March 30, 1981, John W. Hinckley, Jr., using a .22 caliber handgun, attempted to assassinate President Ronald Reagan near the entrance to the Hilton Hotel in Washington, D.C. According to Hinckley's own testimony, his motivation for the assassination attempt had nothing to do with any feelings of animosity toward Reagan, but instead centered on his feelings of love for the actress Jodie Foster. In Hinckley's mind, the bizarre connection between Foster and Reagan came about through Martin Scorsese's film *Taxi Driver*, released in 1976. Having devised a way to put the film on a continuous video loop, Hinckley claimed to

Erica Bain (Jodie Foster) brandishes the gun she initially bought for her own protection (*The Brave One*, Warner Bros., 2007).

have watched it 15 times in a row. He had become obsessed with the relationship between Robert De Niro's character, Travis Bickle, and Iris, the child prostitute played by Jodie Foster. In the trial following Hinckley's shooting spree, Foster provided written testimony that Hinckley had been stalking her and had sent her written messages in an attempt to gain her attention. In a letter sent just three weeks prior to the shooting, Hinckley wrote: "Jodie Foster, love, just wait. I will rescue you very soon." In videotaped testimony provided at Hinckley's trial, Foster was asked whether she had ever seen a message like that before. She replied, "Yes, in the movie *Taxi Driver* the character Travis Bickle sends the character Iris a rescue letter" (Shermer, 2004: 114).

Briefly summarizing the film, Bickle, a depressed, discharged, post–Vietnam U.S. marine, tries to find love by courting a woman working on the campaign of a U.S. senator running for president. When his attention is met with rejection, his thoughts turn angry and violent. He buys a handgun and trains himself to use it with a hidden spring-loaded sleeve holster. Shortly after walking into a convenience store, he finds himself using the gun to kill a man who enters the store and attempts to rob it. He then attempts to assassinate the senator, but when this plan meets with too many obstacles his attention turns to aiding Iris, whom he has recently met when she was wrestled from his cab by her pimp. Unsuccessful in persuading her to quit her life of prostitution, he thinks constantly of rescuing her. He eventually confronts her handlers, killing her pimp and his bouncers. Having been wounded in the act, Bickle is heroized in the media for his courage in busting the child prostitution ring.

Years later, on September 14, 2007, Warner Bros. released *The Brave One*, starring Jodie Foster in the role of Erica Bain. A brief overview of this film reveals parallels with the *Taxi Driver* plot line.

Following a vicious attack in which her fiancé is killed and she barely survives, Erica acquires a handgun for protection. One evening she finds herself in the middle of a robbery shooting at a convenience store and uses her gun to kill the perpetrator before he can kill her. She leaves before the police arrive. The attractions of vigilantism combined with her anger overwhelm her and she succumbs to every opportunity to slay anyone who overtly threatens her, including two punks who sexually threaten her in a subway car. A New York policeman, Detective Mercer (Terrence Howard), is assigned to find those who attacked Erica and killed her fiancé. He also pursues those responsible for the trail of bodies left by Erica and begins to suspect she is involved in these killings. Before Mercer can prove Erica is responsible, she succeeds in finding her attackers and killing all but one. As she struggles with the last one, Mercer arrives. In a starkly illegal but sympathetic act, Mercer gives Erica his own gun to kill the last of her assailants. He then allows Erica to go free and places her gun in the hand of the dead man to fix the blame for the vigilante killings on him. In the final scene, Erica returns home with her rescued dog, which was taken by the attackers on the night of the attack in Central Park.

Taxi Driver and *The Brave One* contain several similarities in character and plot. The characters of Bickle and Bain are both depressed and tormented as a result of exposure to violence—Bickle as an ex-marine, and Bain as a victim of street violence. Both arm themselves with handguns, which they use to kill robbery perpetrators they encounter by accident in convenience stores. Both commit vigilante killings. Both accomplish a rescue—Bickle, the rescue of Iris, and Bain the rescue of her dog. And at the conclusion of each film, both Bickle and Bain escape legal complications relating to their vigilante actions.

Foster is aware of the many parallels between *Taxi Driver* and *The Brave One* and in a very short interview appearing in the "Shock Jock" column of *New York Magazine* published before the release of the film, she explicitly acknowledges two parallels: "It [*Taxi Driver*] was also about a man descending into madness, and about a country and a city repairing themselves after this war nobody believed in" (Hill, 2007). More extensive public comments from Foster on the parallels between the two films are difficult to find because Foster has made it known she will walk out on any interview where John Hinckley is mentioned. And it is difficult to address the controversial issues surrounding the two films without bringing up the Hinckley case.

However, in an American Film Institute interview, apparently given in 2011, Foster speaks in a revealing way about *Taxi Driver* and the Travis Bickle character.

> I think most people would say that Travis Bickle is neither a hero nor a villain but an anti-hero. That was something that was really popular in the 1970s. And all of those great anti-heroes of that era I love very much. He is somebody who is not conscious to himself. And he's on a path he believes is heroic. And he doesn't see consciously the perversion that is underneath it.
>
> Travis Bickle has the personality of a 14-year-old boy. He sees the world in some ways black and white. And what Martin Scorsese is trying to tell you in *Taxi Driver* is that the world isn't black and white. And no matter how hard he tries to put it into those categories it never will be. And in order to make it that way, he has to do terrible, horrible violence—in order to try to inorganically make it black and white.
>
> I think one of the reasons why we grow to love Travis Bickle in the movie is that we all see ourselves in his loneliness. I think we've all been that way; we've all been in a big city surrounded by thousands of people and felt like there was nobody on the earth that knew us or understood us. And *Little Man Tate*—a movie I directed—is all about that, all about being a solitary person. It doesn't matter how many people are around you, the experience you have in the world will always be solitary.
>
> And the great thing about *Taxi Driver* is that Martin Scorsese wasn't trying to make a story about a hero or a villain. He was trying to show the descent of a man who is obsessive and who doesn't know how to get out of his obsessions [Foster, 2011].

Unfortunately, Foster does not address the irony of her involvement in *The Brave One*. She clearly understands the similarity between *Taxi Driver* and *The Brave One* and also understands that the connections between herself, *Taxi Driver*, and Hinckley have gained much cultural notoriety. The inevitable question arises: Why would Foster consent not only to be the star but also the executive producer of a film when she was herself the profound victim of a man who acknowledged being powerfully and, as it turned out, negatively influenced by a similar film?

The irony can be more dramatically pictured by imagining a remake of *Taxi Driver*, in which Foster chooses to play the female lead in place of the Bickle character. Then imagine no one in the media asking Foster any questions about her role in the film. The entire situation presents much to think about, not the least of which is the question of what Foster may have been thinking when she chose to play Erica Bain.

The AFI interview provides the best clues. Foster understands Travis Bickle as an anti-hero character and states that she loves characters of this type. Her affinity for such characters seems to reside in her own struggles against loneliness, isolation, and pain portrayed through these characters. This part of the identification process presents no mystery. But the failure to proceed a bit further down the line of this identification process, the failure to confront the dangerous side in the potential for imitation of the violent coping responses of these characters, seems thoroughly mysterious (if not irresponsible) given her history with Hinckley and *Taxi Driver*.

On the positive side, she may have thought the role of Erica Bain presented a strong female character whose courage Foster viewed as something to admire. Erica overcomes terrible violence and gets on with her life, albeit with deep scars. Similarly, many of Foster's films depict strong women showing great courage in responding to challenging and threatening situations (for example, *Panic Room* [2002] and *Flight Plan* [2005]). And perhaps Foster also sensed *The Brave One* provided her with an opportunity to show that she had overcome any demons the public might imagine had followed her in the wake of *Taxi Driver* and the Hinckley calamity. These are possible explanations for her interest in the film, but *The Brave One* is not simply a film about a victimized woman overcoming great adversity. The core of the film is about the *way* in which Erica responds to her adversity.

Beyond exploring Foster's motivations for involvement, it is also worthwhile to ask a broader question: Why should *anyone* choose to make a film like *The Brave One*? On the one hand, it qualifies as an action-thriller and action films usually enjoy great box-office popularity and international marketing success. Furthermore, its themes of loner action and revenge have a history of success in Hollywood. Why not make money on a tried-and-true formula? On the other hand, the film traffics in a particular version of this formula having a troubled history—an antagonal melodramatic plot structure in which the featured protagonist struggles with trauma and mental instability and engages in violent criminal actions. As noted in the introduction, these kinds of films have a history of unwanted controversy. So why take the risks? And, when choosing to do so, are the risks worth it?

Before beginning a closer comparison of *The Brave One* and *Taxi Driver*, revisiting the events surrounding *Taxi Driver* helps establish further context and the broader stakes of the analysis. Since what I have written about *Taxi Driver* previously makes the relevant points, for convenience I repeat part of it here:

> In the aftermath of the shooting and in the course of the trial, Hinckley's extraordinary obsession with Foster proved to be a tabloid bonanza. But as details emerged, it became increasingly clear Hinckley's obsession was rooted more directly in the character of Travis Bickle and the plot line of *Taxi Driver*. Hinckley had viewed the film countless times and had formed not only an identification with Bickle and an attachment to Foster through the Iris character, but, more important, had adopted the film as a blueprint for how to achieve success and win admiration. He began to view his life as a "movie" unfolding along lines similar to the *Taxi Driver* script.

> The film *Taxi Driver* certainly did not cause Hinckley to shoot Reagan nor did it cause his obsessive attention toward Jodie Foster. But the film undeniably had a powerful influence on Hinckley—in an exceptionally destructive way.

> By choosing to tell the story of a troubled and violent character, and choosing to tell the story predominantly from the point of view of that character, Scorsese chose to amplify the potential for audience response from emotional arousal to various degrees of shock. And by focusing too narrowly on the violent actions of one character, Scorsese failed to develop characters who could provide a challenging perspective toward the protagonist to draw out more fully the tragic quality of his internal conflict. Instead, as in Scorsese's *Raging Bull* (1980), the conflict is rendered melodramatically as viewers are

relentlessly exposed to the protagonist's maniacally heroic/monstrous actions while seeing nothing of the background necessary to understand the roots feeding his madness and giving shape to the all-too-human qualities of both sides of his conflict.

Introducing another analogy, Jake Horsley suggests close parallels between *Taxi Driver* and Dostoyevsky's *Crime and Punishment* by claiming: "Raskolnikov is an intellectualized version of Travis." But Horsley overlooks an important structural difference between these two dramas. Dostoyevsky provides extensive insight into the history and family background of Raskolnikov and brilliantly dramatizes and draws out the tragic quality of his inner conflict through several characters, especially the detective Porfiry Petrovitch. In *Taxi Driver* the genuine inner conflict never materializes for the viewer because Travis never effectively confronts and challenges his perception of himself nor do any of the characters with whom he interacts. The story lacks a Petrovitch, or an Ishmael, as in *Moby-Dick*, and ultimately Bickle's "white whale" remains submerged in the opaque, simplistic shades of the demonic and the malevolently bestial—his own raging bull.

This failure to adequately dramatize the conflict creates an opening needlessly increasing the odds a percentage of viewers like Hinckley will react to the featured protagonist not only by identifying with the loneliness and isolation but also by slipping into a perverse admiration of the seemingly brave choice of violent action.

Had Scorsese found ways to dig deeper into the archeological ruin of Travis Bickle's soul and thoroughly depict the roots of his conflict—perhaps through greater development of contrapuntal and challenging characters—rather than settling for a series of sensationalistic slices of his awkward and violent encounters with others, *Taxi Driver* would have gained more as drama while risking less in potentially harmful audience reactions to its violence.

As it stands, the film's narrow focus on the protagonist and his radical structuring of conflict highlights and sensationalizes violent resolution to a degree lending itself far too easily to the kind of misunderstanding and response exemplified in Hinckley's reactions. Told through a synagonal design of conflict, *Taxi Driver* would have had—with admittedly no guarantees—a better chance to direct the attention of viewers such as Hinckley back on themselves in a potentially productive confrontation with their divided yet human psyches. Instead, the film's narrow and devotional focus on a violent protagonist is too easily construed by vulnerable and marginalized viewers as a blueprint for heroic overcoming of adversity [2006: 263–264].

Picking up this thread from the analysis of *Taxi Driver*, audiences naturally incline toward identifying with featured characters. As David Denby of *The New Yorker* says in his review of the film *Arbitrage* (2012),

"It's in the nature of our relation to central figures in a narrative that we want to identify with them, even if we don't much like them" (2012). When this identification is made problematic, when such characters are shown to do things most viewers would likely reject and abhor, reactions become significantly more unpredictable and potentially intense. Commenting further on identification with star characters, Denby remarks, "It also helps if they look like Richard Gere rather than, say, Lloyd Blankfein" (2012). Similarly, when Jodie Foster portrays a character like Erica Bain, audiences tend to form stronger identifications because Foster projects the image of an intelligent, likeable, attractive person capable of arousing strong sympathies. As in the case of *Taxi Driver*, the potential for problematic identifications with troubled featured characters grows even more risky with respect to audience responses when such characters are placed in a dramatic structure free of strong contrapuntal characters.

In the case of *The Brave One*, the structure is strongly antagonal. Erica and her fiancé appear as beautiful innocents attacked in an unprovoked and vicious way by hoodlums whose motives and backstories are not provided. The attackers appear as cardboard villains who do evil for the pleasure of it. This antagonal good/evil disparity creates heightened outrage in audiences and a strong inclination to sympathize with Erica. Once the direction of sympathies moves toward Erica, the inertial wave of these sympathies carries audiences along with her as she descends into her own dark thoughts and overtly vigilante actions toward those who may threaten her.

It would appear that the character of Detective Mercer progressively fills the role of a contrapuntal character for Erica as the story unfolds. However, as it turns out, Mercer rides a wave of sympathy for Erica as strong as that created within viewers. As a police detective he is ideally situated, much like Petrovitch in Dostoyevsky's *Crime and Punishment*, to challenge every assumption and rationale presented by Erica and her situation. But he ends up doing no more than affirming her convictions and, at the end, assisting her in executing one of her attackers, covering up her involvement, and allowing her to go free.

With this conclusion, the film avoids the deeper and darker issues surrounding vigilantism and thereby presents a simplistic conflict resolution in which the featured character is allowed to complete her revenge. The film makes no attempt to draw audiences into formulating hesitations with regard to the vigilante actions of the protagonist. None of Erica's targets are portrayed as collateral damage. All are seen to invite the fate she hands them. But this is dishonest in its portrayal of life and especially in its portrayal of vigilantism. Reality is never so clear or simple as portrayed in this film. Punishing or slaying the *wrong* person or persons is the most likely outcome of vigilante action, and this likelihood is never broached in the film.

Imagine how much more powerful this film could have been as drama had Erica killed someone she *mistook* for one of her attackers. The burden of the loss of her fiancé combined with her mistaken killing of another person would be overwhelming. Her emotional turmoil in the wake of such events would set up a dramatic structure confronting her and audiences with a more engaging conflict to develop and bring to conclusion. This would have been a film worth seeing.

As it stands, *The Brave One* shows little bravery on the part of its producers even as it courts great risks. It features a character perpetrating several vigilante killings, elicits strong sympathy for her actions, offers no contrapuntal characters adequately questioning her reasoning, emotions, and actions, and instead portrays a character, a police officer, who ultimately supports her vigilantism.

The most important point of similarity between *The Brave One* and *Taxi Driver* consists of a troubled featured character destabilized by trauma—an anti-hero—along with the absence of a contrapuntal character sufficiently realized to draw into question the spirit of the anti-hero's agenda. Featured anti-heroes without adequate contrapuntal voices constitute the primary structural failure of films such as *A Clockwork Orange* and *Natural Born Killers*. These films are among the foremost copycat crime inspiring films, films identified as *reverse* antagonal melodrama. In many respects the anti-hero qualities of Erica Bain are appreciably less inflammatory than the anti-hero qualities of the star characters in these films. She is a victim, shown to be vulnerable, and progresses only gradually toward violence. Nevertheless, members of a viewing audience are similarly left with few obstacles to prevent their imaginations from interpreting Erica's success in violence as endorsement of such actions—even though that may not be the explicit intent of the producers of the film.

Though *The Brave One* contains structural elements and content consistent with films notorious for prompting copycat crime, unlike *Taxi Driver* it has not thus far produced any notable copycat crimes. One possible explanation may be that the featured protagonist is female and the vast majority of copycat crime perpetrators, in addition to mental instability, appear to require a good measure of testosterone. Vulnerable male viewers may not have formed a strong identification with a female character.

Nevertheless, given the risks of its structure and content, it is worthwhile to review the possible reasons for producing this type of film regardless of the star's gender.

1) Is it designed chiefly for enjoyment and escapism? If so, there are other ways of structuring violent conflict for purposes of popular and engaging drama. Why select the type of drama that has already demonstrated potential for inspiring violence?

2) Does it attempt to provoke viewers to reconsider the value of vigilantism by way of palatable packaging as an action-thriller? If this is the explanation, then it must be argued that a film with this structure does audiences a disservice by avoiding the issue of the likelihood that vigilante action in cases of unclear perpetrator identity leads to victimizing the wrong person(s). As will be discussed in the chapter on television, *Hell on Wheels* succeeds in being more profoundly provocative in this regard while also more dramatically engaging with respect to the development of the featured protagonist.

3) Perhaps a film of this type can be a vehicle for the depiction of a strong female character—a woman who conquers fear, overcomes victimization by violent men, and, in doing so, succeeds in restoring a measure of dignity and confidence to her life? But if this is the primary message of a vigilante film with a female lead, it comes at the expense of modeling vigilantism in a way sufficiently positive to leave many viewers' imaginations stimulated with thoughts of the rewards of taking the law into their own hands.

4) Following Jodie Foster's views expressed in the AFI interview, perhaps such films serve the purpose of pulling back the curtain on the secret struggles and hardships of marginalized and/or victimized persons in society in an attempt to increase popular awareness and broaden understanding for the plight of such persons. But there are many ways

to draw attention to such persons and the help they may need. And why feature marginalized persons drawn to violence? Perhaps they are the most troubling to society but featuring their violent actions in a widely distributed film without adequately contextualizing the violence is an act of carelessness that in itself is a kind of violence.

5) Lastly, it would be remiss not to at least mention the old canard that portrayals of violence delivered to those who richly merit it offers an enjoyable cathartic release as viewers identify with the avengers. However, whatever cathartic release may occur through viewing is of a fleeting cognitive quality and, rather than providing a satisfying release of emotions, such entertainments instead impart an emotional charge with no physical release (see, for example, Baumeister and Bushman, 2003).

Despite all the good reasons for *not* making a film such as *The Brave One*, temptation remains high to do so. But the film's all-too-easily achieved thrills and subsequent risks resemble those of a short-lived junk food sugar high and its corrosive consequences. Very little substance remains to feed the head and the heart, not to mention body and soul. What does remain is an archived digital product capable of being accessed for years—a product with strong potential for imparting attitudes churning in unpredictable ways in the heads of consumers who may live too close to the stream of violence and victimization in society. For them, such films function all too readily in ways analogous to the late Senator Paul Simon's soap ads—seductively advertising and selling violence as, in this case, a remedy for violence—and for some, such as John Hinckley, a potential way to make the real world right.

3

The Dark Knight and
a Dark Night in Aurora

Friday morning, July 20, 2012, began with what felt like a sickening blow to the stomach. What struck me was not a fist but news of the theater shootings in Aurora, Colorado. This senseless rampage occurred in the early morning hours at a premiere showing of *The Dark Knight Rises*, the last installment of the Christopher Nolan Batman trilogy. Regrettably, as disturbing as such news always is, it no longer comes as a surprise. In the wake of a long chain of previous deadly assaults—Columbine (1999), Meridian (2003), Red Lake (2005), Virginia Tech (2007), Fort Hood (2009), Tucson (2011), Newtown (2012), Boston (2013), to name only a few of the most notorious instances—such news is now met with reactions such as, "Again? Really??"

My previous book on film and violence, *Our Faith in Evil*, was written in the aftermath of the Colorado Columbine shootings. As a resident of a Colorado town not far from Columbine High School, these shootings, like the Aurora shootings, struck close to home. The shooters were reported to have been impressed with particular violent films such as *The Matrix* (1999) as well as video games such as *Doom*. Violent film and video had, of course, often been accused of being significant influences in mass shootings and other forms of violence. Having studied film for many years, I became interested in evaluating the claims for possible links between screen violence and real violence and especially how portrayals of violence might relate to adolescent violent behavior. In this first book, I concluded that portrayals of violence occurring within particular dramatic structures have a heightened suggestive affect

Opposite: **Batman (Christian Bale) and The Joker (Heath Ledger) (*The Dark Knight*, Warner Bros., 2008).**

on all audiences. Portrayals of violence within particular contexts may also have an especially suggestive effect on a small percentage of consumers vulnerable to forms of mental instability aggravated by trauma or a pronounced sense of victimization.

Focusing on mental instability as the primary explanation for mass gun crimes, however, does not sufficiently motivate society to address the relevant cultural factors. Why do an alarming number of men of marginal mental stability choose to kill? No matter how crazy, angry, or deluded someone may be, acting out always involves a choice. Clearly, persons are deliberately targeted and prized as targets. But how does this extreme way of "coping" with life's challenges become the alternative of choice? And why do these kinds of mass shootings occur in the United States more than anywhere else in the so-called developed world?

Answers require looking beyond issues of mental pathology and toward environmental cues within broader cultural contexts. Princeton professor of sociology and American studies Peter Alexander Meyers had this to say in the wake of the Newtown massacre at Sandy Hook Elementary:

> What joins private fantasy to public violence? How does Adam Lanza's sensory deprivation chamber transport him into a classroom littered with bodies? The missing and unmentionable link is our cinematic culture. Cinematic culture is not just the cult of cinema, but rather a longer wave in the way we live together, a stream of things that have been re-figuring us since the early 19th century. Cinematic culture feeds the enormous reservoir of symbols and subject positions we draw upon for everyday action in public. No one will doubt that Americans—thinking, speaking, playing, killing—now depend to a large extent on a wide range of models that derive from motion pictures [2013].

Meyers does not so much blame motion pictures for violence; instead he views them as mirroring, modeling, and now accelerating a long cultural history of violence (especially gun violence) as a solution to psychological and social conflicts. When a film such as *The Dark Knight* presents a character who appears to have had a remarkable influence on the shooter in the violent attack on the occupants of an Aurora theater, the need for a closer look at cultural context is a warranted step in the process of sorting out what happened, and why. This link between film and action on the part of one individual must be understood as only part of what Meyers calls a "wave"—not only of crimes—but of deeply embedded cultural attitudinal dispositions. When in crisis, individuals draw from the readily available cultural bank of models they feel fit the problems they face while providing the scripts they need for solutions. While examining this particular film will not reveal what caused the shooter, James Holmes, to kill, it will shed light on a fictional character and a virtual world of conflict structured in ways he found highly persuasive. This virtual world modeled the reality in which he thought he was living, the situation in which he found himself, and the violence he saw as the way to resolve his situation. The structure of this type of film invites modeling of portrayed attitudes toward conflict and situation scripting in which adversaries appear as villains, and violent action becomes the means of resolution and liberation of stored emotions. (Compare, for example, the scripting theory research on screen violence conducted by Huesmann, 1988; Huesmann and Miller, 1994.)

But before examining the content of *The Dark Knight*, it should be emphasized that this analysis is not an attempt to show how *necessary* it is that this or any similar film should inspire violent crime. This analysis attempts instead merely to show how *unnecessary* and, therefore, how *unwise* it is—for purposes relevant to drama and entertainment—that the violence of *The Dark Knight* be presented through its chosen structure of character and plot.

When police approached James Holmes while he sat in his car outside the Aurora theater complex after having ambushed those inside, he was asked to identify himself. He responded by saying, "The Joker." (This information was released, controversially so, by New York City Police Commissioner Ray Kelly in a press conference the day following the Aurora shootings). The Joker Holmes referred to is the villain from *The Dark Knight* (2008)—the Batman film previous to the one screening at the time of Holmes's attack.

Holmes not only identified himself as the Joker, his appearance evoked the character. He had dyed his hair bright orange. Although many have pointed out that Holmes's hair would not need to be orange to mimic the Joker from *The Dark Knight* (whose hair is not orange), the comic-book character from which the film character derives is generally pictured with green hair and the choice of orange is similarly unnatural. Orange hair makes a bold statement and imparts a bizarre and clownish image consistent with the way the Joker character presents himself.

The mockery of choosing an audience of the new Batman film while evoking the identity of the villain of the previous Batman film is also very much consistent with the kind of violent stunt the Joker inflicts on Batman and others in *The Dark Knight*. It is also worth noting that, in the first film of this trilogy of Batman films, *Batman Begins* (2005), Bruce Wayne is shown as a child who sees his parents shot dead while leaving a movie theater.

Holmes may also have followed a DC Comics series called *Batman: The Dark Knight*, launched in September of 2011, with new issues released every month thereafter. The third issue in this series shows the Joker using poison gas to kill the entire audience of a late-night television show. In the same issue another character shoots up the audience of an adult movie theater after losing his job.

Holmes appears also to have immersed himself in video games. Reports claim he was obsessed with shooter video games wherein a character is chosen and an identity assumed in an online setting with other participants. Role playing and assuming alternate identities was, therefore, part of the world Holmes had created for himself. Apparently he was familiar with a video game called *Batman: Arkham City* in which the setting for shooters is an abandoned movie theater—the same theater where Batman's parents were shot. This video game was released in October of 2011 and one of the leading characters is the Joker, voiced by Mark Hamill of *Star Wars* fame. It received the "Game of the Year" award in 2011. The popularity of the game was extraordinary, selling over six million units worldwide. The publication *Game Informer* gave it a review rating of a perfect 10 and touted it as "the best licensed video game ever made" (Reiner, 2011).

Through the combination of comic books, video games, and film, the Joker character of the Batman franchise played a significant role in the imagination and motivations of James Holmes—sufficiently so to result in a heinous copycat crime. As mentioned in the introduction, it is beyond the scope of this book to thoroughly examine the phenomenon of copycat crimes. But since the Joker character and *The Dark Knight* had significant influence on Holmes, it is worthwhile to consider the film's structure since certain types of violent films have demonstrated more potential for copycat violence than others.

The Dark Knight superficially appears to be a good fit for the antagonal melodramatic tradition of good/evil conflict. It divides screen time between three main characters: Batman (Christian Bale), Harvey Dent/Two-Face (Aaron Eckhart), and the Joker (Heath Ledger). The Joker is an unusually extreme kind of villain. Unlike city officials such as Commissioner Gordon (Gary Oldman) and District Attorney Harvey Dent, the Joker claims to have no "plan." He likens himself to a dog chasing cars—an automatic reflex of non-partisan disruption and destruction. As arch-villain, the Joker undermines the plans of Gotham's mafia on the one hand and, on the other, succeeds in corrupting the "incorruptible" crime fighter Harvey Dent. The Joker sees himself not only as Batman's nemesis but also Gotham's as he labors to expose the dishonesty and violence in every attempt to assert organizational control.

Of course, the Joker also tries to corrupt Batman, claiming he and Batman are alike, both using force to impose a will having no justification other than its own power to assert control. They only differ, according to the Joker, in that he is less sanctimonious and hypocritical about his use of force. The Joker claims every so-called good Batman accomplishes also delivers a corresponding evil. He illustrates the truth of this conviction by contriving a dilemma for Batman: if he chooses to save the life of one victim he then condemns another to death. This ruse results in the death of Harvey Dent's fiancée, Rachel (Maggie Gyllenhaal), and Dent's facial disfiguration. The Joker finds Dent's weakness by inflicting on him a senseless personal tragedy with the death of Rachel, thereby transforming him into the criminal Two-Face.

For those who have not seen the film, it is worth describing more of the Joker's schemes in order to show how artful and inventive the scriptwriters were in contriving shocking depredations for him to perform. For example, Batman and Gotham face another dilemma when the Joker contrives for the passengers on two ferries—one loaded with criminals for transport and another loaded with citizens of Gotham—each of which have a trigger device for a bomb that will blow up the other. If one set of passengers does not destroy the other, the Joker will detonate bombs, destroying both. Naturally, those on the criminal ferry think they are doomed—presuming they will be regarded as of little value—and those on the citizens ferry think similarly because they see their fate lies in the hands of criminals. The scriptwriters worked overtime on this too-clever-by-far overly perverse arrangement, which ought

The Joker (Heath Ledger) (*The Dark Knight*, Warner Bros., 2008).

to have found its way to the cutting-room floor—especially with the running time at 152 minutes.

The Joker also threatens to bomb a hospital unless an accountant working for Wayne Enterprises is killed. Fearing the threat may be carried out but unwilling to execute the accountant, Commissioner Gordon orders the evacuation of local hospitals, including Gotham General Hospital. After the Joker pays a surprise visit to the one remaining patient in Gotham General—his recent victim Harvey Dent—he exits through a hallway as rooms explode behind him. He is then shown outside the building, casually walking away while holding a detonating device. Explosions continue from the hospital in view behind him, then suddenly stop. He presses a button with no results and looks at the device quizzically. Finally, a last press of the button initiates a further series of explosions, whereupon he flippantly tosses the device aside and continues casually walking away. Explosions continue as an aerial view shows the entire hospital bursting into one huge fireball.

In these and other instances throughout the film the Joker uses humans as hostages and victims, not in response to anything others have done to him, but as bait or fodder in his schemes to disrupt the city, oppose Batman, and create moral dilemmas. The amount of screen time devoted to the Joker and his perverse and fantastic schemes confirms the point made by many reviewers that, while titled *The Dark Knight*, the film is sufficiently the Joker's to warrant a title such as *Day of the Joker*. Even promotional posters, such as the one pictured herein, highlight the Joker while Batman faintly appears in the shadows behind him. Granting the Joker's upstaging of Batman, the film slips significantly from the category of classic antagonal melodrama toward the darker category of *reverse* antagonal melodrama characteristic of the horror genre. Even though Batman re-captures the Joker near the end of the film, the Joker—much like the monster of the horror genre—succeeds in spreading enough chaos, death, and terror to claim victory. Batman emerges from the rubble only to claim a weak Phyrric victory before exiling himself from Gotham while assuming the blame for Harvey Dent's revenge killings for the murder of Rachel.

Films of this type, featuring darkly pathological characters engaged in extraordinary acts of violence, lead the way to inspire copycat crime. They do so more than related dramatic varieties, because they invite— or rather, *sell*, in the manner of seductive advertisement—identification with the perpetrators of violence. As discussed in the previous chapter, the more thoroughly a film features a pathological character, the more it requires contrapuntal characters or viewpoints sufficient to expose the full backstory and inner conflict behind the horror of external actions. This level of development becomes necessary in order to devalorize the motives and seductive powers of such characters. The more devalorization remains inadequately dramatized, the more violence appears liberating and identifications form consistent with the use of violence—as if violence were central to the creation of identity. In this context it is worth returning to Marshall McLuhan and his insight into the connection between identity construction and violence: "Violence, whether spiritual or physical, is a quest for identity and the meaningful. The less identity, the more violence" (Benedetti and DeHart, 1997).

Moreover, when heroized and glamorized villains are given only a quick hint of background, as in *The Dark Knight*, indicating they are victims of abuse and injustice, they are thereby provided a story intended as character development which, in its brevity, may provide for many viewers a rationale for violence. For example, as the Joker threatens a member of the Gotham crime syndicate with a knife, he explains that, as a child, he cringed in a corner as his father beat his mother. Noticing this, his father came over to him with a knife and asked, "Why so sad?" Placing the knife in his mouth and slashing upward at the corners, he said, "Let's put a smile on that face." Marginalized and vulnerable members of an audience, members who have had their own experience of victimization, are left too free to take what is intended as *explanation* for pathology as instead *justification* for violent payback.

Recall that the first film of the trilogy, *Batman Begins*, contains a recounting of the child Bruce Wayne witnessing the shooting of his parents outside a theater. Like the Joker, Batman was traumatized by violence as a child. But the Joker was victimized by his own father whereas Batman and his parents were victimized by a street criminal. This difference could partly account for the difference in their choice of "careers." But the film fails to pursue this difference, leaving audiences with merely the aforementioned suggestive glimpse into the background of the Joker. Consequently, the intensity of his motivations remains obscure and viewers can only react in amazement at his sinister cleverness with no further insight into the dimensions of his pathology. But since no one opposing the Joker thinks to probe the deeper roots of his character, viewers are not led to do so either.

As a result, the Joker progressively emerges as a dead character, a stalled project, more automaton than human, lacking all traces of human empathy. The entire drama is then restricted to the violent conflict structure of man versus machine. The dramatic tension reduces to little more than the Joker as a ticking bomb and Batman as the best hope to stop the detonation. And, in fact, the use of timed explosives by the Joker throughout the film mirrors the machine-like ticking-bomb essence to which he has been reduced. This kind of superficial character development is the norm for action films, which are essentially about making action—that is to say violence—the focus of attention. Character development is incidental to the desired effects. And this is precisely why violent action films of antagonally extreme structure are risky, especially for a vulnerable percentage of viewers.

Exaggerating real life to illustrate real life can serve legitimate purposes of art. But films become irrelevant to the human experience when they exaggerate characters and conflicts to such stark extremes as to lose touch with the complexity of real-life conflict. When this happens, films weaken their role as art imitating life while strengthening their potential as art influencing life. As long as films of antagonal structure with extreme violent content continue to be churned out by writers and producers focused primarily on profit, there will continue to be great potential for negative consequences. These consequences arise not only through the heightened potential for varieties of imitative behavior by a marginal few, but they also arise through the potential for furthering dysfunctional attitudes toward conflict and violence. The viewing public needs to ask more of writers and producers as well as screen critics and reviewers.

That "viewers get what they want" remains a common refrain from producers when answering complaints about violence in action-thriller films. Ticket sales, apparently, serve as sufficient justification of these claims. But this refrain has a rather disarming rejoinder. The following anecdote, borrowed from a professor of communication, identifies the problem:

> A man is playing poker, and his friend, after watching the play for awhile, takes him aside.
>
> The friend says, "Are you so blind you can't see they are cheating you?"
>
> The player responds, "I suspected they are cheating me, but I like to play and theirs is the only game I know of."
>
> And the friend asks, "Have you looked elsewhere?"
>
> After pondering this question for a moment, the player answers, "No. I'm too busy playing" [Smith, 2009: 39].

Viewers are playing the game producers deal because they like action films just as the poker player likes to play poker. But this does not mean a better game cannot be found. Regarding the theme of a better game, would it have been possible to have written a screenplay for *The Dark Knight* that would have saved it from itself? If, for example, the Joker and Batman characters in *The Dark Knight* had really gotten under each other's skin and probed the corners of the psyche down to the level of motivation and the springs of action, would a better film have emerged?

And would viewers such as James Holmes have been led, perhaps, to think more about their inner conflicts and the inglorious stain of violence?

The success of such a potential rewrite, however, in raising the quality of this film is doubtful. The Joker character is too much a contrived cartoon of psychopathology. He has been constructed out of the imaginations of writers searching for villains who can provide the rationale for fantastic crimes of violence to suit the needs of fantastic superheroic saviors. The more preposterous the crime solved and the criminal defeated, the more extraordinary the victorious hero. This kind of comic-book thinking has fueled the recent explosion of serial-killer films and television shows. But the entire serial-killer and mass-murderer genre is a dip into depravity for which there is no defense other than the imagined marketing need for escalation of absurd shock-value violence. The psyches of serial killers and mass murderers may be of interest to psychologists—and for good reason—but the public interest in them reflects more the problem of the cheated poker player than any genuine quality in the game. The solution resides in educating writers on how to become better writers rather than supposing ticket sales necessarily indicate what consumers want. The next chapter, focusing on the film *No Country for Old Men*, contains further discussion of *The Dark Knight* in a comparison and contrast of the two films toward the end of the chapter.

4

No Country for Old Men
A Violent Look at Violence

Like *The Dark Knight, No Country for Old Men* (2007) divides screen time between three primary characters. But among the three, Ed Tom Bell (Tommy Lee Jones), a West Texas sheriff of the 1980s era, is the central protagonist. The film begins with Bell in a voice-over, returns to his actions in sequences throughout the film, and ends with him telling his wife, Loretta (Tess Harper), about a previous night's dream. His opening narration, accompanied by scenes of dry Texas grasslands, tells viewers of his lengthy tenure in law enforcement—having been sheriff of the county since he was 25—and having a father and grandfather who were also sheriffs in the same area. He calls them "old-timers" and marvels at how several of them refused to carry a gun. Bell wonders how they would operate in his times. He then speaks of a boy he sent to the electric chair for killing a 14-year-old girl. The boy claimed he killed her because he had been planning to kill someone for as long as he could recall. He told Bell if he were released he would do it again and that he knew he was going to hell. Bell's response to all this reveals his character, his view of the times, and sets the tenor for the entire film.

> I don't know what to make of that. I surely don't. Crime you see now, it's hard to even take its measure. It's not that I'm afraid of it. I always knew you had to be willing to die to even do this job. But I don't want to push my chips forward and go out and meet something I don't understand. Man would have to put his soul at hazard. He'd have to say, okay—I'll be part of this world.

As Bell narrates these last sentences, viewers see a patrolman on a deserted stretch of two-lane highway walking a handcuffed man to his cruiser and placing him inside. The patrolman drives his detainee back to the patrol offices. But while making a phone call, the man approaches

Llewelyn Moss (Josh Brolin, right) with recovered drug money and a victim of the botched drug deal (*No Country for Old Men*, Miramax Films, 2007).

him from behind, places his handcuffed wrists around his head, and strangles him to death in a struggle on the office floor. Viewers later learn that this tall, ominous, emotionless man is a career hitman named Anton Chigurh (Javier Bardem), employed primarily by drug traffickers. An important part of his arsenal of deadly weaponry includes a penetrating captive bolt pistol (a variety of cattle gun) attached to a tank of compressed air. The bolt pistol's retractable pin, unlike bullets from a gun, leaves no material evidence. After strangling the patrolman, he steals his cruiser and, several miles down the highway, uses the siren on the cruiser to pull over a sedan. Calmly approaching the car with his air compressor and bolt pistol, he asks the unsuspecting driver to step out of the car, places the bolt pistol to his head, kills him, and steals the car to continue his escape.

Also, early in the film, the focus switches to Llewelyn Moss (Josh Brolin), a Vietnam War veteran who lives in a trailer with his girlfriend, Carla Jean (Kelly Macdonald). While hunting pronghorn sheep in a stretch of desert, Moss comes across several dead bodies spread out among a circle of vehicles. One badly wounded survivor slumps in the cab of a truck. Moss recognizes the scene as a botched exchange of drugs for money. Not finding the money, he notices a set of tracks heading away from the scene. He follows them and finds another dead body under a lone tree. Next to the body lies a suitcase in which he finds the money. He departs with the cash. Back in his trailer at night, however, he has misgivings about leaving the wounded man to die and returns to the scene with a jug of water. He finds the man dead just as the Mexicans who own the drugs discover his truck and descend on the area in a four-wheel drive vehicle. Moss barely escapes by jumping into a river. The next evening representatives of those who own the money visit the scene, joined by Chigurh. They find Moss's truck, which he had been forced to leave behind. Apparently preferring to work alone, Chigurh executes the others with a gun he finds on site. He then uses information from the truck to begin tracking Moss.

When Moss decides to run with the money and suffer the consequences come what may, the plot quickly thickens. He becomes the target of a multi-pronged manhunt, with Sheriff Bell and law enforcement as one prong, Mexican drug suppliers as another, and Chigurh—working for the buyers—as the third. Before long, a fourth party joins the manhunt—bounty hunter Carson Wells (Woody Harrelson), also working for the buyers. The buyers have hired Wells to kill Chigurh for the slaying of the two buyers' representatives and also to find Moss and the money. For the remainder of the film, scenes shift from one character to another.

As the chase unfolds, Chigurh leaves a trail of dead bodies while displaying calculating android coolness and a disturbing killer's code of unflinching "integrity." He will not alter for any reason what he contracts or promises to do. Those who get in his way, however, are sometimes allowed the benefit of a coin toss to avoid becoming collateral damage. Like the god of the Old Testament or the cold, predictable yet unpredictable stalk of death itself, Chigurh operates in the world with unwavering adherence to eccentric rules abetted by the random inscrutability of a coin toss. The film builds considerable tension as Bell, Chigurh, and Moss—the primary characters—and Wells as a minor fourth, all chase each other in a game of who gets the money. Through these men's actions and their personal quirks the film generates a disturbing mix of codes, power, fanaticism, violence, and fondness for happenstance—all in friction with a hard reality toward which Sheriff Bell and audiences strain to find an appropriate comportment.

With the elimination of Wells, Moss, and several Mexican drug operatives, the chase eventually narrows to Bell pursuing Chigurh, whom Bell knows is responsible for the trail of bodies from the highway patrolman to Wells. Bell's growing understanding of Chigurh's relentless drive, uncanny elusiveness, and willingness to take extreme but highly calculated risks, forces him toward a choice that daily becomes more obviously one of life and death. He must decide between continuing to track down and confront Chigurh—and most likely be killed in the process—or move along into retirement as planned. But Bell is troubled by the times and his conscience pulls him in the direction of believing people like him are badly needed in the thin line of defense against the kind of violence he sees.

As indicated in his opening narrative, Bell believes he is witness to a new kind of criminal and a new and more perverse wave of needless killing. This view is expressed again, for example, in the dialogue during the scene with the El Paso sheriff after Moss has been killed by the Mexicans.

> *El Paso Sheriff*: It's all the goddamn money and drugs—money and drugs. It's just goddamn beyond everything. What's it mean? What's it leading to? You know, if you'd have told me twenty years ago I'd see children walking the streets of our Texas town with green hair and bones in their noses I just flat out wouldn't have believed you.
> *Bell*: Signs and wonders. But I think once you stop hearing "sir" and "ma'am" the rest is soon to follow.
> *EPS*: Well it's the tide, the dismal tide. It's not the one thing.
> *Bell*: Not the one thing.

With this scene, the film points again to the current state of criminal violence stemming from drug trafficking and raises the question of how those who find themselves on this unconventional battle line are obligated to act. After Wells tracks Moss to the Mexican hospital, he anticipates Moss's demise and says to him, "You think you are, but you're not cut out for this." As it turns out, Wells was not cut out for it either since, as mentioned, he becomes another of Chigurh's victims. Maybe Bell is smarter than either Moss or Wells and knows he is not cut out for it either—meaning the degree of threat posed by Chigurh and the criminal organizations creating the need for killers like Chigurh. This may be the time to back away from a risk out of all proportion to what the sheriff of a small county ought reasonably to be expected to take. But does Bell have a special wisdom and a balanced grasp on how to cope with an overwhelming challenge or is he simply a coward who turns away when the going gets tough? How to answer? The film shows Bell's conscience causing him to ask similar questions.

Toward the end of the film, Bell visits his uncle Ellis (Barry Corbin), a former deputy sheriff confined to a wheelchair since having been shot several years ago in the line of duty. Although living in a shack overrun with cats, clutter, dirty dishes, and stale coffee, Ellis seems solid as a rock. Having learned in a letter from Bell's wife of her husband's plan to retire soon, Ellis asks why he wants to quit. Bell tells him he feels "overmatched." He goes on to explain that he thought God would have come into his life by now, but apparently God wants nothing to do with a man such as him. Ellis waves him off, saying he cannot know what God thinks of him. He tells him about a lawman—another family relative—senselessly killed in 1909 on his ranchhouse porch. The man who shot him, accompanied by several others, sat on his horse and watched him bleed to death in front of his wife. Then the shooter and the others road off. Ellis reminds him that the Southwest has always been hard on people. Just before the scene cuts away, he says to Bell, "You can't stop what's coming. It ain't all waiting on you. That's vanity."

The talk with Ellis appears to redirect Bell's thinking. This scene also opens the film onto broader, more existential questions relating to violence and its seemingly inescapable incursions and cycles within and between different groups and communities. A provocative scene near the end of the film and immediately following the scene with Ellis raises even more difficult questions than those troubling Bell. Returning to her mother's house after her funeral, Moss's wife, Carla Jean, finds Chigurh sitting silently in a chair in the corner of her bedroom. She has not met Chigurh before but immediately knows he is the one who chased her husband. The scene is riveting.

Carla Jean: I need to sit down. [She sits down]. You got no cause to hurt me.

Chigurh: I know. But I gave my word.
CJ: You gave your word?
C: To your husband.
CJ: That doesn't make sense. You gave your word to my husband to kill me?
C: Your husband had the opportunity to save you. Instead, he used you to try to save himself.
CJ: It's not like that. Not like you say. [*Pause*] You don't have to do this.
C: [*Exasperated*] People always say the same thing.
CJ: (*Looking confused*] What do they say?
C: They say you don't have to do this.
CJ: You don't.
C: Okay. (He takes out a coin, tosses it in the air, places it on his knee, and covers it with his hand.) This is the best I can do. Call it.
CJ: I know'd you was crazy when I saw you sitting there. I know'd exactly what was in store for me.
C: Call it.
CJ: No, I ain't gonna call it.
C: [*Sternly*] Call it.
CJ: The coin don't have no say. It's just you.
C: I got here the same way the coin did.
(The sequence cuts to show Chigurh exiting from the front door of the house. He stops on the porch to check his shoes for blood.)

What are audiences to make of this scene? In one sense Chigurh's presence in the world and the violence he brings into it appear to be the result of a coin toss of worldly fate. This worldly fate includes the potential, on one side of the coin, for cooperation and, on the other side, for conflict and violence. The world presents the best and the worst in living and dying. And sometimes it produces men like Chigurh. But is he the result of a coin toss? Is there nothing more to it than that?

Shortly after leaving Carla Jean, the audience sees how Chigurh responds to seemingly chance violence—delivered like the randomness of a coin toss—when his car is broadsided at an intersection leaving him with a broken left arm. As a cold-blooded killer, it would seem he deserves to be killed. And yet, for at least the moment, he escapes justice. He survives the crash, remains calm, takes it in stride, procures the help of two teenagers to put his broken arm in a sling, and limps off to freedom.

What is this odd car crash event meant to tell audiences? That crime pays but the price varies? That only the good die young? That for some reason he did not deserve to die? That he practiced what he preached, took life as a coin toss, and shrugged off misfortune? More than likely this event appears in the film as a way of pointing out Chigurh's conviction that his fate is set by his nature and that his nature has already been decided along with everything else. He believes what he does and what happens to him are the playing out of a cosmic coin toss that determined the events of his life just as if a cosmic mint had coined him, made him who he is, and made everything happen the way it does. To complain or wish otherwise would be futile.

Consider also the role of other chance events in the film. Moss finds the money from the failed drug deal. Did Moss rightly attempt to take advantage of a fortunate opportunity or did the opportunity draw out a flaw in his character that would have led him inevitably to disaster of one form or another? Carson Wells luckily notices where Moss has tossed the suitcase of money at the border river crossing. When Chigurh later gets the drop on him in the hotel, he thinks he can use this information to extricate himself. Chigurh does not take the bait. Was Wells overconfident and not really "cut out" to be a bounty hunter, or was he simply unlucky? Sheriff Bell narrowly misses a direct confrontation with Chigurh at the hotel where Moss was killed. Is Bell's escape from death a fortunate chance event? Or is it all of a piece with his destiny as a man who knows how not to push fate at the wrong moment? Every choice made by the main protagonists carries a string of consequences that, with scrutiny, seems appropriate to it—a kind of poetic justice. But is it really justice? Or is it simply a reflection of the need to find a comprehensible stamp of order and destiny to life that it, in fact, lacks?

The world introduces through its own nature the ever-present potential for the worst. Chigurh apparently sees his own nature and function in the world as set and decided like a minted coin or a completed coin toss. But there is another way of looking at life. Perhaps Chigurh's nature is a work in progress such that, as Carla Jean might express it, he must "call it" himself, heads or tails, killer or not a killer, as if the coin *never lands*, never decides for him. The film poses the question of whether it makes sense to see anyone's life as the result of an originary, destiny-deciding coin toss. Is Carla Jean's fate consistent with having "called it" when she decided to hang out with a man like Moss? Were there no preceding coin tosses? No following coin tosses?

Could it be the case that a person's character and fate are necessarily re-decided every day? When Chigurh uses a coin toss to decide, he nonethe-less chooses that particular way to decide. The French existentialist philosopher Jean Paul Sartre lends support to Carla Jean's insistence that the coin has "no say." Sartre insists that humans are "condemned to free-dom," condemned to choose. Placing responsibility on the coin is a form of self-deception, what Sartre calls *bad faith*.

With so many weighty questions squirming to the surface, *No Country for Old Men* clearly avoids the simplistic shock sensationalism of standard action-thrillers. The film penetrates past the challenges of violence in an escalating war of drugs and money, exposing broader existential questions associated with responding to extreme violence. The killings never resound with cause for celebration, instead leaving audiences with strong feelings of disgust. In this respect, the structure of the film resembles synagonal tragic drama. If pressed, the film could possibly be shoe-horned into the category of antagonal melodrama with hero and villain extremes corresponding to Sheriff Bell and Anton Chig-urh. But Bell is not a hero who saves the day, and Chigurh is, through the guiding eyes of Bell, better seen as a symptom than an individual.

In fact, Bell leads viewers beyond the melodramatization of conflict in his refusal to pursue and confront Chigurh in heroic Lone Ranger style. He follows Ellis's advice, understands that it is not all "waiting on him," and goes into retirement as planned. This ending of the film sug-gests the larger conflict behind the other conflicts consists of society at war with itself. Heightened trends of violence within society suggest a significant measure of social and cultural dysfunction. Solutions for this dysfunction are as much beyond the talents and capacities of an aging county sheriff as any one person's ability to stamp out a brushfire.

Bell grasps the size of the problem and at first sees it as the leading edge of an apocalyptic storm—"signs and wonders"—a level of threat never previously witnessed. The visit with Uncle Ellis enables him to recognize the extent to which the front lines of various forms of societal warfare grind out atrocious acts of violence in every era. The "current times" are always the "end times." If such is the case, "old-timers" like his father have already shown him the path forward, since they have already been through it. Bell's father led the way with a career as sheriff, and Bell has done the same. He has contributed what he can in his time and place and that is all one man can do. And now the time has come for another generation to take the reins and fill the same roles as Bell and his father and grandfather. Genuine progress against violence stemming from varieties of factional warfare within society must proceed as a systemically broad social and cultural endeavor.

As already suggested, *No Country for Old Men* offers further insight into *The Dark Knight*. Like *The Dark Knight* it also divides its time between a triangle of characters who bear comparison with each other. This similarity, however, also draws out more precisely how the two films differ significantly in their treatment of violence through their structuring of conflict.

As discussed in Chapter Three, the structure of *The Dark Knight* conforms superficially to antagonal melodrama, in which the heroic Batman triumphs over the villainous Joker. However, as further noted, *The Dark Knight* edges close to the structure of reverse antagonal melodrama. In this regard, its structure bears comparison with the genre of classic horror in which the monstrous character steals the limelight and dominates the action with attention-grabbing, shock-value antics of violence and mayhem.

But whether regarded as antagonal melodrama or reverse antagonal melodrama, the dramatic structure of *The Dark Knight* importantly separates itself from the structure of *No Country for Old Men*. This separation in structure also parallels, despite similarities in character, a significant difference in the structural treatment of the Joker and Chigurh characters, prompting a difference in audience reception. The exchange between the Joker and Harvey Dent in the Gotham Hospital helps illustrate this difference.

Citing his disfigured face and murdered girlfriend, Dent rages to the Joker that these atrocities were part of his "plan." But the Joker—gesturing to his clown makeup—responds, "Do I really look like a guy with a plan?" He calls the mob, the cops, and Commissioner Gordon "schemers" with scheming plans. But he is no schemer. Instead he shows the schemers how attempts to control their "little worlds" are truly pathetic. He also sees their hypocrisy. If he tells the press a gangbanger or a truck full of soldiers will get blown up, nobody panics. But if he says one little old man will die, then everyone loses their minds. Placing a gun in Dent's hand, he continues: "Introduce a little anarchy, upset the established order, and everything becomes chaos. I'm an agent of chaos." By presenting Dent with the opportunity to kill him, the Joker intends to complete Dent's corruption by demonstrating to him that he is also a murderer. Unable to pull the trigger on impulse, Dent instead pulls a coin from his pocket and, while presenting each side of the coin, says, "You live, you die."

By leaving the decision to a coin toss, Dent, like Chigurh, fools himself into believing he thereby makes chance the deciding agent. Fate becomes the agent, which fits his new understanding of himself as a victim of fate and fate as his new god to worship. This choice, however, amounts to a complete capitulation to the Joker. This is the precise moment when Dent becomes Two-Face and thereby becomes the Joker's tool—which is why the Joker responds to his coin toss with, "Now we're talkin'."

Like the Joker, Chigurh adheres to a fanatical set of private rules. His strict adherence to these rules makes of him a kind of machine, the machinations of which can only be interrupted by the machinery of chance manifested in a coin toss—which, in fact, only reveals what fate has already decided. The Joker's corruption of Harvey Dent into Two-Face reduces Dent to a similar regimen whereby his imposition of precise retributive justice is assisted and absolved by the chance flip of a coin. In this respect, Chigurh and Two-Face—now the Joker's convert—become two sides of the same coin. Both impose their stamp of justice and wryly honor the god of fate who coined them and revealed to them what they were all along.

In *The Dark Knight*, Batman squares off against the challenge of the Joker's evil violence by confronting it as if it were something that could be eradicated through the power of incorruptible law enforcement—represented in the first part of the film by Harvey Dent. But in *No Country for Old Men*, Sheriff Bell refuses to square off against Chigurh because he gradually realizes a solution to the violence is not contingent on the heroism of officers of the law. In *No Country for Old Men* no one person emerges to play savior and rescue the world from its potential for violence and injustice. Instead of pursuing Chigurh to the ends of the earth (as Batman is willing to do in order to stop the Joker), Bell abandons the chase and moves on to retirement. Through the eyes of Bell, audiences look beyond Chigurh and his violence to see a measure of deep social and cultural conflict overrunning the front line composed of particular cases. In this respect, *No Country for Old Men* clearly emerges as a story about the collective psyche, a conflict between social and cultural forces which are significantly out of balance. Through the eyes of Bell and his actions and commentary, all the players and conflicts in the film move from two-dimensional to multi-dimensional complexity, leaving viewers with synagonal vision and no easy judgments or solutions.

By contrast, no one in *The Dark Knight*, including Batman, projects sufficient gravitas and compelling insight to pull audiences along in a progressive broadening of perspective on the characters and events. At the end of *The Dark Knight*, Batman's exile is billed as a heroic self-sacrifice for the sake of Gotham. Audiences are meant to feel his absence as a great loss to Gotham. Viewers understand that Gotham cannot be right without Batman just as Batman understands Gotham cannot be right without Harvey Dent—at least the untainted memory of Harvey Dent—to inspire and rescue the city from its collective quandary. In *No Country for Old Men*, Sheriff Bell's insight brings a sense of loss to the entire societal drama that exceeds the loss to the community with his retirement. The complexity of violence as a social and cultural problem requires more than a superhero, more than a Batman to solve. It requires a society and a culture not at war with itself—a social and cultural challenge which, to one degree or another, has for the most part bedeviled humanity since the dawn of civilization.

In this respect, the title of the film, borrowed from the first line of W.B. Yeats's famous poem "Sailing to Byzantium" (1962: 95), must be understood as presenting a piece of advice for current times. For Yeats, Byzantium symbolizes a civilization of beauty, balance, and cooperation over ugliness, disproportion, and violence. It also signifies a place refusing to neglect the lessons of the past and its "monuments of unageing intellect" contained in stories and works of art having stood the test of time. As Ellis advises Bell, Yeats also cautions readers: Beware of getting lost in the "sensual music" or, in this case, the "violent noise" of the current time. Take note of the past and keep its light close, as Bell does in telling his wife of the dream about his father.

> It was like we was both back in older times and I was on horseback goin' through the mountains of a night. It was cold and there was snow on the ground and he rode past me and kept on goin'. Never said nothin'. He just

71

road on past and he had this blanket wrapped around him and he had his head down and when he road past I seen he was carryin' fire in a horn the way people used to do and I could see the horn from the light inside it. About the color of the moon. And in the dream I knew he was goin' on ahead and that he was fixin' to make a fire somewhere out there in all that dark and all that cold and I knew that whenever I got there he would be there. And then I woke up.

Though traces of the past surely contain many lessons worth preserving and keeping alive when going forward into the future, the next chapter confronts the question of whether every prominent message from the past is benign in its influence on how to go forward.

5

The Book of Eli
A Violent Look at Violence,
Take Two

Venturing any praise for the Hughes brothers' *The Book of Eli* (2010) seems like an act of heresy given the consensus of scorn heaped on it. The chorus of critical commentary discourages even taking the film seriously. Many reviewers have not minced words:

"The script is a calamity, the direction worse."—Nigel Andrews, *Financial Times* [2010]

"Earnestly shallow, machete-and-bow-and-arrow entertainment."— Stephanie Zacharek, Salonwww [2010]

"A synthesis of modern Hollywood-videogame bloodlust and conservative heartland godliness that ... comes off as a preachy Sunday school slog of a marriage."—Nick Schager, *Slant Magazine* [2010]

"Denzel Washington attempt[s] to become a poster boy for black scifi geeks—the only conceivable audience for adolescent trash like this."— Armond White, *New York Press* [2010]

"This futuristic action catastrophe, seemingly collaged together from the lesser works of Vin Diesel, is an affront to anyone with even moderate blood flow to the brain."—Colin Covert, *Minneapolis Star Tribune* [2010]

Based on these assessments, the film conveys little of importance while doling out a supersized portion of gratuitous violence. A superficial body count would not dispel such notions. But scenes from the film linger in the viewer's memory and Atticus Ross's soundtrack powerfully promotes this haunting quality. Cinema in general, while dominated by the image, draws on vocabularies of logos and pathos, thoughts and feelings, as contributors to its effects. The critics above find *The Book of Eli*'s logos weakened and its pathos stunted by crude shock violence. But

73

the haunting quality suggests something more may frame the film and its violence—a level of mythos sliding beneath the surface images. The wash of sepia in the cinematography imposes a slightly unreal quality of dream and myth throughout the film. Much like a dream, myth appeals to layers of perception beyond direct communication and imitates the structure of a dream in bypassing standard logic and everyday temporality. Of course, claims about meta-rational qualities of mythic narrative could reflect little more than hasty inflation of a work that, appearing artful, is, in fact, artless nonsense and "an affront to anyone with even a moderate blood flow to the brain." But this is not the case in *The Book of Eli*.

In his review of the film, Mick LaSalle of the *San Francisco Chronicle* remarks on "Hollywood's current preoccupation with the apocalypse" (2010). The previous year alone includes films of this genre such as *Knowing* (2009), *The Road* (2009), and *2012* (2009). *The Book of Eli* takes place 30 years after a global war has annihilated most of humanity. Those who remain attempt to build a life from the technological fragments left after the catastrophe. La Salle rightly asks "what is with" Hollywood's current preoccupation? But he saves answering this question for another time and instead ends his review with the next obvious question: "Should we be getting paranoid right around now?" Pondering La Salle's question brings to mind Freud's famous remark in reference to dream imagery: "Sometimes a cigar is just a cigar." But this thought should not draw attention from instances when a cigar is *not* a cigar. Apocalypse films may *not* be about raising the alarm for global disaster and the need for honing survival skills. But if the theme of apocalypse does not speak of apocalypse, of what does it speak?

Manohla Dargis of the *New York Times* joins a minority of critics who see a mythic quality in *The Book of Eli* and a less conventional framing of its themes, including its violence. This view emerges when she comments on an early fight scene occurring outside a tunnel underpass: "The arcs of spurting gore appear black, not red. Like all the fight sequences, this one is highly stylized: set inside a tunnel with the camera low and the sky serving as an illuminated backdrop, it looks like a page out of a comic come to animated life." Dargis goes on to speak of the simplification of the imagery and the larger significance of this for understanding not only the style of the film but also how that style informs the content and the broader meaning of the film: "The graphic simplicity of this scene works not only because it's visually striking, but also because it's a part of a meaningful piece in a story in which everything, nature and civilization included, has been stripped away." In this stripping away even the people have been stripped, including the character of Eli (Denzel Washington). As Dargis notes, "Much like the land and narrative he travels through, Eli has been similarly reduced. A loner, he doesn't speak much, even to himself" (2010).

It seems appropriate to find stripped-down people and environments in films featuring the aftermath of an apocalyptic event. But instead of an apocalyptic narrative chosen for its stripped-down characters and landscapes, the key to understanding the significance of these kinds of narratives in the current age may lie in a reversal of emphasis. The primary goal may not be to construct a story of world catastrophe but to tell a human story in a simplified setting. With this as the end, the apocalyptic narrative offers a convenient and arresting means—much like films set in the Old West. Films such as *The Book of Eli* may not be taking audiences to the "end times" so much as taking them to a much simpler time—a time when most of the modern and postmodern technological paraphernalia have been swept away so that it becomes possible to experience life and its conflicts in a more basic way.

The current appeal of apocalyptic films may reside in their response to a collective need for stripping away the overwhelming complexity and stimulation of contemporary life. The experience of mass destruction appeals to many because it feeds a desire to blow away all the competing stimuli and challenges present—and all too present—in the real world. The desire for destruction may not be symptomatic of dissatisfaction with the particular trappings of this complex world so much as an inability to cope with, process, control, structure, and make sense of all its trappings. The technological progress of civilization may have its benefits but it also brings with it sensory and cognitive overload. In this world of overload, the desire for clearing away and stripping down becomes a physical need. Complexity can breed confusion and confusion can breed despair—instigating a scramble to find relief. Films featuring apocalypse fill this need by depicting or implying an act of sweeping destruction, a clearing away, followed by a simplified life in the aftermath. This stripped-down world is not without its challenges, but its conflicts appear with greater clarity and it becomes easier to see what really matters in life.

Now it may be thought, given the possible downside to progress and civilization brought by increasing technological sophistication, that technology itself is the essence of evil, of everything that is wrong or has gone wrong with postmodern civilization. In line with this thinking, it would only be wry poetic justice, then, that a massive catastrophe wrought by high-tech weapons wipe out the contrived technological façade pasted over the world along with the people and culture responsible for that façade. But *The Book of Eli* contains one especially iconic scene suggesting technology itself is not the problem. This scene comes early in the film. Eli sits in the remains of an abandoned house and listens rapturously on an early model iPod to Al Green's "How Can You Mend a Broken Heart." The music device emits not only an echo of civilization and its comforts but also confirms the potential for benefit in technological devices. On the basis of this scene alone it would seem the film suggests technology, in and of itself, is not the undoing of humanity. And this thought raises the question of what more precisely has gone wrong. What does the film say about how humanity lost its way in the search for what really matters in life?

A significant clue for the answer the film gives to this question may be found within its broad structuring and particular depictions of conflict. Superficially, its conflict follows a melodramatic structure wherein Eli functions as the hero or saintly figure, and Carnegie (Gary Oldman) serves as the villain or demonic figure. In a struggle of mythic proportions, Eli must thwart the villain, rescue the damsel in distress—Solara (Mila Kunis)—and return human community to a proper course. This melodramatic theme also comes with religious overtones of sin and redemption as audiences learn fairly early in the film that Eli's "book" is, in fact, the Bible. Eli reveals himself to be a Biblical scholar by reciting Scripture from memory.

Carnegie also treasures the book. But for him it is more than a book. Early in the film he sums this up when he screams at one of his henchmen, "It's not a book, it's a weapon!!" Carnegie believes the words and stories in the Bible contain a great power he can use to draw people together, from which point he can construct a web of influence to enlist others into what he envisions as a plan for better community. The worship the book inspires, Carnegie believes, will create similar worship of those who possess and master its content. For this reason, Carnegie has been relentlessly searching for the Bible because he does not have a copy. Most copies were destroyed in the catastrophe. As Eli recounts in the campfire scene with Solara, "After the war people made it their business to find and destroy any [copies] that the fires didn't get already." He then explains this purge of Bibles by saying, "Some said this [book] was the reason for the war in the first place." And if viewers are to believe Eli, his is the only surviving copy.

When Solara asks how he found his copy he tells her he heard a voice that seemed to come from inside him. The voice led him to where he found the book. Then the voice instructed him to travel west in order to bring it to a place where it would be safe. The voice assured him he would be protected on the journey from anyone or anything standing in his path. The fight scenes and Eli's uncanny talent for flawless aim— with bow, machete, or gun—demonstrate his ability to protect and provide for himself. These warrior talents appear even more stunning when it becomes apparent near the end of the film that he is blind! His miraculous powers seem to warrant concluding he has indeed been assisted by a supernatural hand. Carnegie's earthly and corrupt desire for control, on the other hand, suggests he is influenced by the voice of a lower and darker power.

However, this antagonal melodramatic drawing of characters and plot fails to account for significant parts of the story. Eli's credentials for a saintly role seem less than authentic. He is not the embodiment of his brother's keeper. He kills to protect the book and continue his relentless mission west. Early in the film he encounters hijackers who intend to rob and kill him. He leaves them all dead. He spares a female accomplice but refuses her request for help and leaves her alone on the roadside to fend for herself. Soon after, he watches (hears) in seclusion from an overpass a scene of rape and murder on the road below and cautions himself not to intervene by whispering the words, "Stay on the path. It's not your concern." Similarly, in his departure from Carnegie's town, he leaves in his wake a trail of dead bodies. A Christian might well ask, "Is this what Jesus would do?" For Eli it appears the mission of transporting the book to the mysterious location west is more important than the people he meets on the way. The end justifies any means.

Solara finally awakens in him a feeling for others. At first he refuses to help her leave Carnegie's town, but when two highwaymen assault and attempt to rape her, he intervenes by killing both men. Yet his awakened humanity, if such is the case, does not extend to George (Michael Gambon) and Martha (Frances de la Tour), the owners of the isolated house Solara and he visit after leaving the town. In the scene at their house, while being attacked by Carnegie's men, Solara yells to Eli, "Hey, you know that voice you heard? Did he say anything about this?" Eli confidently calls back to her, "We'll get out alive, both of us." George overhears and asks about Martha and himself. Eli glibly replies, "Didn't mention you." A short time later, George and Martha are both killed. Although these two are portrayed as unsavory cannibals, does Eli's attitude—or that of the voice that speaks to him—reflect an attitude consistent with his book?

Clearly, Eli's role is more of a warrior than a Jesus humanitarian. Yet, while they are driving west in the car taken from Carnegie's men, Eli confesses to Solara that, in all the years of his journey, he got "so caught up in keeping it [the book] safe he forgot to live by what he learned from it." When Solara asks him what he learned, he replies, "Do for others more than you do for yourself." It appears Eli has, indeed, come to an awakening and has, however late in the day, taken a message from the book in sharp contrast to the message and the potential Carnegie sees in the book. But those who 30 years earlier survived the great catastrophe apparently agreed with Carnegie regarding the book. Yet, unlike Carnegie, they feared rather than craved its potential as a weapon. Instead of wanting to preserve the book, they wanted to destroy it.

While superficially the film seems to draw a clear portraiture of human conflict in the melodramatic mold of good versus evil—Eli versus Carnegie—the audience is left with an unsettling deeper question about the clarity of the conflict. Who is right about the book? The crucial conflict may not be so much between Eli and Carnegie (both of whom for different reasons want to preserve the book), but rather between those who want to preserve the book and those who want to forget it. And this conflict is not so easily framed in melodramatic simplicity.

If the book can be understood to have played a significant role in the great catastrophe, can Eli be right to take such pains to preserve it? In preserving the book, Eli may unwittingly play as destructive a role as

Carnegie, preserving the book and its role as a weapon, and ultimately initiating once again the conflict and violence resulting in near destruction of humanity. The supernatural hand guiding and protecting Eli may be less than benevolent. Some hint of the continuation of a dark process of violence is indicated at the conclusion of the film with the image of Solara dressed like Eli and back on the road carrying his backpack and weapons. What has Eli and his book spawned?

If there is a particular message in *The Book of Eli*, it cannot be, as some critics have claimed, a simple homage to Christianity or the Bible. The film clearly suggests that the Bible cannot be relied on to guarantee benevolent human community and that it may indeed be all too reliable as a means for ensuring division and conflict. But the film need not be understood as singling out the Bible or Christianity. A scene near the end of the film lends support to this interpretation. The leader of the Alcatraz community (Malcolm McDowell) places the newly printed copy of the Bible on a shelf alongside copies of the Torah and Qu'ran. Whatever gesture the film may make toward the Bible appears to include the other religions of the Abrahamic tradition.

When directly questioned about whether *The Book of Eli* is a Christian film with an overall Christian message, the Hughes brothers flatly deny the film should be read in this way. They are, in fact, altogether coy about how to read the film. For example, Albert Hughes advises, "There are certain things that are ambiguous about certain questions that I have the answers to for myself, but I want the audience to make up their own minds on. You can't give the audience all the answers. Some people think you should, but you shouldn't, and that's what an audience should do, answer that question for themselves." Allen Hughes is equally sly when he adds, "If you're open minded and you sit back and watch it, maybe watch it again because there are so many subtle things that are happening that are worthy of a repeat viewing" (Woerner, 2010).

As already stated, with the early scene of peaceful music emanating from the old iPod, the film hints that technology is not the problem. Technology is a tool. How technological devices are used determines whether they yield good or bad outcomes. Words are little more than tools and, in this respect, the Bible is also a tool. The meaning and currency assigned to words rather than the words themselves, determine the kind of world they help create. But this is not what Eli and Carnegie

Solara (Mila Kunis) takes to the road with Eli's backpack and weapons (*The Book of Eli*, Alcon Entertainment, 2010).

appear to believe. They see the Bible not just as a tool but as the tool of tools, as the most sacred tool. As such, the Bible transcends being a tool and becomes a fetish. And perhaps this transition and elevation of the book from tool to fetish accounts for its contribution to the division and conflict leading to the apocalypse. Certainly this is one possible reading of *The Book of Eli*.

And suppose you found yourself to be a survivor in the aftermath of catastrophic destruction of humanity and material civilization. And suppose you could take with you into the future only one book for purposes of building a new society. What book would you choose? Could any book guarantee an untroubled future for humanity? Can or should one book serve as the sacred text of texts? And what does your answer say about the value of any one book? What really matters in human community may lie beyond what words and other tools can reliably convey, create, or preserve. Clearly, *The Book of Eli*, in its stripped-down context of mythic iconography, presents complex conflict as it confronts complex questions. Granting as much, the film deserves to be viewed as more than a violent action-thriller. The film's stylized violence emerges from an evolving context which draws the roots—at least the potential *literary* roots—of violence and conflict into question. In raising such questions, *The Book of Eli* merits more respect than it has broadly received in the marketplace of critics.

6

Merry Christmas, Mr. Lawrence
The Ordeal of Loving Your Enemy

Drama consists of actions just as language consists of symbolic actions. Actions disclose motives as texts disclose meanings. Motives present points of view as meanings present perspectives. Points of view define actors as perspectives define persons. Actors shape and are shaped by scenes as persons shape and are shaped by societies and cultures. These parallels mark the logic of connections between drama and language. They also mark the network of associations comprising much of

Maj. Jack "Strafer" Celliers (David Bowie) surprises his captor, Capt. Yonoi (Ryuichi Sakamoto), with an embrace (*Merry Christmas, Mr. Lawrence*, Recorded Picture Company, 1983).

the substance of what American literary critic Kenneth Burke refers to as the symbolic action view of language—or dramatism (1966). For Burke, deeds and words are both *actions*. Action differs from motion because action entails choice and motion does not. Since philosophers contend the evidence is not conclusive, this difference requires the leap of faith that choice indeed differs significantly from mere movement.

According to Burke, every use of language—whether description, interpretation, explanation, expression, or whatever—counts as symbolic *action* because choices are made in the selection of words. A dead body may be called murder, accident, homicide, suicide, manslaughter, self-defense, euthanasia, or many other descriptors. Which term is used calls for a decision, reflects a point of view, establishes a frame, and creates a scene. A different descriptor calls for a different drama. It is in this sense that Burke sees language-using as dramatistic—that is, *inevitably* action and motive oriented—such that words cannot be disentangled from motives and such that reading actions poses similar problems of interpretation as reading texts.

Dramatism meshes nicely with the metaphor of framing, which in dramatic production is another name for staging. The stage, like the frame, is more a mental creation than a physical one. Staging, like framing, is a way of re-contextualizing. It constitutes a certain way of looking, of sectioning off experience and placing it in an observational perspective. And, as has been argued herein, the action of framing or structuring conflict bears crucially on whether conflict results in violence. This chapter examines drama and conflict in relation to dramatistic framing and point of view and illustrates how analyzing the portrayal of conflict in a specific dramatic production may yield general insight into subtle workings of conflict that may otherwise go unnoticed in real life.

Many dramatic productions offer exceptional insights. But with respect to the theme at hand—the inevitability of point of view, of framing, and its role in creating and resolving violent conflict—some candidates are more illustrative than others. The film *Merry Christmas, Mr. Lawrence* (1983) is a fine dramatic example of extreme conflict and capably illustrates the importance of a well-developed ability for flexible framing with regard to conflict management. Although the oldest of the films analyzed in this book, it has been singled out because of the renewed attention brought to it from its relatively recent release on DVD

(2005) and its exceptional treatment—for a war film—of extreme conflict.

The location in time and place for most of the action in the film is Java (part of Indonesia), 1942. War is the most destructive form of human conflict, but the setting for the film—a Japanese prisoner-of-war camp—provides a context for interaction between combatants other than deadly violence. In prisoner-of-war camps during World War II this interaction would, at the very least, consist of various acts of dominance, submission and intermittent defiance. A cinematic portrayal of this cycle would not be particularly noteworthy. But in this film, the arousal of an undercurrent of mutual respect between the four central characters alters the nature of the conflict, creating exceptional drama and providing a key insight into the role of attitudinal framing in structuring conflict.

The film opens with a scene in which a Japanese sergeant, Hara (Takeshi Kitano), attempts to extract a confession from a Korean guard he believes sexually attacked a Dutch prisoner. Hara summons a British officer, Col. John Lawrence (Tom Conti), to witness the episode. Lawrence wants to know what happened and questions the men. When Hara interrupts and berates the men, the Korean guard attempts to commit suicide. Hara approves and encourages him to proceed. Lawrence then moves to intervene but Hara stops him and rages about his tolerance and his attention to explanations. For Hara, what these men have to say is irrelevant.

This incident establishes the primary theme for the film. Hara cannot understand Lawrence's interest in explanations and another's point of view. Consistent with his cultural training, he interprets this interest as weakness. Moreover, Hara regards such sentiment as weakness heaped on weakness because the Japanese view all prisoners as weak for having allowed themselves to be captured rather than taking their own lives. Prisoners are not only treated as prisoners but also as men who are not quite men—men contaminated by a dangerous spiritual impurity.

But Hara nevertheless senses Lawrence is different. Like other prisoners, he exhibits little fear of the Japanese, but, unlike the others, his lack of fear is motivated by a measure of respect rather than hatred. Confused by Lawrence's knowledge and appreciation of Japanese language and culture, Hara grudgingly respects his unusual attitude while despising his empathy and tolerance for others. For Hara, Lawrence projects incompatible traits. This anomaly in character makes it difficult for Hara to deal with him in a routine way.

A new prisoner, Maj. Jack "Strafer" Celliers (David Bowie), enters the camp following a Japanese military court ruling. As a British commando, he faces possible execution, but the court, headed by camp commander, Capt. Yonoi (Ryuichi Sakamoto), releases him to join the other prisoners. Celliers possesses physical qualities and leadership charisma admired by the Japanese culture, so the court is inclined to be lenient with him and spare his life. Yonoi in particular is favorably impressed by Celliers's imposing physical appearance (blond hair and classic Caucasian features) and his defiant but measured manner.

Yonoi's admiration for Celliers suggests a possible homoerotic interpretation, but other factors suggest otherwise. The opening scene—which is not found in the book on which the film is based—is likely included in the film to emphasize the Japanese cultural contempt—at the time of World War II—for homosexuality. This scene, combined with the previously mentioned high regard the Japanese of the period had for persons of Celliers's physical features, prepares the way for understanding Yonoi's admiration for Celliers apart from a narrowly homosexual interpretation. Although the possibility of homosexual undertones in Yonoi's character should not be dismissed, placing too much significance in this interpretation would cloud the complex psychological/cultural quality of conflict within Yonoi.

Despite themselves, Yonoi and Hara feel inclined to grant Lawrence and Celliers a measure of respect. But this inclination only fuels their need to unmask their enemy's traits as ultimately false, as part of a façade concealing weakness and wrong-headedness—the qualities that ought to belong to an enemy. Hara and Yonoi struggle to be free of doubts about their own motives and actions—doubts that would extend them beyond the boundary of their patriotic-militaristic point of view. In parallel inner conflicts, Lawrence and Celliers struggle to continue seeing beyond themselves, to prevent the retreat to entirely personal perspectives—dominated by pain and abuse—leading to profound hatred of the Japanese.

Tensions climb when Yonoi forces the prisoners to attend the execution of the Korean homosexual. In response to the prisoners' lack of proper respect and cooperation at this execution ceremony, Yonoi forces them to conduct the "spiritual cleansing" of a 48 hour fast and confinement to the barracks. The next day, during Yonoi's inspection of the barracks, Celliers openly defies the rules of the fast by eating flowers and manju cakes he has gathered from the jungle. At the same time, the guards find a concealed radio. Yonoi holds Lawrence accountable for the radio and both he and Celliers are taken to the cells.

Later that night, a Japanese aide to Yonoi—acting on his belief that Celliers is an evil spirit intending to ruin Yonoi—attempts to kill Celliers after breaking into his cell. Instead, Celliers knocks him unconscious, escapes, and finds Lawrence in his cell, badly beaten and tied to a post. While fleeing with Lawrence toward the jungle, they suddenly encounter Yonoi. Brandishing the knife taken from his would-be assassin, Celliers confronts Yonoi. But when Yonoi draws his sword and prepares to fight, Celliers lays down his knife and offers only a cryptic smile to Yonoi. Outraged, Yonoi screams, "Why won't you fight? If you defeat me you will be free!" Celliers continues smiling but says nothing. Guards finally arrive and Lawrence, half-delirious from beatings and exhaustion, whispers to Celliers, "Jack, I think he's taken a bit of a shine to you."

The next day Yonoi sentences Lawrence to death as punishment for the hidden radio. When Lawrence protests that he is not responsible, Yonoi agrees with him. In disbelief Lawrence asks, "So I'm to die to preserve your sense of order?" Yonoi answers, "Yes, you understand, Lawrence. You must die for me." Bursting with anger, Lawrence loses control and is restrained and beaten by a guard. Subdued, he finally asks Yonoi, "What'll happen to Major Celliers? You wouldn't execute him for such a crime?" Yonoi calmly states that is "none of his business" but then asks if Lawrence would like to see Celliers before he dies. Lawrence agrees and is taken to a cell next to where Celliers is held—a wall separating them. Here, during the night, they exchange stories about their past.

Lawrence tells Celliers about a woman he met a few days prior to the fall of Singapore. Anticipation of the Japanese landing fills the local residents with great anxiety and merges with the fatalistic mood of the unprepared and outnumbered defending troops. In a foreign place among foreign people, waiting for a foreign enemy, Lawrence feels profoundly lost, his actions empty and meaningless. At the hotel where he is temporarily quartered, he befriends a young Asian woman, telling her what he knows about the timing of the impending invasion. They share an evening in conversation and plan to meet for breakfast. But Lawrence is drawn away in the night when the Japanese attack begins and does not return to the hotel for two days. When he returns, he finds her waiting for him in the same place she was standing when he left her on the evening of their last meeting. He has the sensation she never moved. After this second meeting, they do not meet again. But Lawrence, seeing with more than his own eyes, experiences the point of view of another, which turns the foreign landscape into more than a place and its subjects into human beings.

Celliers describes his relationship to his younger brother for whom he felt shame because he failed to live up to his own standards of stature and behavior. While Celliers is handsome, athletic, well liked, and capable at most undertakings, his brother is short, slightly deformed, introverted, and capable of skills like singing and gardening. The differences between the two produce a tension resulting ultimately in Celliers's betrayal of his brother at a school initiation. True to Celliers's worst fears, the initiation escalates into an ugly mocking. As the other boys ridicule and laugh at his brother for his deformity (a slight hump on his back), Celliers hides in a chemistry lab room, unable to associate himself with his deformed brother. This event, the crowning deed to a long series of smaller betrayals, eats away at Celliers until it finally consumes the blindness causing him to despise his brother. He understands and accepts their differences and the disparities in what they have each come to value. His inability to go on despising his brother makes him question the act of despising anyone—including the Japanese.

Both stories vividly describe the experience of being drawn out of oneself to the extent of understanding another's situation and point of view. In both cases this experience of getting outside the self originates through an unusually strong sense of connection with someone else. In each case this connection stretches the self to see beyond the limits of current personal motivation and experience. The shared stories provide insight into how these two men gained their exceptional ability for seeing beyond themselves and into other people.

Thinking they are doomed for execution, Celliers and Lawrence are brought before Hara. They soon realize Hara is intoxicated on sake. He informs them he has been celebrating their holiday and that, since today is Christmas, he wishes them a Merry Christmas. Without Yonoi's consent, he releases them to return to the other prisoners. Celliers and Lawrence exchange glances, stunned by this inexplicable favor and the acknowledgment of their cultural heritage.

The following morning Yonoi discovers what Hara has done. But due to his liking for Hara, he shows lenience. In order to save face with the prisoners, however, Yonoi realizes he must extract something from them. The tension in the film reaches its apex when, having found the limits of his patience with his conflicting military and personal motives, Yonoi asserts his military motives and demands the entire camp—including the wounded—be brought to the central courtyard. Here he insists he be informed of the number of weapons experts in the camp. When the ranking officer Hicksley-Ellis (Jack Thompson) informs him there are no munitions experts in the camp, Yonoi loses all restraint and prepares to execute Hicksley-Ellis with his sword.

At the point when Yonoi appears ready for the execution Celliers calmly walks from his position at the corner of the assembled men, places himself between Yonoi and Hicksley-Ellis, and faces Yonoi. Frozen with surprise, Yonoi stares at Celliers in disbelief. He finally strikes Celliers, who falls backward from the blow. Celliers quickly rises, approaches Yonoi again, and this time stands face to face with him. Placing his hands firmly on Yonoi's shoulders, he then kisses him on each cheek. Yonoi remains motionless for a long moment, at a loss for what to do. He finally reacts by raising his sword in shock and rage. But he cannot bring himself to strike Celliers. Falling backward, he is caught by two of his men. Other soldiers nearby tackle Celliers and beat him. Celliers has succeeded in turning attention from Hicksley-Ellis to himself, and the scene ends. The next day a new Japanese camp commander replaces Yonoi. Celliers is buried in the ground up to his neck and left to die in the sun.

The film concludes with a scene after the war. Lawrence now visits Hara in prison. Tried and convicted of war crimes, Hara has been sentenced to execution at dawn. He explains he requested the visit from Lawrence because he believes Lawrence is the only person he knows who can help him understand why he is treated differently from other Japanese officers. His treatment of prisoners was intended only to rid them of their "wrong-headedness" and make them better men. Knowing

Hara and his devoted adherence to the practices of his culture, Lawrence understands this to be a sincere pronouncement, however peculiar it might sound to those who were victims of the Japanese military and cultural codes. Grasping the instructive irony in the situation, Lawrence tells Hara he is now the victim of men who think they are right just as Lawrence was the victim of men who thought they were right in the prisoner-of-war camp. Hara shows his understanding and appreciation of this insight by again wishing Lawrence a Merry Christmas.

Although the major conflict portrayed in the film occurs between the Japanese and the prisoners, the greater contrast in character exists between Lawrence and Celliers and the ranking British officer, Hicksley-Ellis. He never falters from intense hatred of the Japanese and shows no inclination or capacity to discover what manner of person the enemy is. This dehumanization of the Japanese makes it possible for him to keep the conflict clearly polarized. For Lawrence, this surrender to hatred is too easy and constitutes too great a dehumanization of oneself. When pressed by Hara for an explanation of the British "cowardliness" in surrender, Lawrence answers that the British do not commit suicide because they want to keep on fighting. Even as a prisoner, he keeps on

Sgt. Gengo Hara (Takeshi Kitano, left) and Col. John Lawrence (Tom Conti) say goodbye as Hara awaits execution at dawn (*Merry Christmas, Mr. Lawrence,* Recorded Picture Company, 1983).

fighting by attempting to bridge the conflict and cultural chasm between them. For Lawrence, this is how the war is really fought—not by trying merely to overcome the enemy by force.

In the book on which the film is based, *The Seed and the Sower*, Celliers comments in a parallel way about the clearing in his feeling about his brother: "I had not been obedient to my own awareness of life." The narrator continues, commenting about Celliers, "Many of his generation, as he, had been condemned by what he called the 'betrayal of the natural brother in their lives,' and could see little in the world around them beyond the hatred caused by their own rejections" (Van der Post, 1983: 149–150).

The human potential for overcoming violent conflict can be measured by the capacity to see beyond self and into others' motivations and personal and cultural genealogies. This capacity also manifests itself in flexible framing—imagining new perspectives, new ways of reading and understanding experience. The broader a personal repertoire of points of view and frames of reference the better the chances for responding to conflict in ways short of violence. But with respect to strategic management of conflict, the most difficult type of conflict to negotiate arises when point of view appreciation and the desire for cooperation are largely *unilateral*. *Merry Christmas, Mr. Lawrence* portrays this type of conflict and strategies for overcoming it.

The side more vulnerable and thereby more inclined toward changing the relational imbalance must take the first step in the process of decreasing polarization. This first step toward broadening viewpoints involves eliciting a measure of respect beyond the respect motivated by fear. In their willingness to show respect combined with the absence of fear and contempt, Lawrence and Celliers challenge the Japanese—with their cultural valuation of pride and competition—to show less fear and hatred toward them. By creating a pattern of respect independent of fear, the possibility opens for a measure of trust. This measure of trust, no matter how small it may seem at the beginning, is a prerequisite for achieving the bit of cooperation necessary for initiating a shift in the rigid framing of conflict.

In the film, a small measure of trust arises through a series of apparently contradictory acts—acts of resistance coupled with acts of acknowledgment and respect. Celliers defies Yonoi's order to fast for two days. But he does not kill the Japanese soldier who has tried to kill him nor does he take the opportunity to attack Yonoi with a knife. While continuing to "fight" the Japanese, Lawrence nevertheless speaks their language and shows knowledge and appreciation of Japanese customs. These acts appear contradictory to the Japanese, who interpret them as vacillations between strength and weakness—acts of hostility and acts of ingratiation. Instead, they are overtures and opportunities for reframing the situation. As the pattern of these acts grows, the Japanese become more inclined to change their interpretation, more inclined to match the strength of the prisoners' actions rather than risk being humiliated— in the sense of having received something greater than has been given. The film suggests that conflict management turns on finding ways to, in effect, compel respect by shaming an enemy whose culture highly values honor and pride.

Celliers and Lawrence make use of their unusual qualities—striking physical appearance in the one case and knowledge of the Japanese language and culture in the other case—to push the potential for destabilizing the status quo connections (or lack thereof) between the warring factions. It is hard to hate and victimize someone respected. But to gain that respect from an adversary requires giving respect—giving it in a genuine way, in a way that does not appear false or ingratiating, in a way that requires seeing from the other side and thereby seeing value in the other side. As pride is so hard to set aside in a conflict, it is best used as an ally in winning respect. This approach to conflict offers the best chance for destabilizing rigid attitudes in those cases where lack of respect and a significant power imbalance exist at the outset.

Although Celliers is put to death for his actions, his death is not by Yonoi's hand. After Yonoi is relieved of command at the camp and before he leaves for redeployment, he visits Celliers, where he lies buried to the neck but still conscious. He approaches him from behind, snips a bit of his hair with a knife, wraps it in a piece of paper, and pockets it. Rising and walking around to face him, Yonoi then performs a military salute, turns, and marches away. Celliers did not succeed in single-handedly winning the war or avoiding his own death, but he did succeed in altering the way in which one Japanese officer framed the enemy.

Another film released many years before *Merry Christmas, Mr. Lawrence* set a remarkable standard. David Lean's 1957 masterpiece, *The*

Bridge on the River Kwai, remains as provocative and compelling for viewers today as the day it was released. Many parallels exist between the two films. Both are set in a World War II Japanese prisoner-of-war camp in southeast Asia. Both feature head-to-head conflict between a rigid camp commander and the de facto leader of the POWs. In each case the conflict between the leaders evolves toward a measure of trust and shared respect. Also, in each film the conflict between the two central characters progresses in the company of an important third party— Col. John Lawrence in *Merry Christmas, Mr. Lawrence* and Major Clipton in *The Bridge on the River Kwai*. Each of these characters plays a role something like that of Ishmael in *Moby-Dick*—providing another set of eyes through which viewers gain additional insight on the unfolding events. Each also has the most memorable line. Only paraphrased above, Lawrence's precise words to Hara are, "You're the victim of men who think they are right just as one day you and Captain Yonoi believed absolutely that you were right. The truth is, of course, that nobody's right." And Major Clipton famously repeats one word at the end of *The Bridge on the River Kwai* as he observes and absorbs the death of the men around him and the destruction of the bridge behind him, "Madness! Madness!"

Both films serve as superb examples of violent conflict framed in the structure of synagonal tragic drama and both were popular in the marketplace. Although *Merry Christmas, Mr. Lawrence* did not win the awards it should have, *The Bridge on the River Kwai* swept the Academy Awards for best picture, best director, best actor, best screenplay, best score, best editing, and best cinematography. This was a year the Academy got it right.

7

Shutter Island

The Ordeal of Loving Your Enemy,
Take Two

Examining a film's critical reception offers information useful in sorting out the range of the film's general impressions on audiences. In the case of *Shutter Island* (2010), directed by Martin Scorsese, the reviews are mixed but mostly positive, though not ravingly so. About two-thirds of critics liked the film while the remainder generally found it to be extraordinarily bad. Mixed reviews, especially where the mixture includes strong negative reactions, suggest the film is complex and worth a closer look. *Shutter Island* is also worth a closer look in relation to dramatic portrayals of violence because it contains scenes of graphic violence some critics have suggested are gratuitous, sensationalistic, and in shockingly bad taste. For example, here is an excerpt from Nick Pinkerton's review in *Village Voice*:

> Daniels flashes back repeatedly to Dachau: a camp Kapo choking in his own blood; a firing line tracking shot popping with squibs like a string of fire-crackers; piled corpses frozen into a horrible sculpture. No violence is unsuitable for aestheticization; at one point in the film's web of visions, the perpetrator of a triple filicide points proudly to her handiwork and says, "See, aren't they beautiful?"—and Director of Photography Robert Richardson's image concurs [2010].

Peter Marsay of *Evangelicals Now* appears to disagree, though in a somewhat backhanded way:

> This all amounts to two plus hours of quality pulp fiction, but from a director so expert a storyteller, it feels perhaps one step too far into style over substance territory. The content features subject matter relating to such real-life horrors as the Holocaust and filicide. On one hand these are not handled gratuitously, and are absolutely integral to the story, but some may find their

juxtaposition with a tale, which is ultimately inconsequential, uncomfortable [2010].

On the one hand, Marsay acknowledges that the graphic violence may be integral to the story but then claims the story is "ultimately inconsequential," thereby suggesting the depictions of the Holocaust and filicide are bizarre when placed within such a trivial context. If true, this would be no small shortcoming for a film.

Mick LaSalle of the *San Francisco Chronicle* saw the film as attempting (but dismally failing) to be a noir pulp thriller in which even the soundtrack becomes offensive:

> If Martin Scorsese weren't aware of himself as a great filmmaker, he could never have made a movie as bad as "Shutter Island." The potential was here for some trashy fun, for a punchy, 100-minute edge-of-your-seat thriller. Instead, Scorsese tries to transform Dennis Lehane's novel into an epic psychological investigation. He stuffs the film with heavy-handed art direction and piles on a ludicrously ominous soundtrack. The soundtrack is a constant reminder of the movie's importance and only highlights its unimportance [2010].

Chuck Aule/Dr. Sheehan (Mark Ruffalo, left) and Andrew Laeddis/Teddy Daniels (Leonardo DiCaprio) pass a guard as they enter Ashecliffe Hospital (*Shutter Island*, Paramount Pictures, 2010).

Several critics note that, despite being a deep psychological investigation, the film lacks the emotional intensity audiences have come to expect from Scorsese. A number of critics place a good part of the blame for the lack of emotional intensity on the choice of Leonardo DiCaprio in the starring role. Dana Stevens of *Slate* is one of the most strident critics on these two points:

> *Shutter Island* is an aesthetically and at times intellectually exciting puzzle, but it's never emotionally involving. The movie is inert, despite the fact that it bombards us with lurid imagery and high-intensity stimuli: frozen Dachau victims, dying Nazis, beautiful child murderesses, abandoned graveyards besieged by hurricanes. Set piece after set piece makes you go, "Holy mackerel," but the entirety of the movie makes you go, "When's dinner?" Leonardo DiCaprio is not without talent, but how did he come to be Martin Scorsese's muse? The type of role Scorsese loves to craft for him is just the sort he's most unsuited to: the anguished but streetwise tough guy with his collar turned up to the wind. Beneath the Robert Mitchum mannerisms and carefully cultivated Boston accent ... DiCaprio still seems like a pudding-faced little boy, alternately sullen and giddy, a little too eager to be loved [2010].

Peter Howell of *The Star.com* also finds DiCaprio less than convincing in a Robert Mitchum impersonation:

> DiCaprio is out of his league in this role. He's just not credible in the scuffed shoes of an alcoholic copper who also bears the psychic scars in World War II of having been one of the first soldiers to liberate the Dachau concentration camp, and to witness the horrors therein. Robert Mitchum would have stubbed out his ciggie on the forehead of a guy like DiCaprio [2010].

But contrary to the conclusions of these and other critics, *Shutter Island* is one of Scorsese's best films due in no small part to the strength of Dennis Lehane's 2003 novel of the same title to which the screen adaptation is remarkably faithful. Appreciating the quality of this film, and particularly its use of graphic violence, requires an adequate understanding of the story it tells. It is not a noir psychological thriller—although it certainly contains elements of that genre. Some critics have noted the film follows in the footsteps of Hitchcock, though failing to rise to the standard set by Hitchcock due to its confused plot strands. However, these various strands or levels of plot and the structure holding them together are precisely what enable the film (and the book) to transcend the surprises of Hitchcockian devices. Lehane achieves an extraordinary weave of genres and layers of complexity, including elements of gothic, noir, mystery, crime-drama, psychodrama, action-thriller, and meta-theater.

Rather than any of Hitchcock's work, *Shutter Island* more appropriately bears comparison to the work of John Fowles in *The Magus* (1965), which was made into a film of the same title in 1968. Both works are situated on an island on which a mysterious man, with an implied Nazi collaborationist past, appears to operate a clinic for the insane. Using highly experimental techniques, including drugs and staged events, the lines between what is real and what is staged become blurred to a depth nearly impossible to untangle. But the meta-theatrical entanglements of each film would not rise to great drama if not also achieving a synagonal structuring of conflict. But unlike the structure, for example, of *Merry Christmas, Mr. Lawrence*, *Shutter Island*, as well as *The Magus*, feature conflict unfolding primarily *within* the featured protagonist rather than between featured protagonists.

Briefly summarizing the plot, two U.S. marshals, Edward "Teddy" Daniels (DiCaprio) and Chuck Aule (Mark Ruffalo) are assigned to visit Ashecliffe Hospital for the criminally insane located on an island in Boston Harbor. They must investigate the unusual disappearance, from a locked room, of a patient who has been institutionalized after drowning her three children. But Daniels quickly develops suspicions about the staff at Ashecliffe, headed by Dr. John Cawley (Ben Kingsley) and Dr. Jeremiah Naehring (Max von Sydow), a German with a past possibly related to Nazi medical experiments in concentration camps. Daniels believes Cawley and Naehring enroll the inmates of Ashecliffe in psychological experiments aimed at mind control, using a combination of treatments with drugs and surgeries. But as events unfold, deeper revelations ensue and, after a series of dreams and hallucinations, Daniels himself appears to be mentally ill and, in fact, just one more inmate at Ashecliffe. Daniels's partner, Chuck, disappears and then returns as one of the staff doctors. He has been helping to stage the storyline of Daniels as a U.S. marshal as part of an experimental treatment to help break through the delusions Daniels constructs for himself as protection from the reality of multiple traumas he has suffered.

Daniels's traumas include having been among the first U.S. troops liberating Dachau, having been part of a massacre of German guards at Dachau, and, following the war, having been the husband of a schizophrenic wife who drowns their three children while insanely believing she is saving them. Following this plot line, Daniels's real name is Andrew Laeddis (an anagram of "Edward Daniels"). His wife is Dolores Chanal (Michelle Williams), whom he has killed after discovering she drowned their three children. Ultimately, Laeddis's treatment is unsuccessful, the staff at Ashecliffe decides recovery is impossible, and he is scheduled for a lobotomy to remove his potential for violence.

With these bare essentials of the plot at hand, it becomes easier to understand why DiCaprio makes an excellent choice for the lead role. Critics are right to point out that he cannot project the tough-guy image of an actor like Robert Mitchum. But the role does not call for that kind of character. Instead, the role calls for a person who has less imposing features and who can project a measure of vulnerability alongside a measure of credibility. This becomes especially clear when Daniels answers to the name "Teddy" instead of "Ed" or "Edward." DiCaprio is ideal for the role and offers an impressive performance, delivering someone who seems sane as well as quite possibly insane.

Once properly grasping the nature of the plot, the soundtrack also begins to make perfect sense. It is, in fact, as Mick LaSalle claims, at times overbearing and intrusive. But as the film progresses, it becomes clearer the scenes unfold from the perspective of Daniels/Laeddis and the hyper-reality of his overwrought imagination. The music reflects and evokes this overwrought condition, is designed to do so, and accomplishes the task brilliantly.

The graphic depictions of violence in the film must also be seen through the lens of the Daniels/Laeddis psychotraumas and the hyper-reality these create for him. Getting inside the Daniels/Laeddis psyche requires exposing the parallels between the traumas he has experienced and the delusions he constructs to protect himself from his memory of them.

Teddy Daniels has no children and his wife died in an apartment fire set by arsonist Andrew Laeddis. Laeddis wants to live in Daniels's world because in that world he did not kill his wife and she did not murder their children. The absence of wife and children from Daniels's world is accounted for by the fire Laeddis set prior to their having children. Daniels/Laeddis has divided the conflict within his psyche into light and dark, good and evil, hero and monster halves. He has constructed a melodrama in which Laeddis is freighted with all the crimes, weaknesses, and failings. But this internal melodrama is contradicted by a larger drama unfolding through Daniels/Laeddis's interactions with other people. If these other people are to be believed in addition to the content of Daniels/Laeddis's growing hallucinations, then the structure of the conflict changes from antagonal to synagonal psychodrama. Understanding the parallels Daniels/Laeddis draws between his traumas discloses the depth of the tragic structure.

Andrew Laeddis was among those American troops who liberated the victims at Dachau. In an act of disgust and rage at the discovery of such inhumane treatment, Laeddis's group of soldiers assemble and execute the German guards remaining at Dachau (this is not Lehane's creation but is based on an historical event). Subsequently, Laeddis feels two degrees of guilt: one for being among those who failed to prevent such tragic human abuse as found at Dachau and the other for having succumbed to emotion and participated in the execution of the guards.

Andrew Laeddis was also the man who married Dolores Chanal. In an act of staggering psychopathology she kills their three children by drowning them in a lake behind their home. Laeddis understands her pathology but kills her nevertheless in an act portrayed as something akin to euthanasia. Consequently, he suffers from two degrees of guilt: one, for not having saved his children from his wife and for not saving his wife from herself, and the other for having chosen to kill her.

But the parallels between Laeddis's two traumas reveal why it becomes so difficult for him to recover and regain his sanity. On the road to this recovery it appears he must face particular facts. If Laeddis acknowledges his wife's crime, her drowning of their children, then he must also acknowledge his feelings that she needed to be killed, like the Dachau guards. But if he acknowledges her illness and accepts his own action and its wrongful nature, then he must also—consistent with the parallels he has constructed in his mind—accept his own shooting of the Dachau guards as a crime.

Furthermore, if he allows himself to see that his wife's behavior was the result of deliberate yet deluded and misguided actions, so also the behavior of the guards may need to be understood as deliberate yet terribly misguided actions. This realization, then, requires an extraordinary shift of his understanding of human motivation and crime. Yet how can such a shift be tolerated in cases of blatant genocide and filicide? Are not these crimes obviously evil, intolerable, and deserving of execution? Are not such acts unforgivable?

Yet if Laeddis's own behavior were somehow wrongful and misguided and he were to acknowledge as much, then does not his own criminal behavior place him in a similar category as his wife and the guards? And would not this wrongful and misguided behavior be symptomatic of the kind of weakness underlying his failures to save the victims at Dachau and the lives of his own children? Doubtless he asks himself what kind of a man could allow such things to happen on his watch? The questions he asks himself may seem harsh, but Laeddis cannot get past being harsh with himself.

But if Laeddis retains a sense of justification in shooting the guards at Dachau, it is not so easy to extend parallel sentiment and retain a similar feeling of justification in shooting his wife. This is the case because he loved his wife. The bond of love gets in the way of feeling justified. And if he were to give in to his feeling of empathy and forgiveness toward the troubled humanity he sees in his wife, he immediately encounters the logical necessity of extending the same sentiment toward the troubled humanity of the German guards. But such a feeling overwhelms his conscience and arouses his moral indignation. What kind of a man sees humanity in such actions?

The more Laeddis edges closer to confronting the reality of his actions and feelings, the more he must acknowledge his own failing and weakness—along with the hard reality of the tragic losses he has witnessed and suffered. These challenges prove too much for him and so Andrew Laeddis becomes Edward Daniels.

Closely following Lehane's novel and its extraordinary weave of psychological conflicts, Scorsese's film masterfully holds viewers in suspense throughout as it remains unclear which character is more real: Daniels or Laeddis. Finally, in the lighthouse scene near the end of the film, the spell of doubt is broken when Daniels realizes his gun is a toy and that Dr. Cawley's goal has not been to lobotomize him. This realization shocks Daniels into accepting that he is Laeddis and, for a time, it appears Dr. Cawley's unusual therapeutic gambit has succeeded. However, in the final scene of the film Laeddis is shown to have regressed back to Daniels and Dr. Cawley abandons hope of curing him.

The film succeeds in offering a near-perfect example of synagonal tragic psychodrama. The conflict projected through the personas of Daniels and Laeddis consists of opposing parts of the self, each with a voice of anguished legitimacy struggling to find balance and achieve a measure of functional stability. Unfortunately, Daniels/Laeddis fails to find that stability and the drama ends tragically. The graphic violence presented in the context of this story is in no way gratuitous but instead plays an essential role in accounting for the intensity of the inner conflict at the center of the drama.

Nor are the extreme instances of violence—the violence at Dachau and the filicide—gratuitously contrived for the sake of shocking Hitchcockian drama. I know from family experience the stark reality of the kind of inner conflict portrayed in this story. One of my uncles—like Daniels, a good and empathic man—was in the first group of Americans to enter Dachau. I saw the pictures he took on that day and understood the lifelong effect it had on him and others who were with him. Another uncle was the lone survivor of a group of soldiers killed in a grenade blast in a foxhole during the Battle of the Bulge. He struggled with PTSD all his life and eventually died of alcoholism. Yet another uncle was married to a paranoid schizophrenic at a time when knowledge and treatment options were much more limited and for whom the consequences for his children and himself were a heavy weight to carry. These kinds of traumas were not uncommon after World War II, and the combination of similar traumas in one individual is not inconceivable. This mix of traumas represented in the Daniels/Laeddis character offers an iconic portrayal of the kinds of challenges faced by many of the post–World War II generation.

In conclusion, the depictions of violence in *Shutter Island* appear in a dramatic context in which they are experienced as genuinely tragic and integral to the story rather than manipulative and superfluous shock-value additions. Consequently, the film and its violence trace an emotional and psychological journey exceeding noir entertainment. From the point of view of dramatic structure in relation to violent content, *Shutter Island* may be Scorsese's finest film, for which he owes a debt to Dennis Lehane's novel.

8

Memoirs of a Geisha
Melodrama or Tragic Drama?

Memoirs of a Geisha is not the most likely candidate for analysis in a book on screen violence. There are no exploding hospitals, warring drug factions, or Mandingo fighters. But *Memoirs of a Geisha* presents another kind of violence—the violence of child abuse, rape, betrayal, bondage, and objectification. These forms of violence can be as deadly as the blood-spilling kind and their treatment in film merits similar attention.

Like *Shutter Island*, *Memoirs of a Geisha* did not fare well with many critics and reviewers. For example, Roger Ebert of the *Chicago Sun-*

The stunningly beautiful Sayuri (Ziyi Zhang) (*Memoirs of a Geisha*, Columbia Pictures, 2005).

101

Times writes of the film: "I suspect that the more you know about Japan and movies, the less you will enjoy 'Memoirs of a Geisha.' Much of what I know about Japan I have learned from Japanese movies, and on that basis I know this is not a movie about actual geishas, but depends on the romanticism of female subjection" (2005).

Eleanor Ringel Gillespie of the *Atlanta Journal-Constitution* writes: "Supersized budget and lustrous trappings aside, 'Memoirs of a Geisha' is basically 'Desperate Housewives' with kimonos and fans.... For the most part this movie is part Douglas Sirk '50s melodrama, part the 'World of Suzie Wong'.... The movie is also a Cinderella story, with its very own Prince Charming" (2005).

Manohla Dargis of the *New York Times* describes the film as a "lavishly appointed melodrama," the story of "Japanese geishas swept up in jealous rivalries." She goes on to acknowledge that "geishas aren't typical sex workers" then adds the caveat "but while serving a new customer every six months certainly sounds less untoward than, say, turning six tricks a night in a day-rate motel, who's kidding whom?" (2009).

Similar comments and conclusions about the film can be found across the board from the *Boston Globe* to the *San Francisco Chronicle*. Others berate the film for its lack of historical accuracy in depicting details of geisha life: "there is no 'bidding' for virgins"; "geishas do not spend their lives looking for a 'danna,'" etc. And it has also been criticized for racial stereotyping of Asians: "the lecherous Oriental man"; "all Asians look the same"—evident in the use of Chinese actresses to play Japanese women.

These criticisms of the film are puzzling. Labeling the story a romanticism of female subjection or a careless distortion of historical and cultural detail counts as a narrowly myopic complaint. Judging the story to be an endorsement of the life of a "sex worker" is even more extraordinarily wrongheaded. Ebert appears especially obtuse, for example, acknowledging his guilt in having found a sense of enjoyment, despite its faults, in a film that "evokes nostalgia" for a way of life that, by his reckoning, glorifies the sex trade, the auctioning of virgins, and the conscription of underage girls. All such criticism falls into the trap of failing to see the forest for the trees.

Ebert, however, makes a step in the right direction when he starts out by asserting, "I know this is not a movie about actual geishas." More to the point, the film presents a penetrating and beautifully wrought account of life with allegorical undertones. What more proof could be required for its generalizing of the human experience than being a memoir of a Japanese woman of the World War II era, written by a contemporary American male? Although the author of the novel (1997), Arthur Golden, interviewed several women who were geishas during the time frame of his novel, he and his own history are nevertheless an ocean, a culture, a generation, and a gender beyond the world of geishas. Those who criticize the film for its inaccuracies in depictions of geisha life and other historical and cultural details of the period misunderstand the nature of the art they are evaluating. It is not primarily an historical or period drama nor even a story about the geisha life, the sex trade, or a gender-specific story relevant primarily to the lives of women. It is a story about Everyman/Everywoman and is, in that sense, relevant to everyone. Having a degree in art history from Harvard with emphasis on Japanese art, Golden probably chose the context of Japanese pre-war geisha life because of his interest and familiarity with Asian and Japanese culture. He likely believed the memoir of a geisha would serve as a profoundly engaging root metaphor for life around which he could weave the kind of universal story he wanted to tell.

The crucial features of the drama center on the structure of the conflicts, the quality of relationships, and the way in which character complicates the conflicts toward tragic outcomes. In this respect, much like a story of mythic quality, historical inaccuracy of minor details becomes largely irrelevant. The fact that Chinese actresses play Japanese women speaking English with a Hong Kong accent only contributes to the universality of the story. Deeply accurate and complete in its representation of universal types of conflicts and predicaments encountered in life, this story also rises to the level of synagonal tragic drama. It presents the tragic vision of life, about which more will be said, the vision that while life contains suffering, hard lessons, and potential ruin, it is not thereby inevitably a kind of hell. Furthermore, *Memoirs of a Geisha* shows how to stay in the mix in a way maximizing whatever chances exist for fulfillment. What more could be asked from drama? But the claim that so many have missed the mark in reviewing this story requires a demonstration of the case.

Much has already been said herein about synagonal tragic drama, but for purposes of examining *Memoirs of a Geisha* a few additional points in particular should be added. Aristotle describes the tragic protagonist as a person with whom it is easy to identify—a person of strong, but not flawless, character. This person encounters obstacles and conflicts on life's path and eventually suffers a downfall precisely through the very trait deemed to be a source of strength (Barnes, ed., 1984). Literary critic Kenneth Burke supplies the notion that tragic actions turn on conflicts designed to be viewed by the audience in largely nonpartisan terms, inducing a measure of identification with all sides of the central relational conflicts (Burke, 1984). And Robert Heilman offers the further qualification that the tragic plot brings the protagonist into profound inner conflict, producing an ongoing dilemma between competing choices, each having authentic claims of legitimacy (1968).

In a broad sense, the story of the passage of the child Chiyo (Suzuka Ohgo) into the woman Sayuri (Ziyi Zhang) offers a poignant and well-chronicled dramatization of life's stages. Chiyo/Sayuri transitions from childhood and adolescent dependency and various forms of constraining, even destructive, subservience to a more open life of liberation, personhood, and pursuit of a path more of her own making. Throughout the film Chiyo/Sayuri models an extraordinary resilience in response to cruel behavior by others and to hard turns of fate. The course of these actions and events bring about three major crises for her. In the beginning sequences of the film she is sold into slavery by her family, then separated from her sister, and finally informed that both her parents are dead and that she will not see her sister again. This complete break with the family initiates the first great crisis of loss and separation in her life.

Later, her encounter with the Chairman (Ken Watanabe) lifts her from despair. Without her knowledge, he makes it possible for her to gain entrance into geisha training. Maturing as a geisha, she acquires status in the world of the geisha trade largely through the kindness and mentorship of Mameha (Michelle Yeoh), the woman chosen by the Chairman to help her. Achieving status in a house of geishas opens an avenue of independence and potential she had not anticipated. She becomes a formidable rival for Hotsumomo (Gong Li) among the favored geishas and a possible successor for Mother (Kaori Momoi) as head of the geisha house. But as her ascendance into this role becomes certain—and along with it the potential for greater independence and freedom to direct her life—the war rips apart the fabric of this world and sends her back into a life of renewed powerlessness, poverty, and subservience. This initiates the second great crisis of separation.

After the war, persuaded by the Chairman's associate Nobu (Koji Yakusho), Sayuri chooses to return to her life as a geisha and renew her hope of gaining the attention of the Chairman for whom she has kept a secret love. But a triangle of tensions between Nobu, the Chairman, and Sayuri eventually leads to a self-destructive incident with an American financier and the death of her hopes for a future with the Chairman. This initiates the third great crisis of her life, powerfully symbolized in the film when she releases the Chairman's handkerchief into the wind on the cliff above the sea. As she stands near the edge of the cliff she confronts the ultimate choice of suicide or resuming her life. Again, she overcomes adversity and moves on.

Each of these three crises represents the loss of hope for the kind of connection with others Sayuri desires—a connection characterized by genuine mutual trust and care. With each loss Sayuri finds the strength to hang on, resurrect herself, and continue striving toward finding that connection with others—a connection represented most powerfully by the kind of love she sees the Chairman as capable of giving her. This persistent striving toward greater liberation from subservient and abusive relationships functions as a primary theme in the film and is symbolically conveyed and emphasized when Sayuri's nature is likened to that of water—a comparison first made in the film by Mother. Water has the ability, with time, to wear down stone and iron and will eventually find its way through the smallest crack in a pottery jar. But the combination of Sayuri's water strength pitted against misfortune and cruel behavior on the part of others does not suffice to place the film in the category of tragic drama. The structure of the drama emerges in Sayuri's conflicts with others, in which, through Sayuri's eyes, none of the characters arouse abiding outrage.

Sayuri models the ability to see from another's angle. For example, she realizes as Hotsumomo flees the burning house after their fight, that she, too, has lost a love—a loss in which Sayuri's actions played a role. At that moment Sayuri wonders if she is on a path to become bitter and tormented like Hotsumomo. She begins to see but for the Grace of God she may become Hotsumomo. In that flash of understanding she must also forgive Hotsumomo and thereby guides the audience to do the same. The measure of audience identification with Hotsumomo induced by Sayuri's reflection broadens Hotsumomo's character and precludes stereotyping her as a villain. Sayuri's thoughts also prompt the troubling question: What accounts for the difference between one person's response to terrible loss and another's response?

Similarly, Pumpkin (Youki Kudoh) does not descend to the role of a simple villain. Pumpkin's revenge against Sayuri near the end of the film appears to be the work of jealous villainy. But when experiencing the depth of Sayuri's pain in the loss of the Chairman, which Pumpkin deliberately brought about, viewers simultaneously gain a sense of the equal depth of Pumpkin's loss—a loss brought about when Sayuri accepted Mother's appointment to become the heir to head the geisha house. In that moment Sayuri took from Pumpkin the one thing she most wanted in life. Sensing the magnitude of Pumpkin's loss, Sayuri lets go of hatred and the cycle of revenge and is left with only dissipated blame and a profound sense of loss. This blameless sense of the tragic is an intense and complex emotion and is far removed from the emotions aroused in fairy tales such as *Cinderella*—to which *Memoirs of a Geisha* has been disparagingly compared—where, at the conclusion, the doves peck out the eyes of the jealous sisters in fulfillment of Cinderella's vengeful wishes.

Even the Baron (Cary-Hiroyuki Tagawa), in his cruel sexual assault on Sayuri, does not fulfill the function of a villain in the story. Again, Sayuri sufficiently overcomes the incident such that it does not become emotionally crippling for her to the point that she develops an obsession for revenge. Consequently, the Baron slips past becoming an abiding outrage and villainous force in the story. Dramatically, the encounter with the Baron serves the purpose of revealing to the viewer the range of possibilities hanging in the balance for Sayuri between the Baron, the Doctor, Nobu, and the Chairman. These contrasts help to further appreciation for what the Chairman symbolizes for Sayuri and why she cannot give up striving for the kind of life and liberation he presents and represents.

By portraying the actions and reactions of the cast in ways precluding the categorization of particular characters as one-dimensional villains, the story follows the pattern of development of tragic drama consistent with Kenneth Burke's criterion. The conflicts of tragic drama elicit a significant measure of non-partisan proportioning of sympathies on the part of the audience. Identification transcends a gravitational pull to one side and spreads inclusively outward such that none of the characters function as deserving scapegoats. But viewers need not be brought to identify with all the characters equally.

In the film, as well as the book, the main lines of tension and conflict eventually emerge between Sayuri, Nobu, and the Chairman. These lines of relational conflict also mirror lines of internal conflict within each of these characters. The internal conflicts, in Heilman's terms, consist of authentic claims of competing motives within each of the characters.

Nobu, for example, appears as an essentially good man who struggles within because of his inability to give of himself. He fears loss in general and loss of control in particular. He feels a strong attraction to Sayuri but cannot abandon himself to love any more than he can let go of his fear—specifically his fear of loss of control in his world of business interests. But the war brings with it the realization of his greatest fear in the complete loss of his business. After the war, his desperate need to rebuild his business again clouds his attraction to Sayuri. He comes for her partly because he has feelings for her but more so because he needs her to help him manipulate the Americans into providing the financing necessary to rebuild. Because insecurity dominates his motives, stability becomes his primary need and so his first order of concern lies in the degree of control he can create through his career life. Sayuri represents the love he needs in his life but, nevertheless, she remains of secondary concern to him and so she functions for him more as a tool than a person. She senses this and knows that if she falls predominantly under his control she will likely continue to be used by him and thereby not gain the kind of liberation in love she seeks. Nevertheless, near the end of the film, the competition between Nobu's motivation for love and motivation for work—and the inability to negotiate the two—begins to tear him apart.

From Sayuri's point of view, Nobu's attention toward her creates a significant inner conflict because, on the one hand, she cannot trust him due to his divided nature, his dominating need, and thereby his inability to give in a way that also looks out for her best interests and fulfillment. On the other hand, he has possibly been instrumental in saving her life through his efforts to provide a safe place for her during the war and has in other ways shown her kindness and loyalty while never doing anything to harm or shame her—unlike many other persons in her geisha world. So she feels a sense of indebtedness to him which complicates her desire to free herself from him in order to keep open the possibility for gaining the kind of liberation she has always sought. In this regard, Sayuri's relationship with Nobu symbolizes the broader ongoing conflict within her between greater liberation and ties of friendship, loyalty, and obligation.

The Chairman's inner conflict becomes fully apparent only at the end of the film when his motives are more clearly revealed. But hints of his inner conflict appear earlier when he tells Sayuri of the sense of indebtedness he has toward Nobu for having saved his life by shielding him from an explosion. This and other subtle actions demonstrate that the Chairman sacrifices his own feelings for Sayuri in deference to his sense of obligation toward Nobu. These actions flow from his magnanimous nature. But because he refuses to allow himself to see Sayuri's attraction to him, he fails to recognize the pain his generosity toward Nobu causes Sayuri. Nor does he fully realize the sense in which he effaces and even betrays himself. His great strength of character, his generous heart, begins to function as weakness rather than strength.

This same irony, whereby an admirable character trait leads to tragic loss, occurs also with Sayuri. Her inner struggle between her desire for liberation, which she sees as possible through the Chairman as her benefactor, her danna, and her sense of obligation toward Nobu and reluctance to betray him, leads her finally to a desperate and self-destructive decision. She consents to a sexual liaison with the American in the hope that this act will turn Nobu away from her. This act betrays her deepest sense of integrity and ultimately shames her in her own eyes as well as in the eyes, or so she believes, of the Chairman. However wrong it would have been for Sayuri to become Nobu's danna, giving herself to the American was, for her, a worse mistake. After Pumpkin's treachery she quickly understands this. Her sense of her own failure, her strength in love and desire turned to weakness, helps prevent her from heaping rage and blame on Pumpkin for her betrayal by bringing the Chairman instead of Nobu to the scene of her rendezvous with the American.

In a parallel way Nobu's inner conflict leads to the same irony of downfall through what initially appears to be strength of character. His strength lies in his business acumen and his focus and determination to succeed in the world of commerce. This business acumen and determination also combines with his sense of fairness and loyalty in transactions. But this strength is his undoing in the realm of human relations insofar as it overwhelms and obscures sensitivity to his own and others' emotional needs and relational predicaments. He finds he can function in the controlled marketplace of exchange, the marketplace of corporations and geisha houses, but not in the unpredictable and often unruly community of human suffering, resentment, joy, and surprise.

It can be fairly claimed, then, that the love triangle between Sayuri, Nobu, and the Chairman presents characters conforming to tragic drama. They are all characters portrayed in ways eliciting significant measures of identification and sympathy from the viewer, each imbued with a particular kind of nobility of character, and each brought, through

Sayuri (Ziyi Zhang) contemplates the loss of the Chairman (*Memoirs of a Geisha*, Columbia Pictures, 2005).

the fate of their mutual entanglement and character strengths, to a point of tragic collapse and despair.

In the end, however, Nobu fails to rise above his despair as a result of his inability to let go of his obsessions, give and forgive. He fails to achieve in his actions the creation of relationships based on genuine care and concern for others whereby it becomes possible to attain the kind of liberation to make a life of one's own. Sayuri possesses this kind of generosity of spirit, evident in her ability to rebound without resentment from the cruelty of others, such as Mother, the Baron, Hotsumomo, Pumpkin, and the American. But she also intuitively senses she cannot attain the quality of life she wants without finding her way to another (or others) who can also genuinely care for her with a love free of control and manipulation. From the day she met the Chairman on the bridge she sensed he was the kind of person who could offer that kind of connection and unconditional giving. In this regard, *Memoirs of a Geisha* transcends the level of a romantic love story to become a love story of and about human relations in general and the path to personhood, liberation, and self-actualization—a path achieved only through the labor of finding and creating genuinely caring connections with other people.

Altogether, *Memoirs of a Geisha* is a story to be seen as neither an historical drama about nor an endorsement of the geisha way of life—in the limited sense of the word as a "sex trade." Even after the scene on the cliff where she releases the Chairman's handkerchief into the wind, Sayuri's decision to return to her geisha roots, while being an affirmation of life, is neither affirmation as endorsement of geisha life nor acceptance as resignation to that way of life. It is only an acceptance of the circumstances of her fate, the fact of her geisha training, with the recognition that, through these circumstances, she will go forward, like water, with a faith that life may, in some inscrutable way, still bring her fulfillment and liberation.

But there is a sense, also, in which the geisha life serves expansively as a metaphor or allegory for life in general. Just as the geisha must not give her heart to a particular man, so also in life everyone may do well to remember that the heart must not be given up for possession by another. Ultimately, the heart belongs to life, and the deepest love must be love of life. And that love will bring with it the faith that life's inexhaustible potential for value will find a way to bring fulfillment.

The fact that the story ends happily does not transform it from tragic drama to a fairy tale. While, in one sense, the "heroic" Chairman "rescues" the threatened "damsel," each more rightly rescues or liberates the other. In the film, this is indicated in the last scene when both Sayuri and the Chairman confess a sense of shame in their actions and thereby acknowledge their mutual mistakes. Through their shared confessions they create measures of equality in love and respect. In the book, the mutual love and regard between the two emerges in a way confirming Sayuri's faith that the Chairman's quality of love for her liberates rather than constrains her. She decides it will be best for both of them if she moves to America. Although the Chairman knows this will mean they will see much less of each other, he nevertheless supports her in the decision and helps her to make the move. And this move only furthers Sayuri's growth as a woman into the personhood of making a life through choices of her own, a move enabled by the Chairman's genuine care for her and what she believes is best for herself.

Nevertheless, the hard lessons of Sayuri's past bring with them an awareness of the ever-present potential for future hardship of one kind or another, which precludes the simplistic and complacent view that life is finally a fairy tale with justice served. Life always remains potentially too harsh and unpredictable to be a fairy tale. But *Memoirs of a Geisha* reveals that despite inscrutable violence—whether abuse, rape, betrayal, bondage, objectification, or worse—the world always presents possibilities of fulfillment for resilient, persevering, and generous water-like natures.

PART II

Violence in Popular Television— Early 21st Century Samplings

9

The Sopranos
(1999–2007)

Of the multitude of screen dramas in the post–World War II era, one in particular, an iconic film, stands out as marking a point in time when a palpable reversal of fortune transpired in the traditional cultural hierarchy of mythic figures dominating the landscape of American culture. Patrick Goldstein refers to it as "the first modern American film." Roger Ebert presciently claimed, "Years from now it is quite possible that [it] will be seen as the definitive film of the 1960s" (2002: 86). Not only did it become the definitive film of the '60s, it launched a wave of successors and imitators as its ethos gripped the American imagination. It piqued individualist aspirations but did so in a striking and newly liberating way. Having written previously on this particular film (2006), that commentary and the introduction to it are worth paraphrasing here in establishing the context for examining the subject of this chapter—the most popular television crime drama of the last decade, *The Sopranos*.

If the United States was an individualist culture prior to World War II, it was only marginally so compared to the postwar period. The war initiated enormous social upheaval throughout the world as the majority of able-bodied men around the globe were uprooted from parochial lifestyles, forced to join ranks across race, class, and religion, and shipped out to foreign places where they confronted more strangeness and diversity in a few months than previously would have been encountered over many years or even lifetimes. This upheaval of humanity mixed, shuffled, and, in some cases, shattered social and cultural norms in the United States and around the world.

Following the turmoil of war, the economic boom of the 1950s and '60s accelerated individualism in the United States beyond anything foreseeable in the decades prior to the war. Fostered by democratic

114

political and capitalist economic culture combined with technological advances in media (e.g., television), individualism took root in the United States more than anywhere else in the world.

This individualism consisted primarily of a new emphasis on acquiring an identity apart from family or group affiliation—an identity unique to a personal self and for which that self is entirely responsible. And in the decades of the 1970s and '80s, class, race, ethnicity, gender, and age—while still socially significant—became much less so with regard to social status than ever before. Identity became more a personal achievement than a hereditary or social happenstance. Not surprisingly, in this social climate of individual recognition, the outlaw, the maverick, the criminal, the celebrity, the millionaire, the sports superstar, the social stand-out, the exception to the rule—in whatever form—gained social capital in having achieved a distinctiveness apart from and in addition to any ties to a group.

As a result of this continuing emphasis on identity formation separate from group membership, some observers of the American system view it as an adolescent culture—a culture perennially frozen in adolescent motives and adolescent angst. The teenage years belong to the period of exaggerated identity crisis—the period of separation during which becoming a self, an individual apart from parents and siblings, becomes an engrossing fixation. One of the clearest and most tempting ways to demonstrate individuation and separation from the system of values represented by the family is to engage in rule-breaking, consensus-breaking, or law-breaking behavior. But for many adolescents this period of identity formation becomes stressful and emotionally taxing and, rather than realizing itself through modes of individual self-actualization, it plays out through membership in a new group. Such groups include the anti-conformist, high visibility trench coat and gothic clubs and, at the extremes, the outlaw credentials of urban gangs or the quasi-tribal notoriety of skinhead neo–Nazi groups.

Consistent with the value placed on formation of a distinctive identity, the United States places a premium on innovative thinking—the kind of thinking summed up in a late 1960s phrase made popular—appropriately—in a television commercial: "thinking outside the box." Although intended to suggest transcending routine and ordinary approaches to problems, applications of the phrase may, through extension of its logic, widen to include thinking outside the box of norms and rules, beyond the boundary of codes and laws, and straight into the "outside" of criminal behavior. In a society of rampant individualism some impatient players may be tempted to "think outside the box" of its most basic laws—especially when the going gets tough or the opportunities get easy.

In America, the slippery slope leading from "thinking outside the box" to criminal behavior is sometimes lubricated by an additional slipperiness derived from over-extension of the logic conveyed in the famous 1970s bumper sticker: "Question Authority." It has become easier in the United States—more than in any other place in the world—to openly think, speak, and produce art in ways that show the traditional hero/villain alignment of the "authorities" and the "criminals" in reverse order to the extent that the "criminals" become the heroes and the "authorities" become the villains.

Within the conflict structure of drama, the criminal resembles the monster. The monster is a creature whose mere appearance often portends evil and the unnatural. But the monster, like the criminal, is not without appeal. Each exhibits a quality of freedom breath-taking in its radical departure from standard constraints and norms of society—a freedom seductive in its seeming drive to break taboos, to think *radically* outside the box. Members of society conforming to its rules may secretly admire the freedom from restraints exemplified in the criminal, and, to that extent, the criminal becomes a kind of hero. Rejecting the well-worn and often slow path to respectability, the notorious criminal finds a shortcut to heroic status in the myth-making machinery of a culture placing high value on individualism and self-actualization.

In deference to the increasing postwar identity needs among adolescents and young adults, the Hollywood filmmaking industry, along with the comic-book industry, increased production of a variation of the antagonal melodramatic plot structure. The criminal and the outcast exchange places with the establishment hero. The agent representing communal authority—usually the corporate leader, the politician, or the police—emerges as the villain, as, for example, in *Chinatown* (1974), *The Gauntlet* (1977), and *L.A. Confidential* (1997). Or an agent of the system, such as the mayor, may be portrayed as merely quasi-villainous by playing into the hands of an agent designed to symbolize pure evil (for example, a serial killer) as in *Dirty Harry* (1971). The outcast and outlaw legends—to be distinguished from the persons—of Jesse James, Doc Holliday, and Billy the Kid provided steppingstones along the path to 20th century popular hero loners, ranging from Sam Spade to The Man With No Name to Rambo.

The individualist, non-conformist narrative increased in popularity in the 1950s, taking full flight in the '60s, and has remained the dominant popular narrative into the 21st century. In a culture with identity strongly rooted in forms of self-actualization and self-expression rather than group association and group achievement, the challenge of adolescent identity crisis easily extends into adult life. This may understandably give the illusion of a culture stuck in adolescent modes of angst. But, more precisely, this culture evolves its own social pattern of recognition and exchange which, in many ways, emerges as a beneficial progression. Collective valuation of individual autonomy has its rewards through increases in social equality, individual liberties, and human-rights protections. While acknowledging these benefits, however, one need not overlook losses in social cohesiveness nor grant that every artifact pandering to individualistic culture necessarily contributes beneficially in cultural progression.

With these considerations in mind, insert into the American postwar social milieu the film *Bonnie and Clyde* (1967). This film marks the cultural turning point where the outlaw rises from secondary to primary celebrity status. Criminal protagonists become not only the stars but are portrayed—unlike previous films featuring gangsters and criminals—with considerably broader strokes of glamour and sympathy. *Bonnie and Clyde* was not unprecedented in raising criminals to star status. Some inspiration came from previous films such as Joseph H. Lewis's *Gun Crazy* (1950). But it brought a list of significant changes to a genre previously belonging to the "B" shelf of Hollywood films. Its innovations included featuring top Hollywood stars (Warren Beatty, Gene Hackman) and superb cinematography while achieving wide distribution (on its second run), good reviews, and great press (including making the cover of *Time* magazine). Its audacity surprised many and its success confounded most film critics and industry pundits.

The story is based on the lives of the famous East Texas outlaws Clyde Barrow and Bonnie Parker and their bank-robbing adventures throughout the Southern Midwest during the early 1930s. Like several other criminals and gangsters of the 1920s and '30s, Bonnie and Clyde attained a measure of favorable celebrity in the popular culture of the times because the banks they robbed were the same banks involved in foreclosures on failing family farms. Building on the Robin Hood folk-hero status of the real Bonnie and Clyde, director Arthur Penn and producer/star Warren Beatty increased the likelihood of audience identification by adding winsome Faye Dunaway to co-star.

In her book on crime films and society, Nicole Rafter rightly insists that the success of the film—in terms of its desired effects—depends vitally on viewer identification with the main characters. Rafter argues, "The key factor in the movie's success was the way viewers empathized with Bonnie and Clyde. That audiences were able to identify with what were, after all, two long-dead punks arose from the scriptwriters' skillful downplaying of the characters' negative traits and emphasis on their virtues" (2000: 156). In support of this assertion, Rafter notes that Bonnie and Clyde are portrayed with heroic traits—brave and inventive, sensitive to each other's vulnerabilities, and defiant in the face of certain death.

The conclusion of the film achieved legendary status, eclipsing the level of folk-hero fame attained by the real Bonnie and Clyde. Arthur Penn's slow-motion camera combined with real-time sound effects and squib technology (small charges wired to explode with simulated blood) added a shockingly realistic and graphic whiplash effect—an abrupt, bullet-punctuated end to the couples' quiet afternoon drive. The slow-motion, extended, blood-splattering conclusion leaves no doubt it is specifically designed to resolve any ambiguous sentiments on the part of audiences toward Bonnie and Clyde through the outrage aroused toward their brutal executioners. With this ending, the ambiguities in their character traits are sacrificed and redeemed through a fate parallel to that of depression-era farmers—victims of a system that failed them, abandoned them, and finally ambushed them in a cruel and deadly trap.

The problem with all of this arises from the fact that the characters and events are of a piece with the tinseled, reductive, and ultimately tedious form of antagonal melodrama structuring the conflict throughout the film. The failings of character evident in the protagonists' alter-ego shadows are, in fact, nothing more than reflections of what is intended to be understood as the ugly and evil system that created them.

A sinister and malevolent corruption permeates this system which makes it, rather than its criminals, the proper target for audience outrage. This theme played well at the time the film was released in 1967—a time when the radical politics of the counter-culture had emerged in protest of a perceived epidemic of evils ranging from racism, sexism, colonialism, cronyism, militarism, capitalism, fascism, deception, corruption, and moral bankruptcy—to name only the most glaring of the New Left accusations leveled against the system now pejoratively labeled The Establishment. Bonnie and Clyde reflected and fueled the structuring of the political and cultural conflict of the era in the mold of antagonal melodrama—a structure incapable of leading the way toward desired changes. Instead, popular framing of the conflict in highly antagonal terms of right and wrong, good and evil, ensured the eventual breakdown of the leading political youth organization, Students for a Democratic Society (SDS), and facilitated the logic resulting in the dissolution of SDS and the terrorism of splinter groups, such as the Weather Underground.

No one should be persuaded to believe identification with characters in a film will *not* be accompanied by a substantial tendency among viewers to approve of their attitudes and actions—not to mention their words and dress. Faye Dunaway's outfits, for example, inaugurated a popular clothing trend among women in the months after the film's successful re-release. And though it may be the case that some viewers identify with the criminal in antagonal, noir-styled melodramas to the point of imitation of violent behavior, that possibility in itself, while significant, does not constitute the primary cause for concern regarding such melodramas. The broader concern lies in effects playing to and preying on the entire viewing audience—the arousal of emotions associated with victimization combined with attitudinal conditioning toward oversimplified, inflammatory structuring of conflict with violent resolutions.

The American public, as a consequence of the influence of a strongly individualistic culture, is prone to form identifications in the right persuasive circumstances with anyone who stands out from the crowd. But films pandering to this susceptibility through depictions of glamorized gangsters acting out scenes of graphic violence through contrived, oversimplified conflict do not need to be lauded as examples of great filmmaking—as in the case of *Bonnie and Clyde*. Such films may

119

present a temptation similar to junk-food confections, but in the long run they only give individualistic culture a bad reputation—a reputation it neither needs nor deserves. But if this is the case, what rightful place in the cultural future do crime dramas have?

Films of the anti-heroic crime genre have consistently filled theaters and garnered awards and critical acclaim, as several films from prominent American directors such as Francis Ford Coppola, Martin Scorsese, and others have demonstrated over the decades since *Bonnie and Clyde*. The American Film Institute ranks Coppola's *The Godfather* (1972) #2 on its list of all-time greatest films (*Bonnie and Clyde* ranks #42). So it is not surprising that HBO's airing of the first episode of *The Sopranos* in January of 1999 met with success and continued for six seasons, becoming the most popular and financially successful series in the history of cable television. The following analysis discusses how precisely *The Sopranos*, apart from its similar popularity, succeeds as a crime drama where *Bonnie and Clyde* and many previous crime dramas fail.

Tony Soprano (James Gandolfini) (*The Sopranos*, Home Box Office, 1999–2007).

Much has been written in commentary about *The Sopranos*, not merely as a crime drama but as a notoriously *violent* crime drama. Among the many options, Open Court's Popular Culture and Philosophy series contributes *The Sopranos and Philosophy*, which presents a surprisingly readable and rewarding range of essays. The subtitle of this volume—"I Kill Therefore I Am"—cleverly situates the essays in the philosophical genre while drawing attention to the fact that violence emerges as a crucial element in the television series. This violence makes the series especially controversial. The brutal and graphically portrayed murders taking place in virtually every episode, many of them committed by the series star character, Tony Soprano (brilliantly portrayed by James Gandolfini), provide a troubling context against which to weigh the responses from major media outlets offering adulatory comments such as these:

"The best show on TV"—*Wall Street Journal*

"Television at its best"—*Denver Post*

"Just plain brilliant"—*Variety*

"One of the most profound dramas in the history of television"—*Washington Post*

"The best drama in the last half-century of TV"—*Newsday*

"TV's richest and most intriguing adult drama"—*TV Guide*

Why all the praise for a show featuring so much violence, especially in a culture where criticism of media violence has been a mantra in the last several decades? In the words placed on the back cover of *The Sopranos and Philosophy*, "Is there something ethically or psychologically damaging in the fact that millions of TV viewers regularly identify with a murderer?" Perhaps those who enjoyed *The Sopranos* have some answering to do. If so, this commentary may help.

Although most of the essays in *The Sopranos and Philosophy* volume complement each other, two in particular establish an interesting tension between ways of characterizing the series as a genre. Mike Lippman (2004) argues that *The Sopranos* contains the elements of classic tragic drama consistent with Aristotle's famous definition. Kevin Stoehr (2004, 2006), however, argues that the series takes its inspiration from and conforms to the primary features of classic noir melodramas of the pre- and post- World War II era. While there may be room to debate some overlap, these two genres are not thoroughly compatible. This incompatibility prompts the question: which better describes the kind of drama presented in *The Sopranos*? And how does the answer to that question inform concerns about the portrayal of graphic violence and its potential effects on audiences?

The Case for Tragic Drama

In making the case for tragic drama Lippman argues that Tony Soprano fits the profile drawn by Aristotle for a classic tragic hero. To qualify as tragic, the featured protagonist's plight must succeed in arousing emotions appropriate to tragedy—emotions Aristotle names as *eleos* and *phobos* (usually translated as "pity" and "fear"). As previously discussed, in order to arouse such emotions in the audience the protagonist must possess certain traits for eliciting identification. These include, especially, a quality of character permitting the audience to sense that the protagonist, while starting from high station and fortune, is similar to themselves with respect to virtues and vices and that what misfortunes descend are disproportionate to what is deserved. Furthermore, the tragic fall the protagonist undergoes transpires through self-initiated events set in motion by actions rooted in a character flaw clearly distinguishable from simple depravity. Consequently, the hero follows a trajectory neither of a good and innocent man going from good fortune to bad nor a purely evil man going from bad fortune to good. The tragic hero corresponds to what Lippman, following Aristotle, refers to as "the man in-between"—a man of average virtue experiencing a fall in fortune and having a hand in his own demise. With these conditions met, the audience can fear for the fate of the protagonist, as they would for themselves in a similar situation and experience empathy insofar as misfortune is beyond what may be deserved.

Having set forth these parameters of tragic form and character, Lippman then proceeds to show how Tony Soprano fills the requirements. As a mob boss, Tony qualifies as a man of "high station and fortune" but he also exhibits qualities inviting common comparison. For example, Lippman explains, "Despite being a cold-blooded killer, Tony does have a set of values that distinguish him from your typical Mafia psychopath and that permit the audience to look upon him with compassion" (2004: 149). These values include the "family values" of honor, loyalty, and responsibility associated with his two families—his wife, Carmela (Edie Falco) and children and his Mafia brotherhood. Tony provides and cares for his family. He presides over traditional Sunday family dinners, attends daughter Meadow's (Jamie-Lynn Sigler) soccer games, worries about son Anthony Jr., "A.J." (Robert Iler) and his lack of motivation for school, and generally attempts to be a responsible father. He also attempts to be a dutiful son to his mother, Livia (Nancy Marchand). Sensing her limitations with advancing age, he makes plans to establish her in a senior community apartment where she will have prepared meals and be more closely watched. Similarly, Tony respects and, at times, even appears to love his business associates, especially his nephew and top "soldier" Christopher (Michael Imperioli), whom he treats like a son and heir-apparent.

These family values are tribal values clearly reserved for the Mafia tribe and contrast sharply with the devaluing of the larger society beyond the tribe. This contrast results in a stark "us vs. them" division between the larger society and the crime society of Tony's mob tribe. The tension between family norms and the norms of society repeats itself in the knot between Tony's two families and the tension surrounding his attempts to reconcile them. As Lippman points out, this tension is especially evident in the episode titled "College" from the first season. Here, Tony accompanies Meadow on a trip for interviews at several New England colleges. His sweet paternalism turns rancid, however, when, unbeknownst to Meadow, he spots a man hiding under witness protection for having ratted on the family, stalks him, and brutally strangles him.

The division between family man and crime lord creates cognitive dissonance in the audience—a dissonance further fueled by Tony's strengths and likable qualities weighed against disturbing shortcomings. Lippman lists these as including philandering, hypocrisy, racism, bullying, narcissism, and a proclivity toward remorselessly using deadly violence. Nevertheless, the combination of these qualities leads Lippman to assess Tony as neither good nor evil and to conclude: "Clearly, Tony fits Aristotle's model of the tragic hero as a 'man in-between'" (2004: 150).

According to Lippman, Tony also fits Aristotle's tragic profile with respect to the tragic flaw. Lippman rightly understands that this tragic flaw must not be confused with Tony's obvious moral failings. If Tony's fall were to be associated with these failings, the audience would not feel much empathy for him. Instead, his difficulties must be seen to emerge from a more admirable side of his person—an aspect of character that also, through his own actions, contributes to his troubles and demise. Lippman argues that while "physically manifested in his panic attacks," Tony's flaw "is his inability to successfully live up to his conflicting moral roles and responsibilities" (2004: 151).

In season one, for example, the vulnerable side of Tony appears in his nurturing attitude toward the family of ducks having taken up residence in his swimming pool. When they fly away he feels (without fully realizing it) an unusual sense of loss that, combined with his panic attacks, compels him to consult a therapist. The psychiatrist, Dr. Jennifer Melfi (Lorraine Bracco), prompts him to see the ducks as representing his family. Their departure, then, signals his fear of the loss of his family. These fears are fueled when Tony's efforts to gain rapport with his mother and Uncle Corrado "Junior" (Dominic Chianese) are met not only with contempt but eventually an attempt on his life, which fails only by a stroke of luck. Additional complications presented by his nephew Christopher and his wife and kids (Meadow is preparing to "leave the nest" for college) exacerbate Tony's sense of alienation and mounting potential loss. His dutifulness toward his two families meets challenge and resistance at every turn. Consequently, he begins to feel himself on the edge of failure in every aspect of life that has meaning for him.

As it turns out, the choice of therapy only contributes to the crisis between himself and his mother and uncle. When they accidentally learn of his treatment sessions they perceive this to be a sign of weakness and a possible security leak that could threaten the family business. Lippman interprets Tony's tragic conflict with his mother and uncle as something that could have been avoided were it not for his own choices—choices which, ironically, were motivated by his attempt to avert such a crisis. Much like Oedipus, argues Lippman, Tony contributes to his own family conflict through an act designed to forestall such conflict.

The theme of family conflict, especially involving murderous intentions and actions, lies close to the heart of most Greek tragic drama. Aristotle believed conflict between family members heightens the tragic emotions of *eleos* and *phobos* because everyone can easily identify with the family and because the conflict festers within what normally serves as the primary zone of comfort and support. As Lippman points out, the dramatic tensions in *The Sopranos* feature conflicts within the families rather than between the families and the larger society. The series focuses on growing conflicts between mother and son (Livia and Tony), uncle and nephew (Corrado and Tony; Tony and Christopher), father and children (Tony and A.J.; Tony and Meadow), and an assortment of tensions and feuds within the business family—usually centering on the theme of sell-out or betrayal (as in the case of "Big Pussy" Bonpensiero [Vincent Pastore] at the end of season two).

Given the combination of the elements outlined above, including especially the arousal of *eleos* and *phobos*, the "man in-between" stature of the hero, the tragic flaw, and the family conflicts, Lippman concludes that *The Sopranos* is best understood as an instance of classic tragic drama. Even though the first season ends untragically (with Tony apparently having overcome his most pressing conflicts and difficulties), Lippman nevertheless rightly presses the point of tragic undertones:

> For Aristotle, a tragedy does not need to end badly. The mere intention of family members to do violence against each other is enough to make a tragic plot.... Despite the fact that Tony's career continues to rise, the climax[es] of each subsequent season ... all emphasize Tony's failures to succeed in his non-business life. He fails as a friend, father-figure, and husband. His Mafia lifestyle will not allow him any way to avoid disaster.... Therapy may allow us to pretend that Tony is redeemable, but even from season one we learn that Tony's personality and lifestyle will make it impossible for him to escape his destiny. In the end, Tony is bound to fall [2004: 155–156].

Even though this assessment was published before the final season of *The Sopranos*, it remains accurate regarding the trajectory of the series and especially so on at least one interpretation of the final episode. The abrupt cut to black at the restaurant as the immediate family gathers suggests "lights out" for at least Tony if not the entire family.

Although Lippman's case for placing *The Sopranos* in the genre of tragic drama seems on the surface to be adequate and persuasive, it nevertheless contains a number of holes and loose ends, suggesting something less than an ideal fit. For example, does Tony really exhibit the stature of a classic tragic dramatic hero? Are his broad moral failings so easily swept aside in favor of the tragic flaw theory of his impending fall?

The Case for Noir Drama

In describing one of the defining elements of film noir, Kevin L. Stoehr points to a creeping "devolution or dehumanization" of the main protagonist—a devolution "usually characterized by an internal descent into immorality and even amoral indifference" (2004: 40). He goes on to note, "Such a descent is almost always occasioned by external forces (such as victimizing villains or the cold whims of fate), but the suffering or fall of the protagonist is amplified in most cases because of his or her own moral ambiguities and psychological weaknesses" (2004: 40).

Though this description closely parallels the description of the tragic hero's flaw and fall, an important difference exists in the quality of the noir hero and in the dominant features of his or her world, or the world as he or she sees it. Rather than a person of high stature and average moral virtue, the noir hero belongs more properly to the category of anti-hero, having, at the outset of the drama, already suffered a kind of fall into average or diminished status while also having slipped into questionable moral virtue. Furthermore, the noir anti-hero understands the milieu, the world in which he or she operates, as essentially threatening and inhospitable to life—a milieu in which traditional social values, including the value of life itself, are diminished if not entirely lacking. As Stoehr puts it, life becomes a struggle of *"sheer survival* in a world gone wrong" (2004: 40).

Tony Soprano fits the description of the noir anti-hero. While having the stature of a mob boss, he nevertheless belongs to the fallen criminal fringe of society. And, contrary to what Lippman claims, Tony falls short of being a man of average virtue. Rather, he continually appears as a man of badly compromised virtue accompanied by few if any feelings of remorse. His apparent good side consists of haunting desires to have the American dream of a happy family man in a successful business and a willingness to abide by certain family rules to achieve that dream. He fails to see the hypocrisy in his decision to break broader social rules and laws while expecting those around him to adhere honorably to the narrower family code. This is not mere moral relativity or ambiguity. It amounts to egotism *cum* tribal centrism that divides the world into a sharply defined struggle between us and them.

Tony struggles against the persistent attitude projected by his mother, "It's all a big nothing" (as Livia expresses to A.J. in the second season episode "D-Girl"). But the emptiness of his life—the arbitrariness and meaninglessness of his daily interactions—constantly asserts itself into conscious awareness. As a physical manifestation of this awareness, his panic attacks drive him to therapy, where Dr. Melfi challenges him to unearth his deeper insecurities and growing dissatisfactions. Tony's mob life is a symptom of, as well as an ongoing contributor to, his contempt for lawful society and his sense of creeping hopelessness that life has anything of quality to offer him.

Taking a cue from 19th century German philosopher Friedrich Nietzsche, Stoehr defines this broad negative attitude toward life as *nihilism*. For Stoehr, nihilism of character and scene—the alienation from a set of values in the anti-hero and the corruption of traditional values in society—comprise the key elements of film noir. This individual and collective disintegration operates for the noir characters in their perceptions, regardless of what the truth may be about themselves or the larger society in which they live. In Tony's case the encroachment of this general nihilism into the fabric of life does not stop at the boundary between society and his tribe. The pressure from the society in the form of law enforcement (however corrupt and arbitrary in its application) combined with the in-fighting of mob family factions leaves Tony with an incessant anxiety about the presence of a rat—a betrayal from within the tribe.

This concern on Tony's part emerges in the first episode of season one when Tony speaks to Melfi of his admiration for Gary Cooper as "the strong silent type." Tony laments the corruption of values within the mob. In times past "made men" would take jail time rather than rat on an associate. Now, according to Tony, guys "have no room for the penal experience" (Yacowar, 2007: 22). This fear of betrayal becomes reality when Tony discovers that "Big Pussy" Bonpensiero has been cooperating with the FBI. His execution aboard Tony's boat in the last episode of season two ("Funhouse") reinforces the need for vigilance among the remaining members of his crew and confirms their strong sense of encroaching corruption.

As already mentioned, the fear of corruption and betrayal extends not only to business associates but to the blood family. In season one, Tony's mother and uncle betray him and in the remaining seasons he experiences constant concern about his immediate family as Carmela seeks divorce, Meadow pursues law school (and potential further disillusionment with his criminal ways), and A.J. slips into apathy and indifference toward him and everything else. At every level of life—society, business, family, and self—Tony experiences alienation, disintegration, and loss. The accumulation of events through the final season takes him eventually back to the empty swimming pool at his house that the ducks abandoned long ago, in the first episode. The inability to achieve any form of healthy community imparts a profound sense of nothingness. His trajectory through the series leads Stoehr to conclude, "Tony comes to revel in his own resentment, self-loathing, alienation, duplicity, fragmentation, and general life-negation. Like mother, like son" (2004: 46).

Tony's fall transpires through forms of self-imposed blindness and flawed reactions to events. For these reasons Stoehr finds that Tony and *The Sopranos* conform nicely to the tradition of film noir—with perhaps a postmodern flair for self-fragmentation and semi-conscious capitulation to decay:

> If Tony had been consistently unaware of his moral failings due to sheer ignorance or irrationality, then we could fault him at most for being little more than an instinctual animal, wreaking havoc whenever his appetites are aroused. But with a growing recognition of his need for therapy and reflection, Tony shows himself to be worse than a merely savage animal. Tony's increasing neglect of his moral character and its required cultivation is done self-consciously, with an awareness of the conventional importance of values as well as the traditional difference between right and wrong. Therapy has taught him to strive for self-knowledge, but he has instead become true to the very worst aspects of himself.... He substitutes psychology for ethics to suit his own selfish purposes. Subsequently he continues to feel lost amidst the moral wasteland [2004: 47].

Stoehr's analysis of Tony's character as a morally bankrupt antihero with a dash of anxious self-reflection in a bleak and corrupt social landscape exposes the weakness of Lippman's account of *The Sopranos* as classic tragic drama. But Stoehr's assessment also leaves nagging questions. Is the social landscape of *The Sopranos* entirely nihilistic? Do all the main characters fit the description of moral compromise and corruption?

A Genre Beyond Film Noir and Nihilism

At one point in his discussion of *The Sopranos*, Stoehr expresses the idea that, viewed from a crime drama or outlaw social perspective, the series presents an ongoing tension between heroes and villains. But while external villains make their appearance and exit, the dominant tension turns inside. For example, Stoehr remarks, "While the *external* villains in Tony's life change from season to season, the *internal* villain in his life remains ever-present: his inability to take account of *his own* moral decline, even while obsessing about the weaknesses of others" [emphasis in original] (2004: 46).

Melodrama acquires noir shades when the hero, portrayed as hard-boiled and morally ambiguous, projects an anti-heroic image (for example, Humphrey Bogart as anti-hero in *The Maltese Falcon* [1941]). This image nevertheless emerges as heroic when cast against a character or characters portrayed as unequivocally evil. Antagonal psychomelodrama turns to shades of noir when the internal conflict in the featured character swings toward the dominance of the morally dubious or malevolent end of the scale (for example, Edward G. Robinson in *Scarlet Street* [1945]).

Weighing these varieties of melodrama, *The Sopranos* would appear to fit the category of noir psychomelodrama insofar as the featured protagonist, Tony Soprano, qualifies as an anti-hero whose weaknesses of character contribute to increasing sociopathic decline unmitigated by redeeming actions. However, as Stoehr points out, speaking in general of the genre of film noir, nihilism as a collapse of traditional values permeates not only the psychic interior of the hero but also the exterior scene, the social fabric within which he or she functions. "Nihilism [of film noir] signals not only the collapse of values (both within and without) but also the loss of personal unity or wholeness" (2004: 42). Consequently, the cast of primary characters in film noir productions seldom includes anyone who provides a challenge to the anti-hero's way of framing self and world. The nihilism of film noir generally projects a dark (if not disturbing) cynicism toward life, while providing few (if any) reasons for hopefulness or optimism about the human condition.

The broad nihilism of film noir, however, does not entirely mesh with the dramatic structure of *The Sopranos*. One of the primary characters, Dr. Melfi, offers a compelling contrast to Tony Soprano and the ensemble of Mafia characters. Melfi offers a lifeline for Tony—as well as the audience—to the larger and more complex society beyond the constricted boundaries of crime families. In fact, Melfi is such an important piece of *The Sopranos* series that, without her, the drama would be essentially altered into something quite different—a drama centered within the tradition of film noir, perhaps to the extremity of reverse antagonal melodrama.

At various points in the series, through the help of Melfi, Tony seems on the edge of a breakthrough insight that might help him turn his life around. But, invariably, he misses the chance, turns the insight in a way reinforcing or facilitating his old ways, and falls more deeply into the morass of his life of decadence and crime. As the series progresses, others who appear to have a chance of escaping Tony's circle—such as his wife, Carmela, and his son and daughter as well as his nephew Christopher—all get sucked back into the crime life through combinations of turns of fate and poor choices indicative of weaknesses of character.

Dr. Jennifer Melfi (Lorraine Bracco), a character of admirable virtue (*The Sopranos*, Home Box Office, 1999–2007).

Having accepted Tony as a client, Melfi also exposes herself to the corruption of the mob. Rather than helping him toward a better life, it seems possible that she may be led down a spiraling path toward her own moral decline and, perhaps, ultimate demise at the hands of the mob. In writing of the second season, Maurice Yacowar, for example, comments on her growing compulsive behavior and alcoholism:

> Melfi's disintegration proves Tony destructive. Under his unintentional influence even someone of Melfi's sensitivity, knowledge, wisdom, and both psychological and moral self-awareness proves helpless. She breaks down from trying to bridge the abyss between Tony's charm and his evil [2007: 114].

But, with a decisive episode in the third season ("Employee of the Month"), it becomes clear who Melfi is and the quality of character she presents in the face of intense temptation. In this episode, Melfi is brutally raped in the stairwell of her office parking garage. The rapist is apprehended but then released on a legal technicality (a misplaced evidence kit). Melfi later discovers him working at a local fast-food restaurant where his employers, oblivious to his connection with the rape, have honored him as "employee of the month" because of his good work habits. The help of her ex-husband, her son, and a lawyer proves insufficient to bring the rapist to justice.

Melfi understands that by soliciting Tony's help she could, if she wanted, have the rapist "squashed like a bug." In a session with Tony following the rape, she breaks down as Tony consoles her while inquiring about her bruises and her damaged knee. At this point she's strongly tempted to reveal to him what happened but ultimately resists, telling him she fell down a flight of stairs. She conquers the desire for illegal justice and thereby avoids what could have been one major step toward the descent into complicity with Tony's world and his antagonal attitudes toward life and society. Despite this decision Melfi remains vulnerable to Tony and his world as she decides to continue seeing him as a client instead of following the advice of her own therapist. He tells her that in seeing Tony she succeeds only in enabling a hard-core sociopath. In remaining episodes Melfi's commitment to help Tony progressively wanes until, at the end of the last season, she finally chooses to abandon the task, apparently convinced by a recent clinical study that sociopaths are beyond therapeutic intervention.

Summarizing Melfi's predicament regarding her rage toward the rapist and her decision to withhold taking revenge, Yacowar points out her close call and its broader symbolic implications: "If this elegant psychiatrist cannot control her anger then that other great experiment— civilization—will also have failed" (2007: 138). On the one hand, Tony symbolizes a primitive and fanatical tribal consciousness, breaking the world into polarized factions of good and evil relatively positioned along the axis of "us" and "them." On the other hand, Melfi represents a more evolved social consciousness—what Yacowar refers to as "civilization." This consciousness aligns with a complex understanding of justice, one that appeals to and applies law with a more even and inclusive compass.

While the dichotomy of good and evil dividing Tony's world might seem to stand the scale of good and evil on its head, from Tony's point of view the factions of good and evil are clear and radically polarized. Within his clan, members are either with him or against him and any ambiguity concerning loyalty will, in his eyes, quickly reduce to a betrayal meriting a response of deadly violence. In this sense his picture of society and the world is highly antagonal and melodramatic, which further suggests the possibility that *The Sopranos* is a variety of melodrama. The series would, perhaps, fit the profile of classic melodrama if Melfi were the featured protagonist pitted against Tony as the villain. But since Tony is the featured protagonist and, as discussed, a man of compromised virtue, then Stoehr is correct to place *The Sopranos* more in the tradition of noir cinema. However, since Melfi models a character of admirable virtue and, in her actions and in her therapy sessions, provides a lens through which to weigh and assess Tony's character, the audience is presented with a drama qualifying as something less than the blunt nihilism of film noir.

Insofar as Tony presents a character dividing the world into melodramatic extremes (however self-serving or tribal-serving that may be) and insofar as Melfi presents a character who casts light on the limitations and outright destructiveness of Tony's code and worldview, then *The Sopranos* constitutes a drama profoundly questioning antagonal polarization as an ethic of life. A good part of the indictment of this ethic of life, recalling Melfi's brush with rage and desire for deadly vengeance, relates to questioning order enforced through vigilante (as opposed to due process) violence. Within this antagonal melodramatic ethic, identifying someone as a threatening evil removes all restrictions for the use of deadly violence—indeed, it strips individuals of humanity and categorizes them as fit for slaughter.

Since *The Sopranos*—through the dramatization of Tony's world view—draws attention to antagonal structuring precisely in order to question that mode of structuring and responding to conflict, it calls for a another label. The reflexive nature of this drama—as melodrama fixing a critical eye on itself—places it in the category of reflexive or synagonal melodrama.

Synagonal melodrama resembles tragic drama in its depiction of conflict as complex. It ultimately induces identification with all sides of multi-layered conflict. Through identification with Tony, antagonal alignments form early in the series as viewers see how he deploys such alignments. But as the series progresses, these alignments come under pressure and eventually collapse for viewers.

Synagonal melodrama resembles noir drama in this case by featuring a troubled hero (or anti-hero) who exists in a world perceived to be fallen due to the decay of tradition—a perception which leads the anti-hero to the edge of despair. But contrary to what Stoehr maintains, the despair and nihilism ("It's all a big nothing") Tony feels is not so much a result of a descent into moral relativism as a confrontation with the complexity of moral choice. Tony must constantly face the fact that *life is much more complicated than he would like it to be*. He nevertheless interprets this complication as a sign of the decay of the "old values"—the simplicity of antagonal alignments and clarity of action. His awakening to complexity, symbolized by his panic attacks, prompts him to seek the help that turns up in the person of Melfi.

Looking toward literary tradition, Herman Melville's *Moby-Dick* counts as one of the most prominent examples of reflexive melodrama. Given a classically melodramatic reading, the white whale appears as the symbol and embodiment of evil, a demonic will bent solely on destruction and against whom Ahab's heroic dying efforts are directed. But the tale, as Melville tells it, finally elicits a viewpoint from which the whale appears as the unfortunate victim of Ahab's misguided and fanatical persecution. What functions as evil in *Moby-Dick* turns out to be more the *idea* of evil, the notion of deadly defilement operative in Ahab's worldview, which includes his self-understanding. This idea of evil and its scapegoating effects may well be what Melville wants to single out for exceptional attention in his story.

Insofar as the whale becomes heroic, the hero/villain roles of Ahab and the whale are reversed. But this reversal is not a simple reversal within melodramatic form. Instead the reversal accomplishes a radical reversal of reader orientation. It succeeds in altering antagonal structure by placing the structure itself in question. When Ahab, as scapegoater, follows the fanaticism of his conviction to the point of making himself a victim for the whale, the entire mechanism of scapegoating is itself exposed and brought into question.

In *The Sopranos*, Tony is Ahab and the whale is the shadow side of himself lurking below the waters of his conscious horizon. Tony's family—his kin, business associates, and Melfi as a kind of Ishmael— sail together on Tony's *Pequod*, or ship of fate. Melfi gets out alive but the others go down with the ship. Like Ishmael, Melfi helps tell the story of Tony's shadow (whale) side—the side that has him troubled about who he is and what he is doing to the degree that it threatens the essence of who and what he is. Like the white whale for Ahab, Tony's shadow side seems to him to be evil, something which threatens his power, identity, and purpose. But, also like the white whale, this shadow side of Tony may be something he fears for wrongful reasons. It may be instead, as Melfi attempts to lead him to see, a good he ignores or per- secutes perversely at his own expense. Like Ahab before him, even though he seems to actively seek the whale he also actively hides from it. Through every opportunity of encounter with the whale, Ahab chooses to cast a harpoon into it just as Tony chooses to sabotage his personal growth every time Melfi leads him to the door of self- awareness.

Following the tradition of reflexive melodrama, *The Sopranos* is an American masterpiece. It minutely details, in every aspect of life and relationship, the destructiveness of the polarized structuring of conflict inherent in exclusionary tribalism, "us vs. them" logic, and "take no prisoners" violence characteristic of the antagonal melodramatic organ- ization of the world and its associated meaning of evil. This type of drama also illustrates the close parallels between external conflict and internal conflict and the sense in which it can be difficult in such cases to draw lines between drama and psychodrama.

Effects of the Portrayal of Violence

Given the stark realism of the presentation of mob personalities and mob life in *The Sopranos*, one of the more controversial elements of its production emerges in its depictions of violence. The question may arise among many viewers: Why should *The Sopranos* be considered high art when it traffics in graphic, gratuitous, shock-value sex and violence? The answer to this question, as has been argued throughout this book, turns on contextual factors. Dramatic context shapes the way portrayed violence may be experienced by an audience.

Stanley Kubrick offers a particularly apt description of the mechanism of antagonal melodrama:

> Heroic violence in the Hollywood sense is a great deal like the motivational researchers' problem in selling candy. The problem with candy is not to convince people that it's good ... but to free them from the guilt of eating it. We have seen so many times that the body of a film serves merely as an excuse for motivating a final blood-crazed slaughter by the hero of his enemies, and at the same time to relieve the audience's guilt of enjoying this mayhem" [Bailey, 1972: 22].

In synagonal tragic drama, on the other hand, evil is never so clearly depicted that it can be readily assigned to one or the other side of the featured conflict. Led to see measures of legitimacy among the sides of conflict, the audience experiences the tragic dimension of violence. Similar to synagonal tragic drama, synagonal melodrama elicits emotions inconsistent with a celebratory experience of violence. In the case of *The Sopranos*, every instance of the depiction of violence throughout the entire series occurs in a dramatic context eliciting a strong sense of revulsion and sadness rather than celebration or vindication. Violence in *The Sopranos* occurs in contexts designed to generate dramatic irony whereby the audience sees with insight beyond the perspective of any one character—insight invariably exposing the destructiveness of violence in the lives and relationships of the perpetrators. In this regard the series is a monumental achievement in the degree to which it places a magnifying glass on every minute caustic ramification of mob-family tribalism—a tribalism moving on waves of narrow partisanship, coercion, extortion, and violence.

For example, in the previously mentioned episode titled "College" from the first season, Tony takes his daughter, Meadow, to New England for college interviews. The strangling of a man who ratted on the mob family is then placed in the context of this fatherly activity. The jarring conjunction of these two events creates cognitive dissonance in viewers which then contributes to the process of drawing viewers toward deeper questioning of identification with Tony and, also, deeper questioning of identification with his way of structuring the relationship between his families and the larger society.

Similarly, nudity and sexually explicit scenes occur in contexts revealing the way in which the attitudes and behaviors of the protagonists degrade the experience of the body and objectify women. The explicit language often used in the series also contributes toward the overall achievement of dramatic irony by exposing how the choice of crude language works invidiously to degrade the quality of the experiences and relationships within and around the two families.

The Sopranos presents a disturbing realism of violence. But, unlike graphically portrayed violent antagonal melodrama, the series offers realism that is admirable in the thoroughness with which it avoids the pitfalls of trite effects as it exposes the inescapably corrosive side of violence. The series is especially commendable in consistently disclosing how the facile deployment of murder in the service of short-sighted gain fundamentally links to life attitudes serving only to repeatedly spawn sadness, nihilism, and despair. *The Sopranos* demonstrates how television drama may transcend the usual fare of violence for the sake of shock-value ratings appeal with violence framed in ways coaching deeper insight into the complexity of life's choices, challenges, and conflicts.

10

Boardwalk Empire
(2010–)

The success of *The Sopranos* no doubt weighed persuasively in the minds of HBO executives when pondering the merits of a proposed series based on Nelson Johnson's book *Boardwalk Empire: The Birth, High Times, and Corruption of Atlantic City*. The book presents a history of Atlantic City during the Prohibition era, detailing the criminal operations of the Atlantic City treasurer Enoch L. Johnson (no relation to author Nelson Johnson). It also helped the decision process that Terence Winter backed the project as creator, writer, and executive producer, since Winter served as a writer and executive producer for *The Sopranos*. When Martin Scorsese agreed to join the crew for the series and direct the pilot, all switches were set for rolling full steam ahead in production of the show. Funding was never a problem for the series and, consequently, important pieces fell into place, including a star cast featuring Steve Buscemi as "Nucky" Thompson (the character based on Enoch Johnson) and sets and production standards equaling those of feature films. With this kind of backing and talent (and considering the praise given herein for Winter's *Sopranos* and Scorsese's *Shutter Island*), it would seem the HBO series *Boardwalk Empire* could not fail as quality drama.

Nevertheless, Winter and Scorsese clearly do not understand what was achieved in *The Sopranos* and in *Shutter Island*, respectively. The failure of their work in *Boardwalk Empire* gives clear indication that the quality of the dramatic structure of these previous screen dramas was likely an accident with respect to their artistic choices and not a structure achieved through their conscious efforts and designs. *Boardwalk Empire* regresses into the glamorization of criminal figures and the skewed dramatic structure of reverse antagonal melodrama, wherein anti-heroes

Margaret Schroeder (Kelly Macdonald) falls prey to the corrupt temptations of Enoch Thompson (Steve Buscemi) (*Boardwalk Empire*, Home Box Office, 2010–).

occupy center stage and emerge as celebrities in the absence of adequate contrapuntal characters.

Again, it should be reiterated that violent dramas featuring anti-hero types need not include shining contrapuntal heroes as if to offset the potential for immoral or unethical messages. For the sake of engaging conflict and adequate framing of violence, such dramas do, however, require interaction with persons of sufficient insight and strength of character to force a confrontation by anti-heroic characters with the side of themselves they have succeeded in burying. Lacking such confrontations, these dramatic forms fall into the category of drama Aristotle described as "simply odious," whereby corrupt characters succeed in corruption or go from corruption to further corruption, including the corruption of other characters.

Although it may be possible to question the moral influence of such dramas, that is not the issue of focus in this critique. Instead, the issue concerns quality of conflict and the context conflict provides for the portrayal of violence. Stories of neutral or corrupt characters descending into corruption and greater corruption in violence against each other cannot provide engaging conflict because witnessing corruption versus corruption traffics in merely shock-value violence and voyeuristic pleasures. When primary characters progressively appear as scoundrels and the primary conflicts as treachery between crooks, viewers are deprived of dramatic conflict in which anything of genuine value is at stake. Furthermore, as discussed in the chapter on *The Brave One*, viewers are inclined to identify with featured characters in a drama and this inclination may generate strong yet hazardous identifications among marginalized viewers.

In his insightful inquiry into contemporary film titled *Cinema of Excess: Extremes of the National Mind on Film*, Mike King draws from Aristotle when identifying the kind of balance necessary for maintaining quality drama when highlighting extreme characters. Referring to Aristotle, King describes what must be kept in mind:

> His instincts for good drama are made all the more clear when he says that "Those who employ spectacular means to create a sense not of the terrible but only of the monstrous, are strangers to the purpose of Tragedy." This distinction between the terrible and the monstrous is perhaps one of the sharpest tools he bequeaths us in our examination of extreme cinema. The terrible for Aristotle has to provoke pity and fear, as he defines them, while the monstrous—and here we will also use the term "grotesque"—is mere titillation [2009: 12].

With respect to the terms used herein, the "terrible" aligns with the synagonal and the tragic while the "monstrous" aligns with what has been called reverse antagonal melodrama. Dramas of this reverse antagonal type may escape a dilution of genuine dramatic conflict, not by re-scripting reductively back in the direction of traditional hero/villain narratives, but by re-scripting productively toward synagonal psychodramas. In psychodrama the primary conflict lies in competing motives and desires within the anti-heroic character; these internal personas are then drawn into greater confrontation by a contrapuntal character serving as catalyst. Dr. Jennifer Melfi, for example, serves this function in the dramatic structure of *The Sopranos*.

In *Boardwalk Empire*, the character who comes closest to serving a contrapuntal function is Margaret Schroeder (Kelly Macdonald). She begins as a member of the Women's Christian Temperance Union

(WCTU) but eventually becomes the mistress of Enoch Thompson (Steve Buscemi). Unlike Melfi, who is tempted to accept help from Tony Soprano but refuses, Margaret moves progressively deeper into the web of Thompson's corruption as she eventually becomes his wife—even after learning of the extent of his corrupt dealings and how he arranged her previous husband's murder. All of the characters in the series, including Margaret, fall like wounded aircraft in a descending spiral which they—or anyone around them—seem incapable of interrupting. The scriptwriters miss (as of the end of season three, the time of this writing) a great opportunity to construct a powerful conflict around the relationship between Margaret and Enoch. Adequately seizing this opportunity could have led to cracking open the psyches of both characters by deepening their internal conflicts and self confrontations. Focused penetration into the psychology of these two characters and drawing them into greater conflict with themselves, not to mention each other, would have raised the drama to the level of complexity and balance of *The Sopranos*.

Instead, *Boardwalk Empire*, as is routinely the case with anti-hero–centered crime dramas, dwells too thoroughly on the sensationalistic elements of sex and violence. It panders to the pleasures of key-hole peaking into the lives of nasty, brutish people whose behavior would be of little interest were it not for the saucy mix of power and money with sex and violence. This kind of material may provide a guilty pleasure in the gratification of human tendencies to be drawn to the spectacle of train wrecks and analogous human disasters, but these diversions do not come without associated cultural costs—namely the deadening of sensibilities toward genuinely engaging conflict and drama. The Golden Globe Award for Best Dramatic Series given for the first season of *Boardwalk Empire* has not been repeated for subsequent seasons, indicating that even the capricious Hollywood Foreign Press Association tired of the show's descending spiral.

The question of what counts as great drama, drama worthy of nominations and awards, is, of course, an interesting and important issue touched on above when mentioning Aristotle's distinction between the terrible and the monstrous. The postmodern culture of America has seemingly lost its way on this issue. To illustrate the point, imagine a story with a plot roughly like this: Once upon a time an ordinary guy is born into a family of thieves, extortionists, and drug runners who kill those who get in their way. He remains apart from this life for a while but, as a young man, he falls in with the temptations of money and power offered by his family and takes up a leadership role. Eventually becoming thoroughly corrupt himself, he threatens and kills members of his family and builds a nefarious empire on their bones and those of many others who get in his way.

Now imagine a slightly different version of this story: Once upon a time an ordinary guy is born into a family of thieves, extortionists, etc. He remains on the edge of his family life for a while, participating in a branch of their criminal activity. As part of a long-term strategy, his family persuades him to enroll in law school to better learn how to use the law to their criminal ends. At law school, however, he struggles over how to proceed with his life because he both hates and grudgingly admires his father. But, eventually, he becomes a deputy attorney general and indicts, prosecutes, and jails members of his family. All of this transpires at great cost to himself and his immediate family.

Each story portrays conflict between blood relations and within family networks. In light of Aristotle's opinion that conflict between family members presents potential for the most profound and engaging kind of conflict, it would seem both stories are candidates for great drama. But this overlooks an additional requirement that Aristotle sets forth. The chief protagonist must be a person whose fate audiences can be brought to care about. Tony Soprano's ongoing struggle with himself dramatized in Dr. Melfi's sessions and in his dissatisfaction with his life contrasts with the character of Nucky Thompson. Nucky clearly enjoys his life and appears to live without internal conflict. The scene in the final episode of season two, when he kills former associate Jimmy Darmody (Michael Pitt), memorably illustrates not only Nucky's lack of critical introspection, but also the pride he takes in having neither introspection nor regrets about his actions. The following excerpt from this scene begins with Nucky and Jimmy facing each other in the pouring rain, with Eli and two of Nucky's men watching. Nucky has just answered Jimmy's question about who will kill him by pulling a gun from his coat and saying he will do it.

Jimmy: My first time I vomited after. Two days straight. Second time I didn't even think about it.

Nucky: ... so f***ing stupid...

Jimmy: Just try to make yourself calm.

Nucky: You had everything going...

Jimmy: Breathe, Nuck...

Nucky: ...your whole life...

Jimmy: You'll get through it. All you got to worry about is when you run out of booze and you run out of company and the only person left to judge you is your ... (*his words are cut off as Nucky shoots him in the face. Nucky then walks over to him as he lies in the rain, choking on blood, but not yet dead.*)

Nucky: (*Standing over Jimmy, pointing his gun at him.*) You don't know me, James. You never did. (*Speaking emphatically, punctuating each word*) I AM NOT SEEKING FORGIVENESS! (*Nucky then finishes him with another bullet to the head.*)

Boardwalk Empire, like the first version of the crime story given above, cannot count as great drama because it does not present great conflict. In the first version crime story no great conflict arises either within the family members or within the psyche of the protagonist who starts out as the ordinary guy. The killing of members of the crime family counts more as despicable quarreling among a band of scoundrels rather than great conflict since they fight only over *how* to go forward not *whether* to go forward with the family criminal business.

In the second version of the story, however, conflict between family members becomes significant and engaging when blood ties pull members together and competing values pull them apart. When adding to this mix a lead character with whom audience members can strongly identify—a character with weaknesses but also a significant measure of admirable strengths—and an opposing character with some admirable traits within the family, the result is engaging and memorable drama.

The attempt to make great drama from stories such as offered in the first version above requires a dramatist, having constructed no basis for engaging conflict, to assume the mantle of an alchemist and somehow transform lead into gold. However, the Academy of Motion Picture Arts and Sciences and the American Film Institute appear to believe that Francis Ford Coppola managed such an alchemical feat. The first story, outlined above, roughly describes the trajectory of *The Godfather*. The Academy awarded it Best Picture in 1972 and the AFI currently ranks it as the second greatest film of all time. But if persuaded by the analyses herein, the Academy and the AFI mistake fool's gold for gold.

Cinematic portraits of crime families are easy to make and view because crime families offer copious fodder for violence as explosive and magnetically irresistible as a train wreck. *Boardwalk Empire* joins a long list of previous crime dramas selling out to the pornography of corruption and failing to offer engaging conflict. This failure, even with the talent of experienced writers and producers, proves that it is not so easy to take crime drama material and make it into good drama, as was successfully done in the case of *The Sopranos.*

11

Breaking Bad
(2008–2013)

In its first season, *Breaking Bad* scored highly with critics and audiences and has since increased in acclaim and popularity with each season. As another crime series centered on the lives of criminals, it has been compared favorably with *The Sopranos*. Unlike Tony Soprano, however, the lead character in *Breaking Bad*, Walter White (Bryan Cranston), begins as a law-abiding citizen and then moves into crime. He is motivated to do so after discovering he has inoperable lung cancer. This news overwhelms him because it comes in addition to his wife's pregnancy with their second child and the cerebral palsy illness of their first child, teenage son Walter Jr. (RJ Mitte). Faced with his family needs, combined with the extraordinary expense of cancer treatment and unlikely favorable outcome, he feels pressed to find some way to provide for his family in the event of his death.

While doing a ride-along one day with his brother-in-law Hank Schrader (Dean Norris), who is a federal drug enforcement agent, Walter recognizes a former student of his, Jesse Pinkman (Aaron Paul), leaving the scene of a crime. The crime scene turns out to be a methamphetamine lab. Being a high school chemistry teacher, Walter's wheels begin turning. He succeeds in enlisting Jesse's help to create his own lab to make and sell meth around Albuquerque. By doing so, he believes he can earn the money he needs to pay for his medical expenses and leave a substantial nest egg for his family.

Initially, the meth plan seems simple enough. Cook the meth, sell it, and bank the money. But all three steps lead to complications which Walter, due to his inexperience in the criminal drug world, is ill-equipped to anticipate. Nevertheless, while obviously intelligent, Walter also proves to be tough, resilient, and a quick study at figuring out the

Jesse Pinkman (Aaron Paul, left) educates his former science teacher Walter White (Bryan Cranston) in the ways of the drug world (*Breaking Bad*, AMC Network Entertainment, 2008–2013).

protocol required for surviving in the underworld of drug trafficking. For each setback encountered he finds resourceful solutions—solutions, however, which leave a growing trail of dead bodies.

This kind of plot—an ordinary man "breaking bad"—contains extraordinary dramatic possibilities, as many great storytellers of the past, including Dostoyevsky, have discovered and explored. As with *Boardwalk Empire* and the relationship between Enoch and Margaret, the relationship between Walter and his wife, Skyler (Anna Gunn), presents grand opportunities for riveting internal conflict paralleling external conflict. Although growing pressures between Walter and Skyler are an important element of interest early in the *Breaking Bad* series, Skyler, like Margaret of *Boardwalk Empire*, resists at first but slowly descends into the role of accomplice with Walter. Also like Tony Soprano's wife, Carmela, Skyler finds herself increasingly cornered, compromised, and co-opted into the growing circumference of Walter's corruption and madness. Consequently, the tension between Skyler and Walter gradually loses kinetic potential and, along with it, the steam to pressure Walter into confronting the ugly person he is becoming. The potential for internal conflict never materializes for Walter or Skyler.

Similar to *Boardwalk Empire*, the characters descend into deepening spirals of corruption and deadly crime. Viewers are left wondering why they should continue watching. The only thing left to find out relates to the degree of ingenuity required to continue a life of crime reaping only blood-stained rewards and rising risks for a man and wife who, even if they caught a break, would not deserve it. With Skyler and other characters failing to provide serious contrapuntal braking action on Walter's runaway train to hell, the deadly violence he engineers assumes a progressively uglier appearance until those who may have begun the series rooting for his success are left breathless at the scene of an enormous train wreck. But the wreck is too predictably sick to evoke pathos. Instead, viewers are likely to be left with a sensation similar to having single-handedly eaten a bag of donuts—it seemed like a good idea going down but ends up not sitting well.

These reservations regarding *Breaking Bad* aside, there remains an even more troubling element of this dramatization of crime. Methamphetamine is among the most dangerously addictive, potentially life-wrecking and life-threatening illegal drugs in underground circulation. Basing a television series on the manufacture and sale of this drug presents high potential for downside effects. This concern rises especially when the show plays loose in depiction of niceties of the manufacture, distribution, and money laundering sides of such operations. *Breaking Bad* too often provides provocative information regarding these details.

For example, in one episode Walter, Jesse, and two other accomplices devise a scheme to steal a chemical they need from a rail tanker. This episode tracks the entire process of the theft from beginning to end along with the ruse used to delay the train while the tanker is drained. In another episode, Walter and Jesse conspire with a house fumigation business to use a series of vacated and quarantined houses as temporary meth labs. The depiction of these particular schemes in a television show may not necessarily provide blueprints that criminal (or pre-criminal) minds in the real world may be able to use, but they undoubtedly provide inspiration for creative thinking along similar lines.

Beyond the copycat potential, another concern arises from the general idea of "breaking bad" for methamphetamine manufacture. Contrary to what producers of the show may imagine, a few viewers may still exist in television land who may not know how easy it is for someone in a legitimate business, such as house fumigation, to adapt the business to criminal operations for the purpose of making a sideline fortune. Stimulation of creative thinking in the business of methamphetamine manufacturing by "advertising" examples of it on widely viewed prime-time television amounts to another set of prompts for meth production that neither communities nor police need. This point gains additional force when considering that mere profit and amusement serve as the primary purposes for such television shows.

Showtime's *Weeds* (2005–2012), featuring marijuana, was a similarly edgy and questionable experiment in entertainment values. But possession of small amounts of "weed" has been legalized in some states. Methamphetamine is not marijuana. It is something else entirely. The manufacture and sale of it is a far more corrosive societal problem than marijuana use (though the effects of marijuana in current superbud strengths is nothing to ignore, especially in the teenage market).

Viewing entertainment portrayal of crime more generally, the American appetite for amusement derived from television shows presenting minute details of crimes seems voracious given the long-running success of the *CSI* franchise. In *CSI* and the *Miami* and *New York* spin-offs, the technology of crime-scene investigation stars in such spectacular fashion that the lead characters disappear into the background—in the latter two cases, though, not without an assist from poor casting and weak writing. The fad of crime-scene investigation has become so popular that many public high schools now offer an elective class for basic training. But the prospects for creating future generations swamped with law-enforcement cadets and crime-scene investigation experts courts a Faustian bargain. Potential also exists for training future criminals in the art of avoiding detection.

For example, after senselessly murdering a defenseless ten-year-old girl in Colorado, one 17-year-old student of CSI techniques attempted to avoid detection by dismembering her body and then burying her parts. His attempt to avoid detection failed only when his mother grew suspicious of his behavior and called the police (Pow, 2012). This is just one case, but it illustrates the potential double edge of using CSI technology for purposes of entertainment.

Breaking Bad offers an analogous kind of unnecessary information and stimulation in the entertainment world in addition to the risks presented in its framing of violence. As a case in point, the surviving member of the two Boston Marathon bombing suspects, Dzhokhar Tsarnaev, posted the following tweet on January 16, 2013: "*Breaking Bad* taught me how to dispose of a corpse." No evidence exists that Tsarnaev actually disposed of any corpses using the method depicted in this series, but the kind of impression the show made on him clearly emerges in this tweet. As all evidence now indicates Tsarnaev's participation in the Boston Marathon bombing and subsequent gun battles, he need not be understood to have been merely expressing a joke in this tweet. Other tweets on *Breaking Bad* include the comments, "Daaam cuuuh walter forced it this episode" (August 26, 2012) and, just two days before the bombing, "It [*Game of Thrones*] is a good show but breaking bad we can relate to a little bit more, I like meth" (April 13, 2013) (Amira and Becket, 2013). Friends of Tsarnaev have reported how shocked they were to learn of his involvement in gun battles and bombings. According to some, he seemed quite normal—pleasant, friendly, and unlikely to even know how to use a gun. But now it is fair to ask to what extent a television show such as *Breaking Bad* may have contributed to his attitude toward conflict and the choice of violence as the preferred means for achieving whatever change he wanted to see in the world. Too little is known at this time to make too much of the possible influence of the series on Tsarnaev, but it can be safely said it applied scant braking action to thoughts of crime and violence.

Breaking Bad's creator, Vince Gilligan, explains that his motivation for creating the series grew from his desire to experiment with a character who radically changes in the course of the series. His thoughts about the nature of the change consistently gravitated toward the progression of a character from nice guy to really bad guy. How bad is Walter White? When asked if there might be a fifth season for the show, Gilligan replied, "It's hard to write a character that dark and morally ambiguous. I'm going to miss the show when it's over, but on some level, it'll be a relief to not have Walt in my head anymore" (Silverman, 2011). Those who have never seen the show may have good reason to take consolation in the show's departure. Walter White will not be in fans' heads anymore. At least not until the reruns start and the box set DVDs are released.

12

The Following
(2013–)

Given the entertainment industry's evolution toward increasing extremes of violent drama and depictions of violence, there would appear to be no end to the lengths producers of screen dramas will go to up the ante of shock-value violence in order to grab the attention of viewers and compete in the ratings game. A similar "arms race" continues to unfold regarding the featured criminal in crime dramas. Here is a quick tour through the history of this race and its escalatingly violent criminals.

1) On the lowest rung of the ladder resides the ordinary criminal—the pickpocket, the shoplifter, the jewel thief, the train robber, the bank robber, the sting specialist, the con artist, and an assortment of other creative variations. But such ordinariness quickly becomes banal and persists strictly for the pedestrian tastes of more conservative viewers.

2) Raising the bar of intensity requires moving on to the *professional* criminal—such as the pre–World War II gangster. Hollywood has mined the motherlode of thugs and gangsters of the Prohibition era for all they are worth and continues to squeeze more out of it.

3) Old-style gangsters then give way to *crime networks* or mafias—good for extensive mileage touring the gutters of mob practices in racketeering, extortion, gambling, prostitution, and drug running. While crime family dramas still attract some interest in the entertainment industry, they have become somewhat clichéd in the current marketplace.

4) The next level ascends to the serial killer pathological criminal or *psychopath*. He (almost always a "he") commits gruesome murders not for profit, but for pleasure. This type of criminal offers endless fodder for dramatization because he need not be constrained by boundaries of reality. His limitations exist only at the far edges of the imaginations of

scriptwriters—most of whom can outperform the perversity of real-life psychopaths any day of the week. But screen psychopaths are now a dime a dozen, so the true warriors of the arms race are moving on to more sophisticated weaponry.

5) The next step rises to the *professional* psychopath, such as Hannibal "the Cannibal" Lecter. It no longer suffices to be merely crazy. To win the lead role in a crime drama now requires being deliciously, intelligently, crazy. And it is even possible to win Best Actor for the role, earn kudos from the Academy for Best Picture, and be selected by the Library of Congress for inclusion in the National Film Registry for "cultural, historical, and aesthetic significance." Writers and producers of crime dramas were heartened by the heights members of their profession had reached with *The Silence of the Lambs* (1991), but also a bit dismayed. In the corridors of the industry the question reverberated: What now?

6) Creative minds began churning again and answers did not come easily. But all that was needed was to follow the progressive logic of the arms race. What could be better than a professional psychopathic serial killer? How about—serial killer *squared*? Thus, *Dexter* (2006–) was born, Showtime's award-winning series about a serial killer who kills only serial killers, a professional psychopath on the side of justice. This fantastic upward ratcheting of the crime drama liberates audiences for the grandest of Grand Guignol pleasures—watching the machinations of one psychopathic killer as he tracks another, eventually delivering a delicious and richly deserved demise. As might be expected, based on the analyses presented herein, *Dexter* has proven to be a highly stimulating confection for viewers and especially for a small percentage who have found it stimulating enough to inspire them to copycat crimes. This list of victims plots a global trail from the United States to Canada and across the Atlantic to Norway. And these are only crimes resulting in killings clearly traceable to influence from the *Dexter* series. The list does not include assaults and other aggressive actions short of killing. At this writing, the *Dexter* series is still running, so this list of copycat crimes may see additions as the club of Dexter imitators remains open for auditions [Claustro, 2007; *Vancouver Sun*, 2008; Heilbron, 2009].

Opposite: FBI agent Ryan Hardy (Kevin Bacon, left) seeks to silence his adversary, Joe Carroll (James Purefoy) (*The Following*, Fox Broadcasting, 2013–).

The Dexter character is not based on anyone in real life. The significance of this fact, when weighed against the trail of copycat crimes, reveals a disturbing trend. The creative imaginations of scriptwriters, pressured by the crime drama arms race, produced a fantasy character, a vigilante psychopath, in such compelling richness of detail as to stimulate and inspire a host of imitators. Dexter copycats are yet another confirmation—in this case a sad confirmation—of the many ways in which life imitates art. And these examples provide yet another opportunity for consumers to re-evaluate the question of whether their appetites for perverse and shocking violence are worth the risks—not only in relation to copycat crime but, at least as importantly, in relation to their own psychic health and the health of their communities. Fans of the *Dexter* series, as well as many other series discussed herein, must weigh what viewing does *for* them against what it does *to* them.

Returning to the history of the crime drama arms race, surely, with *Dexter*, it would seem scriptwriters have come to the end of the line. What could top professional psychopath serial killer squared? But it would be a grave underestimation of the perverse genius of the creators of crime dramas—genius now exceeding the perversity of any real life psychopath—to suppose they are not up for the challenge. And it would be a further underestimation to suppose the lure of profits and awards so predictably following bold efforts in this genre could fail to squeeze out new ideas. But still, the question must be asked: Now what?

Consumers did not have to wait long for an answer. The setup for the Fox cable network series *The Following* (2013–) is highly predictable in its shocking escalation of the crime drama. What could be better than professional psychopath serial killer squared? The *professional psychopath serial killer crime family*!!—an entire network of loonies working lovingly together to wreak deliciously wicked torturous slaughter on those who have done nothing to deserve it!

The Following moves a little in the direction of traditional oppositional tensions between hero and villain but does so in a slightly noir fashion, featuring a tainted hero. Kevin Bacon plays Ryan Hardy, an FBI agent collecting disability due to a pacemaker in his heart, delicate mental equilibrium, and a problem with alcohol. But the FBI brings him back as a consultant on the case of Dr. Joe Carroll (James Purefoy), a former professor at Winslow University specializing in the instruction of romantic literature and especially Edgar Allan Poe.

It turns out that Prof. Carroll, who has escaped from prison, is responsible for Hardy's pacemaker, having punctured his heart with a weapon before being taken prisoner by the team of agents led by Hardy. Apparently while teaching romantic literature at Winslow, Carroll busied himself with a night shift as a serial killer, torturing and killing 14 female students. Before being recaptured by agent Hardy, Carroll succeeds in killing another female (who had survived a previous assault by him), coordinates a ring of "followers" who are equally psychopathic and admiring of his talents, traumatizes his ex-wife (who, by the way, has had an affair with agent Hardy), arranges for one of his followers (who happens to be the ex-wife's nanny for her young son, Joey) to kidnap the son and take him to a secret location—all while instructing another follower to murder three women in a sorority house as two other followers bicker over sharing guard duty on Joey. (Whew!! Prof. Joe Carroll makes Hannibal Lecter look like a doddering couch potato.)

While all of this is happening, Hardy is also assaulted by a man in an Edgar Allan Poe mask. The masked man manages to escape only to later douse a man on the street with gasoline and set him on fire. Viewers later learn this victim, who appeared to have been picked at random, is instead a literary critic who gave Prof. Carroll's recently published novel a bad review. As if this were not enough stimulation, viewers are also treated to alternating scenes of sexual encounters between those in charge of kidnapped Joey, and the torture of a woman randomly kidnapped from a convenience store and held hostage in the basement. All of this barely brings the summary of events up to the end of episode three.

Clearly, the executives at Fox have taken the gloves off when it comes to going after their share of the crime drama pie. Series creator, Kevin Williamson, wanted a show that would be "gory," "controversial," and appeal to a broad audience. He has thus far succeeded in two out of three of these goals. Viewer following remains to be adequately assessed but Fox describes the new show as a "hit."

Unsurprisingly, critics from many of the major newspapers lavish praise on this parade of lunatic behavior and dead bodies for being relentless in terror and suspense. However, a few critics express serious reservations with the show's enthusiastic renderings of gore. Referring to the show, *Wall Street Journal* critic Nancy Dewolf Smith, for example, asks, "Is it a case of a serial-killer cliché too far?" (2013).

This mess of a television series from producers with puny talent and lamentable motives wrings forth a concluding prayer: Forgive them, Edgar Allan Poe, for they know not what they do. But such forgiveness may prove difficult when, in an era of extraordinary access to information and education, crime dramas are mindlessly escalated to the point where their creation itself becomes a crime.

13

24
(2001–2010)

Kevin Williamson, the series creator of *The Following*, claims to have been mightily inspired by Fox Network's series *24*, and especially by the Jack Bauer character. Williamson is reported to have said to an interviewer, "Sometimes I lie awake at night and cry for Jack Bauer!" (Maerz, 2013). Consequently, Williamson resurrected a part of Bauer in his character Ryan Hardy. And for Williamson, the depredations of serial killers, though not in the same league as terrorists, were at least in the same ballpark. While Hardy hails from the FBI, Bauer serves with the Counter Terrorism Unit (CTU)—and terrorism still trumps all other forms of extreme violence.

The arrival of *24* on the television scene in the fall of 2001 represents a fascinating bit of timing, while provoking a number of difficult questions. The show was scheduled to premiere on November 6, 2001, less than two months after the harrowing events of September 11. The first episode had been filmed and concluded with a terrorist parachuting from an airliner and then detonating a bomb, blowing it apart, presumably killing all on board. In the aftermath of September 11, series producers Joel Surnow and Howard Gordon believed Fox executives would never allow the show to air and would probably postpone or even cancel the entire series. But Fox executives regrouped and, sensing the sudden heightened relevance of the series, worked with the production crew, re-edited the first episode to reduce the shock effect of the airliner explosion, and risked allowing the show to premiere on the scheduled date. Two months later, Kiefer Sutherland won the Golden Globe award for best actor in a television drama series. Fox ordered the second half of the series into production and *24* continued for another seven seasons (Sepinwall, 2011). The popular success of *24* confirms the correctness of

155

Jack Bauer (Kiefer Sutherland), director of field ops for the Counter-Terrorist Unit, gives his all in a one-man crusade against terrorism (*24*, Fox Broadcasting, 2001–2010).

Fox Network's decision from a marketing point of view. The events of September 11 apparently worked in the opposite direction of what was anticipated, boosting viewer interest in the series rather than obviating it.

But all that glitters is not gold. Although *24* is stylistically unusual—each episode follows the events of one 24-hour period—and its production values equal those of a feature film, its dramatic structure is no more innovative than an old-fashioned cowboy matinee cliffhanger. And the featured cowboy is of similar character. Jack Bauer may struggle with a few inner demons but he always shows up as a red-blooded American Lone Ranger out on the streets identifying the bad guys and taking them out as best he can with whatever plodding help he can secure from CTU and government officials. But mostly, like the marshal in *High Noon* standing alone to protect a town, Jack works single-handedly to thwart terrorists—protecting politicians, cities, the government, and the entire nation from deadly attack.

In the wake of September 11, the writers of *24* were hell-bent on creating a counter-terrorist character who would not let slip past him the slightest clue indicating the nature and source of a potential attack on the United States and its citizens. Nor would this counter-terrorist hero fail to use any means at his disposal, including torture, to stop a planned attack. On these points Jack Bauer does not disappoint. As Kiefer Sutherland portrays him, Jack Bauer spares nothing of himself in stopping a threat. Similar to Batman's dedication in *The Dark Knight Rises* when told he has "given everything" for Gotham and he replies, "Not everything. Not yet," Bauer is prepared at every moment to give everything he has, including his life, to protect his country. And in every season, the plot boils down to situations where Jack's body and soul are all that stand between security and complete disaster. By the eighth season, given all the threats he has faced down and all it has cost him, viewers must marvel at why he does not shout, "Hey, can anybody in this country step up and give me a little help? How many times do I have to save you all from annihilation so you can carry on watching your TV shows at night?"

All of which raises an intriguing question: Why would Americans, in the wake of the events of September 11 and its enormous personal and national losses, choose to sit down at night and watch a television show depicting similar threats and attacks on American lives and property? Admittedly, interest has risen with regard to issues of national security. But becoming a *24* fan and routinely watching extreme dramatizations—the sabotage and meltdown of a nuclear power plant; the launching of a nuclear missile at an American city; a VX nerve gas attack at a shopping mall; the assassination of the president; the detonation of a suitcase nuclear bomb near Santa Clarita, California; suicide bombings; the commandeering of a missile-equipped submarine; and a foreign special forces strike inside the White House—all seems somehow disturbingly peculiar.

It is almost as peculiar as eating popcorn and watching simulations of friends and neighbors threatened, attacked, tortured, and killed. Indeed, Bauer ends up torturing his brother and arranging for the execution of his father when they become involved in a terrorist plot. Granted, the current era is the era of reality television and the ushering of stories straight from headlines into the production studio, but where does the line ultimately get drawn between violent reality and violent entertainment?

The current ease with which everything in the real world—not to mention everything in every corner of the imagination—moves into the screen world is nothing short of astounding. But even more astounding is the failure to acknowledge and confront the equal ease with which simulations of life in the screen world tend to move into the real world. The dramatization of a terrorist detonation of a nuclear weapon in a Los Angeles suburb cycles back into minds and communities where it continues to reside—and not without consequences. Presuming that some benefit may derive from heightening awareness and vigilance against terror fails to take into consideration that media repetition of screen images from the September 11 attacks was more than sufficient to set the entire nation on edge and keep it there for several years. Doubtless, most people alive at the time of these attacks will never be quite the same again regarding vigilance toward terrorism. The country has been on edge and continues to be on edge. Why air television dramas pushing it over the edge?

Aside from piquing hyperactive alert reflexes, other consequences from the depictions of terrorist threats in 24 include promoting misconceptions about the nature and degree of threats, boosting paranoia toward particular ethnic groups and nationalities, fueling—all too explicitly—the imaginations and aspirations of potential terrorists and pathological individuals, and, last but not least, advancing misconceptions about the use of torture as an interrogation technique.

In fact, the depiction of torture for purposes of interrogation incited national controversy during the heyday of 24. Late in 2006, Brigadier General Patrick Finnegan of West Point Military Academy thought it was time to pay a visit to the producers of the show and made a trip to the set in California. He was motivated to do so because, as an officer and a teacher at West Point, he had personally witnessed how the promotion of torture on the show had a negative impact on young troops and cadets. Commenting on the situation to *New Yorker Magazine*, Finnegan referred to the show's producers and the depictions of torture stating, "I'd like them to stop. They should do a show where torture backfires.... The kids see it [torture] and say, 'If torture is wrong, what about 24?' The disturbing thing is that although torture may cause Jack Bauer some angst, it is always the patriotic thing to do" (Buncombe, 2007).

Having spoken to soldiers in Iraq, David Danzig of the non-profit organization Human Rights First referenced torture scenes in *24* when he reported, "For young soldiers, there is a direct relationship between what they are doing on their jobs and what they see on TV" (Buncombe, 2007). Civilians and military leaders were not only concerned about the effects on troops but also about the effects on the reputation of the United States in foreign countries. Though television does not reflect official policy of the United States, it does project what many foreign viewers interpret as American popular attitudes and unspoken military practices. And Jack Bauer's attitude projects clearly when he speaks to a terrorist under interrogation, "You're going to tell me what I want to know. It's just a matter of how much you want it to hurt." This is tough talk and plays well with audiences looking for no-nonsense heroes, but it also plays loosely and obliquely in ways the producers of the show cannot control and in ways for which they would doubtless want to assume no responsibility. But producers' responsibilities include more than attracting and entertaining an audience.

These responsibilities were again in evidence when, during the fourth season of the show, public criticism of the portrayal of Muslims, voiced by the Council on American-Islamic Relations, forced Fox Network to broadcast a series of public-service announcements affirming a non-prejudicial position toward Muslims. As the producers and writers of the show took increasing liberties with sensitive subject matter for purposes of amplifying dramatic intensity and controversy, detachment from real-world concerns and potential unintended effects also increased. The show's success and popularity fueled the notion that viewers were on board, that no wrong could be done, and that growing demands for dramatic innovation in the show progressively trumped what were perceived to be marginal real-world concerns—which is not to suggest that a measure of this attitude was not in place from the beginning.

All told, the success of *24* swept producers and writers for the show into a wave of confidence from which they believed nothing could or should stand in their way. In doing so they conjured threats that even real terrorists had not yet imagined. In fact, potential terrorists at home and abroad were probably taking notes and thanking American television for assistance. The next chapter explores this theme and similar concerns in further detail.

14

Homeland
(2011–)

Imagine this: You turn to your favorite cable television channel on a Sunday evening and find the first episode of a new crime-drama series titled: "Death in the Schools." The series tells the story of an emergency police detail assigned to investigate and stop a string of drive-by shootings of children assaulted in playgrounds or on their way home from school. The perpetrators appear to be a small group of youths whose motives for the crimes remain unclear but give evidence of being sociopathic. The police receive tips, but in most cases too late to prevent a slaughter of innocent children. As school security increases to respond to the threat, the perpetrators expand their killing spree across a wider area. When coalitions of viewers concerned about depictions of this kind of violence voice complaints, the writers and producers of the show answer by saying they have only taken inspiration from newspaper headlines and cite specifically the shootings at Newtown, Connecticut. How would you respond to this new television series? Will the next step be a television series based on a serial killer whose favorite target is elementary school classrooms? And will child actors be employed and rigged with squibs to simulate bullets entering their bodies? And will their peers be allowed to watch them portray their own deaths on prime-time television?

How and where will lines be drawn between the purposes of drama and entertainment and the practice of ripping story material from news headlines as a means of fulfilling those purposes? If, in the wake of September 11, Homeland Security is concerned about the possibility of terrorists acquiring and detonating a nuclear weapon in a major city, is that concern grist for dramatization as well? And if the answer is yes, is it necessary to show such a detonation occurring in the suburb of a major city

CIA operative Carrie Mathison (Claire Danes) suspects war hero Nicholas Brody (Damian Lewis) of being brainwashed against the United States (*Homeland*, Showtime, 2011–present).

in the United States as was depicted, as mentioned in the previous chapter, in an episode of *24*? As news teams go the way of turning a day's tragic events into live televised drama (as in the now-infamous aerial coverage of the O.J. Simpson car chase) production teams go the way of *inventing* events they believe could become the next day's headlines. Where does this escalation end in pursuit of entertainment for prime time?

An even better question might be: When do viewers stop following this escalation and start dropping out? Regarding this question, one of the problems to be considered relates to the fact that a person must be of a certain upward age to be able to experience this escalation as escalation. From the time of Hitchcock to the current era has been a multi-generational span and the full extent of the relatively rapid changes are not automatically appreciated by everyone. The good news is that escalation of violent screen drama cannot continue forever. At some point the cultural training in attitudes toward violence grounded in popular antagonal dramas will suffer a fate similar to cigarettes and sugar-laden junk foods. What the head gets served is just as important, if not more so, than what the body gets served, and, eventually, the collective coma induced by consumption of violent media confections will require broad attention.

Meanwhile, another current television series requires attention. Cuing on the success of *24*, Showtime launched *Homeland* in October of 2011, with two executive producers on board who had worked on *24*. Seeking a different angle for escalation, *Homeland* amplifies the paranoia generated by the counter-terrorist theme of *24*. It does so by borrowing an effective theme from the Cold War years—betrayal. The only thing worse than a terrorist attack from the outside is one from the inside. The notion of a former patriot and good soldier assisting foreign terrorists against his own country constitutes the kind of threat guaranteed to hijack American imaginations. With regard to its potential as an action-thriller, then, the critical and popular success of *Homeland* should come as no surprise. Like *24*, the series is cleverly written and well cast and well acted by series stars Claire Danes and Damian Lewis. *Homeland* swept the table for the 2012 Emmy Awards for Outstanding Drama Series and Lead Actor and Actress in a Drama Series and did the same for the 2013 Golden Globe Awards for Best Television Drama Series and Best Actor and Actress. On technical execution and production values *Homeland* appears flawless. But it fails in concept.

The series plot centers on a United States Marine, Nicholas Brody (Lewis) captured by al–Qaeda. Through the efforts of key al–Qaeda operative Abu Nazir (Navid Negahban) Brody experiences Stockholm syndrome, identifies with his captors, and takes up their cause. Nazir makes arrangements for it to appear to the U.S. military that they have discovered and rescued Brody. Brody returns to America a war hero, receives a shower of praise, and eventually wins election to the U.S. House of Representatives. Meanwhile, CIA operative Carrie Mathison (Danes) returns from a posting in Iraq where she has learned from an informer that a captured soldier has been "turned" by al–Qaeda. Mathison suspects Brody but her superiors at Langley doubt the reliability of her source. And, even if correct, other captive marines remain on the list of possible suspects. But Carrie is certain of her source and has a strong intuition that Brody is the one. So the game is on as she attempts to verify her suspicions.

One noteworthy piece of Brody's brainwashing includes his conversion to the religion of Islam. He conducts his daily prayers beyond the eyes of his family in a corner in his garage. Series producers understand the potential volatility of Brody's conversion on both sides of the equation—Muslim and non–Muslim viewers at home and abroad—and make an effort to depict his practice of the faith in ways not overtly linking it to an agenda of violence. But this amounts to an exercise in futility when having written a character such as Brody, who has been "turned" and now sympathizes with terrorist actions at the same time he converts to Islam. The underlying message is clear—the equating of Islam, Arab, and terrorist—and the difficulties with this message abound. Intentionally or not, *Homeland* succeeds in exacerbating this dubious association. The show suffers from this failure and has drawn fire from Arab-American commentators as being the most Islamophobic show on television (Aleaziz, 2011).

The concept of the show is also problematic in another important respect. It shifts the target of terrorism from attacks on American buildings and infrastructure to attacks on individual American political figures—specifically the vice-president of the United States. Abu Nazir wants to kill Vice-President William Walden (Jamey Sheridan) because he holds him responsible for the death of his son, Issa, and 82 other children killed in a drone strike. Walden appears on American television, taking credit for the United States, claiming the drone strike hit Abu Nazir's compound and that any claims to the contrary are lies for purposes of discrediting the United States.

A list of the many things wrong with this plotline must include the notion that a top government official would, with full knowledge of the truth, announce on television that a drone had struck a terrorist compound when, instead, it had struck a school full of children. It could, for the sake of argument, be granted that a top government official is not above publicly lying. But it should be too much to ask for viewers to believe such an official could also be stupid enough to think that in the current era of media appetite for scandal the truth would not eventually come out, in which case the political cost for the administration would be high. Whether or not anything similar to this event and cover-up has ever occurred, the depiction of such a possibility in a television show in the wake of the events of September 11 projects a cynical view of national politics at a time when the entire country still suffers from terrorist paranoia.

Moreover, the *Homeland* shift of al–Qaeda targets from United States real estate and infrastructure to high-ranking political figures counts as an escalation outpacing al–Qaeda itself. Granted, al–Qaeda strategists should not be underestimated in the lengths to which they may be willing to go in order to create havoc in the United States. But consider how perverse it is that a television show designed as action-thriller entertainment should imaginatively conjure types of threats that have not yet materialized and depict them in great detail for the diversion of American audiences.

The answer that such threats may be all too real meets the response that (1) they need not be exploited for purposes of entertainment and (2) they need not be advertised and mapped on globally distributed HDTV, and (3) some things are better left unspoken (or, in this case, untelevised). Making Americans aware of real threats ought to be the work of Homeland Security not *Homeland*. Politicians in Washington have enough to worry about without television shows pointing fingers at them and, in effect, saying to al–Qaeda and other terrorist groups, "Hey, wouldn't these guys who have been responsible for drone strikes make good targets themselves? And if you can't get at the president, why not try the vice-president or any number of other key government personnel?"

Obviously, al–Qaeda and other anti–American terrorist groups do not need American television to provide action maps for them. The point is not so much that television serves in such cases as a source of sensitive information but rather that particular government officials in the United States do not need to be draped with giant red targets and an arrow pointing at them as a reminder to not forget these guys when one is angry at America. These shows also do not stop at the reminder but add something more, such as, "Just in case you're short on ideas, here's one way to go about it." To get another sense of this problem, how would American troops in Afghanistan feel if a television show at home ramped up viewer excitement by showing ways of killing soldiers that had not yet been used by insurgents?

In the final episode of the first season, Brody dons a suicide vest as part of an Abu Nazir plan to kill Vice-President Walden and anyone else who might be nearby. The device malfunctions and the vice-president leaves the area of the trap without knowing what might have occurred. But Nazir remains determined. The second season develops Walden's character more thoroughly and reveals him to be such a despicable, arrogant, ruthless, power-grabbing troll that viewers feel obliged to jump through the screen to aid Nazir and Brody in killing him. By late in the second season, though, Brody has, through Carrie's efforts, been "returned" and is now back to being a patriot. But Nazir holds Carrie hostage and uses her to coerce Brody to again do his bidding, since Brody has now discovered he loves Carrie. Nazir's plan this time requires the serial number of Walden's remotely controlled pacemaker. Brody manages to secretly enter Walden's office, get the serial number from his pacemaker kit, and transfer the information to Nazir before Walden enters the office. Shortly thereafter Nazir accelerates the pacemaker, inducing a heart attack. Walden collapses, helpless. As Brody watches, he informs him, "I'm killing you." Since Walden is now about as popular in viewers eyes as Osama Bin Laden, they likely stand and cheer as Walden dies and Carrie is released unharmed by Nazir.

But the question is worth asking: Should the producers of *Homeland* be proud to have contrived a confluence of character and events sufficient to cause American audiences to applaud the assassination of the vice-president of the United States? And a more harrowing question needs to be asked: Would the producers still be proud and would Americans still cheer if a foreign terrorist and a mentally stressed ex-marine acted in vigilante fashion to assassinate the vice-president of the United States in real life? And consider whether any such vigilante agents could be trusted to have learned the facts to a degree of certainty as to carry out such an execution with unimpeachable moral authority. Would not their assumption of certainty give cause for other Americans to be just a little uncomfortable with the potential for anarchy should such certainty in action become the model for other vigilante operators?

One often-overlooked but significant difference between the virtual world of television drama and the real world of flesh-and-blood drama resides in the ability to design the world of virtual characters and events in a way enabling viewers to attain a kind of omniscience. If every viewer placed themselves in Brody's shoes, would they, should they, have enough confidence in the unerring quality of their judgment to do what Brody did? Even with Carrie's life on the line? Television dramas all too easily construct illusory attitudes about clarity of vision in the real world that the real world rarely, if ever, permits. And when these limits of real life and real perception are not adequately dramatized in the virtual world, violence becomes far easier to justify.

Both Brody and Carrie are flawed heroes, each struggling with mental instability. Brody suffers from Post Traumatic Stress Disorder and identity confusion resulting from his captivity, torture, and subsequent manipulation by Abu Nazir. Carrie suffers from bipolar disease, which causes her to experience spells of manic energy resulting in over-reactions and loss of judgment. But these frailties stand in contrast to Nazir and Walden, who appear as simple villains, ugly and perverse. Accordingly, *Homeland* belongs in the category of reductionistic conflict characteristic of antagonal melodrama. Its violence polarizes, inducing either outrage or applause. Nazir's role becomes especially clear in the exchange he has with Carrie while he holds her hostage.

Carrie Mathison: [referring to *Nicholas Brody*] He's smarter than you think.
Abu Nazir: You love him, too. We have that in common.
M: We have nothing in common.
N: Sometimes, when you are breaking a man, an emotional transformation takes place. For me with Nicholas, it was quite powerful. It really was a kind of love.
M: You're never going to leave this country alive.
N: I know. And I don't care.

M: Bullshit!

N: You can't even imagine that can you? Believing in something bigger than you, more important than you. We are at war. I am a soldier.

M: You're a terrorist.

N: Imagine you are sitting down to dinner with your wife and children. Out of the sky, as if thrown by an angry god, a drone strike hits and destroys all in your house. Who is the terrorist?

M: It's the last day of Ramadan. A young man enters a Shia village pushing a cart full of candies and toys. He waits in the school playground for all the children to gather and he reaches back and flips a switch.

N: We fight with what we have.

M: You pervert the teachings of the Prophet and call it cause. You turn teenagers into suicide bombers.

N: Generation after generation must suffer and die. We are prepared for that. Are you?

M: Whatever it takes.

N: Really?! With your pension plans and organic foods, your beach houses and sports clubs? Do you have the perseverance, the tenacity, the faith? Because we do. You can bomb us, starve us, occupy our holy places, but we will never lose our faith. We carry God in our hearts, our souls. To die is to join Him. It may take a century, two centuries, three centuries, but we will exterminate you.

M: Like I said, you're a terrorist.

The decisive word in Nazir's last lines is "exterminate"—a word often associated with the destruction of vermin. This word appears in close connection to the words, "We carry God in our hearts, our souls." Few viewers will fail to connect the dots leading to the conclusion that God also guides and directs this "extermination." Prior to these last lines, the writers are careful to have Carrie say to Nazir, "You pervert the teachings of the Prophet." But for those who have not read and do not know the Quran, how are they to tell? By every measure provided in the series—including Brody's strange conversion to Islam alongside his conversion to terrorism—the Quran does not fare well.

Any debate concerning the merits of Islam and the Quran is well beyond the scope of this book. But regardless of the merits, *Homeland* does little to dispel and much to excite mistrust of Muslims and the religion of Islam. Common sense should dictate the timing is not right for this kind of message—especially when it is difficult to see anything more at stake in advancing this message than the desire to put viewers on the edge of their seats for action-thriller entertainment. This is not to say the subject of terrorism cannot or should not be explored in screen dramas. But in the current time it becomes imperative to do so through a more complex structure—a synagonal structure of conflict that would reduce the risks of furthering fears and provoking celebration of violence while increasing the chances for making violence a less attractive option for managing conflict.

As indicated in the "Death in the Schools" scenario for a television show with which this chapter opened, the boundaries for dramatic productions continue to be pushed to the point where they begin to seem non-existent. The liberties of freedom of speech and lack of censorship in the United States have moved past the protection of rights and charged in the direction of engraved invitations to say and present anything if it can be used to market a product or make a buck. American culture is now a victim of its own license. The only thing standing between this culture and further escalations of shock violence would appear to be the willingness of individuals—producers and consumers—to acknowledge the power of media and take responsibility for that power by adequately weighing the potential consequences of media productions and distributions.

15

The Walking Dead
(2010–)

Drama needs something to fuel or heighten conflict. For the producers of television dramas confronted with schedules to fill, the choice of what device to use in order to heighten conflict can be challenging. The important thing is that it be effective in attracting an audience and lend itself to extended dramatization in the potential to accommodate new characters and new scenarios. These requirements lend themselves, in turn, to a specific approach to dramatization: wherever possible—simplify, simplify, simplify. And when the concept has been simplified down to where the levers and gears of drama can be reduced no further, gold has likely been struck for appealing to large segments of the prime-time marketplace.

Wanting to ensure the success of a new series as much as possible, AMC's producers were persuaded to accept a story concept that had already been field tested—at least within a particular demographic comprising a good percentage of the potential audience. The concept came from a successful comic-book horror series titled *The Walking Dead*. The horror genre has often shown strength in the television ratings competition but this concept came with an added bonus. The writer of the comic book, Robert Kirkman, had chosen an apocalyptic backdrop in which technological civilization has been largely destroyed and population centers reduced to ghost towns. AMC producers understood apocalyptic drama had been popular of late, but was this particular concept combining horror and apocalypse ready from prime time?

Following the likely thought process in creating *The Walking Dead* story helps in assessing the elements of its appeal and how the producers may have viewed its potential. Since the comic-book series differs in some details from the television series, this analysis of the dramatic

The walking dead (*The Walking Dead*, AMC Network Entertainment, 2010–).

choices involved should be understood to relate only to the thought process that likely transpired in assessing the potential and shaping the theme of the series for television.

With the choice of an apocalyptic backdrop for the series, other elements of the drama could be reverse-engineered into place. The first problem needing to be solved concerned the apocalypse itself. Some explanation must serve to rationalize its existence. *The Walking Dead* producers liked the virus as culprit—an easy choice when needing to account for apocalypse. But a virus cannot be seen coming and its head cannot be blown off with a shotgun. So it lacks as a target when trying to keep the conflict action oriented. A virus serves well as the agent of apocalypse, but something else is needed for spiking dramatic action and creating visible horror.

Vampires had reached a peak in current horror popularity, for which examples are too numerous to list. But the zombie was a category of the monstrous having shown promise in the past and it still seemed to possess untapped potential ready to be exploited. It seemed well suited as the perfect candidate. The zombie is ugly, relentless, and already dead so it presents itself visually as cognitive dissonance—a walking contradiction of life and death. But its "life" is only an illusion deriving from its animation. Its "death" dominates and nicely renders the zombie as pure evil because the zombie, as the "living dead," functions much like a virus—an agency specializing in spreading sickness and death.

The question then becomes, who is infected with the zombie virus and who is not? Viewers learn at the end of season two, *everyone* is infected with the virus. But only when people are bitten by a zombie or killed do they become zombies, or *walkers*. So despite everyone being infected, the line between living humans and undead zombies remains clear. This escalation of the downside of death is noteworthy. Death becomes *doubly evil*: not only evil because it ends life but evil because death lives to spread more death.

The choice of the zombie as enemy enables the dramatist to work within a conflict frame with a clearly identifiable evil (a virus alone is too hard to *see*) and, therefore, a conflict frame of a highly polarized and value-weighted nature. With its apocalyptic setting, *The Walking Dead* presents a simplified *frontier* landscape where conflict becomes basic and abundant. The zombie apocalypse trims away excess population, leaving small groups—as in the Old West frontier—reduced to struggling for survival with only a few tools and limited supplies. This zombie drama serves as the new version of the Hollywood western, especially the wagon train sagas beset by swarms of attacking Indians. And as historian of westerns Philip French explains, the Indian of these early westerns is the "faceless symbol" of evil, an "all-purpose enemy ready at the drop of a tomahawk to spring from the rocks and attack a wagon train" (1977: 79). *The Walking Dead* is a western for the 21st century, wherein the zombie replaces the Indian with the advantage of being a more politically correct reincarnation of faceless evil.

But the zombie—like the Indian of early westerns—is only the background enemy who pulls humans together where, inside their wagon circle, the real conflict takes place between competing human groups. In other words, the zombie—like the Indian—does not even rise to the level of an engaging enemy but operates only as an intermittent but persistent nuisance to pockets of human community. But the simplification achieved by the choice of the apocalyptic landscape demands artful writing in order to avoid the worst kinds of tropes of dramatized human interaction. Unfortunately, inside the wagon circles of *The Walking Dead* tired old stories of human virtues and vices play out in crude simplicity—just as they did in the early television western *Wagon Train* (1957–1962). Joined by other early television westerns such as *Gunsmoke* (1955–1975), *Bonanza* (1959–1973), and *The Virginian* (1962–1971), these series were not really westerns—drawing from difficulties and conflicts of the Old West—so much as they were morality plays, disguised in western dress. They drew their material from contemporary issues and presumed to offer commentary relevant to these issues. *The Walking Dead* treads dangerously close to similar pitfalls, squandering its apocalyptic potential for frontier drama in exchange for bland preaching and trite storylines while hoping the zombies will rescue weak writing with well-timed scary violence.

The series begins from the point of view of Rick Grimes (Andrew Lincoln), a sheriff's deputy, who is shot pre-apocalypse while attempting to stop a crime and taken to a hospital, where he falls into a coma. He wakes from his coma to find the hospital in ruins and the countryside full of zombies. While searching for his wife and child, Rick encounters two other survivors, Morgan (Lennie James) and his son, who bring him up to date on the bleak situation. Rick eventually finds his wife, Lori (Sarah Wayne Callies), and their young son, Carl (Chandler Riggs). Adding a few others along the way, this small group heads, logically enough, for the Center for Disease Control in Atlanta, Georgia. Fending off zombies along the way, they reach the CDC to find only one doctor remains on the premises. He does not have good news for them and holds out little hope for a cure for the virus creating the zombies. The CDC's emergency-power generators fail due to lack of fuel, which initiates an auto-destruct sequence causing evacuation of the complex. Can things possibly get any worse for Rick Grimes and company? Well, yes. His best friend and police partner, Shane Walsh (John Bernthal), has been romantically involved with his wife while he was in the coma and now a tense love triangle has developed. But Rick is a steady guy and refuses to give voice to his rage despite all the bad luck.

However, in season two, Rick is forced to kill Shane in self-defense. Shane then turns into a zombie and attacks Rick, who is then saved when his son shoots the Shane/zombie. By season three, Rick's wandering group settles into an abandoned prison, convenient for keeping the zombies out of the way. But Lori, pregnant by Shane, goes into labor, has a hard time of it, and requires a Caesarean operation. She dies giving birth to the baby and then, as if that were not bad enough, turns into a zombie and must be euthanized by her own son.

Near the prison lies a small settlement of survivors in a town called Woodbury. Perhaps these survivors can offer help and make prison life a little easier? No such luck. Led by a tyrant called "the Governor" (David Morrissey), these folks prove to be unfriendly. The socializing does not go well and, before long, the Governor and his cohorts lead an attack on the prison. Having to fend off crazy humans as well as zombies, Rick realizes his group needs more weapons. He takes a remaining operational vehicle and, along with his son and the sword-wielding Michonne (Danai Gurira), drives to his hometown where he believes he can find more guns.

After arriving in town, Rick and Carl encounter Morgan again, who has now lost his son to the zombies. Most of this episode consists of Rick trying to talk Morgan out of his deep depression and Carl risking zombie attack by trekking off alone to hunt for something in the streets. But what parent would let their kid wander off alone in a zombie-infested town? It turns out the poor judgment belongs to the writers, since they appear to have needed an opportunity for the stoic Michonne to play mother and demonstrate the zombies had not yet robbed her of sentiment. Michonne follows Carl to a building which houses the remains of a bar and restaurant, where she discovers he wants to retrieve a family picture hanging on the wall. Lucky for Carl (and Rick, the careless father!) that Michonne tagged along because Carl encounters zombies at the bar and restaurant. Michonne dispenses with them in a very unmotherly way.

And so it goes. Whenever the numbing morality play lags a little too much, zombies spring from behind the rocks, just like Indians used to do, and provide a spate of good old-fashioned slaughter to spice things up. The dramatic trope of the faceless enemy is a bit too convenient for good drama. But it is conveniently just right for the gratuitous conflict necessary for generating endless opportunities for gratuitous violence. And there is nothing like a de-faced, dehumanized human to make a viewer feel good about shotgunning the head off an ugly body.

Some commentators on pop-culture phenomena such as *The Walking Dead* are inclined to look through the veneer of the show, in this case the zombie veneer, and search for how it must represent some dark corner of fear in the collective psyche. In what ways, for example, do the particular characteristics of the zombie reflect the fears of people in contemporary culture? As the theory goes, whatever monster or villain may be chosen by the dramatist reveals an important aspect of the current cultural context. But a strong case can be made for not reading too much into such choices. As argued herein, the choice of how conflict is *structured* is more significant, informative, and influential than the choice of a particular enemy or threat and what that enemy or threat may be read to symbolize at a particular cultural moment.

French's notion of the "faceless Indian" provides guiding insight. The faceless enemy functions like unminted coin—only, say, of negative value. Viewers may place any face on it they want, any personally relevant exchange value, so long as the coin represents the enemy, the "Other." This enemy may appear differently in the psyches of different viewers. This process becomes especially problematic when unminted coin, following the scripting of antagonal melodrama, gets minted in the real world into the "coin" of particular despised persons or groups thereby facilitating their dehumanization into zombie fodder fit for violent disposal. The "enemy" is idealized as perfect villain and then realized through its discovery in various real-world instances. Then welcome into the world another copycat criminal.

Recreating the frontier landscape, simplifying the civil and cultural environment down to rock-bottom basics, can be a legitimate thing to do and can provide the basis for good drama. But the nature and quality of drama and any violence it may contain, depends on *how* this simplified context is created and the way that choice influences the structure of the conflict evolving within it. Simplifying context while also simplifying conflict and adding a quantity of violence is a risky, artless, and easy thing to do. And being easy while also retaining potential to attract an audience makes it a tempting thing to do from the point of view of television writers and producers. And apparently, judging from the series renewals in the case of *The Walking Dead*, such productions may be as easy to watch as catching a virus. But viewers should keep in mind that catching a virus may not be the only way to become the walking dead.

The Wire
(2002–2008)

David Simon, the primary creative force behind the HBO series *The Wire*, has been writing crime drama since 1990. Two of his books have each inspired television dramas: the first *Homicide: Life on the Street* (1993–1999), a crime drama produced by NBC; and the second, *The Corner* (2000), a six-episode HBO miniseries docudrama relating the true story of a West Baltimore family living in poverty and struggling with drug addiction and drug dealing. Both books were the result of leaves-of-absence Simon took from his work as a journalist for the *Baltimore Sun*, for which he covered the homicide and narcotics beat.

Detective Shakima "Kima" Greggs (Sonja Sohn) and Detective James "Jimmy" McNulty (Dominic West); reflected in the glass: Russel "Stringer" Bell (Idris Elba) and Avon Barksdale (Wood Harris) (*The Wire*, Home Box Office, 2002–2008).

Simon spent a year researching for *Homicide* by observing daily operations in the Baltimore Police Department Homicide Division and traveling with officers on police calls. He immersed himself in a process of similar daily observation as part of his research for *The Corner*, which he co-authored with Ed Burns, a former detective in the Homicide and Narcotics Divisions of the Baltimore Police Department. Simon's career as a journalist, his leave-of-absence research, and his friendship with Burns combined to give him unusual insight into multiple facets of the city of Baltimore and its most chronic problems. Many of the characters in *The Wire* are based on persons drawn from the experiences of Simon and Burns, and all of the stories are based on real-life events. This tightly constructed parallel with real life gives *The Wire* a powerful documentary quality, as the show shines a spotlight into dark corners of the city of Baltimore and the problems its citizens, police force, and politicians struggle to overcome.

Structured as docudrama, *The Wire* poses an interesting question in relation to its depictions of violence. The introduction touched on the issue of realism, of art reflecting life like a message sent straight from reality to the screen. Producers of this kind of drama may see themselves as performing a public service by drawing attention to particular social problems. They might account for their art in the following way:

> I'm holding a mirror to reality. If you don't like what you see, don't blame me. What I'm showing is out there and it is all of a piece with what we in human community have created for ourselves. Don't tell me my depiction of that reality is corrupting or dangerous. The reality itself is the danger and I'm only the messenger bringing you the wake-up call.

In defense of the violence, drug crime, and other types of corruption portrayed in *The Wire*, Simon and Burns would likely be in agreement with this line of reasoning. Granting as much, what sense does it make to castigate a film like *Taxi Driver* while at the same time, as will be done next, praising *The Wire*? Is not the eye of the camera peering into the violent corners of Baltimore in *The Wire* analogous to the camera of Scorsese recording the violent actions of Travis Bickle? The short answer is "no," these exposés are not the same. The difference between them illustrates once again the importance of structure in relation to depictions of violence.

As already discussed in Chapter Two, the narrative thread of *Taxi*

Driver traces only one strand of what should be seen as a complex tapestry. No contrapuntal characters of sufficient depth and clarity appear on the scene to force Bickle into direct confrontation with himself and what he has become. As a result, members of the viewing audience who may, for reasons relating to their own history, identify with Bickle are presented no clear opportunities for self-examination and self-critique. Instead, they are left largely unencumbered in a process of identification which may all too easily devolve into heroizing the "star" of this story and glamorizing his violence.

The Wire, on the other hand, follows many threads of a complex weave and, consequently, places in the path of viewers' visions many cross threads which obstruct the possibilities for viewers forming clean and clear identifications. All of the main characters are portrayed as complicated human beings, each having strengths and weaknesses in relations with others. These characters are also shown in relation to social and bureaucratic contexts challenging their strengths and weaknesses in ways constantly testing the limits of their self-assessments and their internal qualities and conflicts. Contrapuntal contrasts and probings of character continually play out through episodes of *The Wire*. Within this type of synagonal unfolding of narrative it becomes impossible to view depictions of violence as anything other than abhorrent, tragic, and unnecessary.

A particularly good example of contrapuntal structuring appears early in the first season of *The Wire*. Lead homicide detective, James McNulty (Dominic West), and his partner, William "Bunk" Moreland (Wendell Pierce), interrogate a member of the Barksdale drug ring, D'Angelo Barksdale (Lawrence Gilliard, Jr.). D'Angelo is the nephew of the head of the drug ring, Avon Barksdale (Wood Harris). They suspect D'Angelo of involvement in the murder of a state's witness used in his recently concluded murder trial. The witness provided testimony against D'Angelo and the detectives are certain he was killed by the drug ring with D'Angelo's knowledge if not his direct involvement.

During the interrogation D'Angelo admits nothing and claims to know nothing about the murder. McNulty and his partner speak to him as if they fully understand his predicament in relation to his uncle and that he had no part in the murder himself. They want nothing from him other than a letter of condolence to the children of the victim's family.

They inform D'Angelo that the victim's wife had already passed away and the children are, therefore, orphaned. They also explain to him how unnecessary the murder was in light of the fact that he had escaped prosecution at his murder trial and the witness, therefore, posed no further threat. The execution of the witness served only the purpose of payback and intimidation of potential future witnesses.

Pressing D'Angelo further, McNulty shows him a photograph of the three orphaned children. At the sight of the photograph D'Angelo begins to sense the weight of what has happened, breaks down, and agrees to write the letter. The detectives reassure him the letter need convey only his sympathy and no admission of involvement. As D'Angelo finishes the letter, the attorney provided by his uncle Avon arrives and drags him out of the interrogation room, reprimanding him for writing the letter. Detective Kima Greggs of narcotics, who observed the interrogation, then remarks to McNulty about the tragic situation of the orphaned children. McNulty smiles and replies that the children in the photo belong to his partner and that the deceased witness was not a family man.

This entire scene reveals many things in a short space of time. Viewers see two sides of D'Angelo—his loyalty to his uncle and his initial toughness in the face of interrogation. Then viewers see his capacity for guilt in relation to what the drug ring is capable of doing and his capacity for empathy for its victims. Similarly, McNulty shows capacity for empathy by sensing a heart behind D'Angelo's stone-faced façade while at the same time displaying his own toughness by using his empathic instinct in a manipulative way, albeit in the service of law enforcement. *The Wire* consistently draws out these complexities of character, these double images of the human dimensions of character, in ways resonating as true to life.

The lines of conflict in *The Wire* are also not limited to the opposition between cops and criminals. Within the Baltimore Police Department McNulty must deal with the wrath of Dept. Commander for Operations William Rawls (John Doman). Rawls despises him because he brought the attention of a judge to the lack of investigation of several unsolved homicides relating to the Barksdale drug-trafficking ring. Tensions also arise between the deputy commissioner Ervin Burrell (Frankie Faison), certain City Hall politicians, and McNulty's investigative detail when drug money appears to be finding its way into political coffers.

On the criminal side, the Barksdale group faces opposition from Omar Little (Michael Kenneth Williams) and his small group of armed robbers, who take money from street drug operatives.

These lines of conflict among the cops, bureaucrats, politicians, and criminals also crisscross as members of City Hall are suspected of doing favors for Avon Barksdale and Omar agrees to cooperate with the police against Barksdale. In addition to these sets of conflicts, viewers are provided significant glimpses into the personal lives of the key players and their domestic conflicts. These conflicts only escalate through what both the cops and criminals do for a living, including especially the risks they take.

Few shows in the history of film or television succeed as well as *The Wire* in doing justice to the complexity of conflict between official and criminal factions in a large city. Good guys and bad guys emerge in the narrative but everyone has a story which, as it unfolds, obstructs easy categorizations of characters. The personal stories of the characters also play against the larger backdrop of the city and its Gordian Knot of intersecting and often conflicting interests and factions. This larger context makes it possible to penetrate more thoroughly into the deeper truth of motives that, on the surface, might appear flatly contemptible.

In *The Wire* nothing is simple and, consequently, the dramatic structure and portrayal of conflict emerge as thoroughly synagonal and multi-perspectival. Depictions of violence are sobering because the victims always have a strong flesh-and-blood identity, as if they were persons viewers knew personally. And because of the texture of the writing, viewers do, in fact, know these victims personally. In this sense, *The Wire* builds a viewer's repertoire of virtual experience with a quality nearly as textured, diverse, and informative as real-life experience.

An especially good example of the quality of this virtual experience appears in the last episode of the first season when events push D'Angelo's conflicted nature to the forefront of the action as McNulty and his detail close in on the Barksdale drug ring. D'Angelo has been caught transporting a kilo of uncut heroin for his uncle Avon. Never comfortable with his inherited career, he attempts to plea bargain with assistant state's attorney Rhonda Pearlman (Deidre Lovejoy) for an escape from his life of crime. McNulty and his partner, Moreland, seek information about the string of murders committed by the Barksdale gang as a result

Jimmy McNulty (Dominic West) listens to testimony in the interrogation room (*The Wire*, Home Box Office, 2002–2008).

of attempts to eliminate anyone who might be able to incriminate Avon Barksdale. Photos of the bloodied victims include Wallace, one of D'Angelo's underlings who had, with D'Angelo's approval and assistance, attempted to escape the drug ring and finish his education. After seeing the photos, D'Angelo is sickened and angry. The concluding dialogue in this scene reveals not only D'Angelo's inner conflict but also the complexity of the social and family matrix from which he has emerged.

> *D'Angelo Barksdale:* You don't understand, man. You all don't get it. You grow up in this shit. My grandfather was Butch Stanford. You know who Butch Stanford was in this town? All my people, man, my father, my uncles, my cousins—it's just what you do. (*He picks up the photo of Wallace showing a bullet hole in his head and stares at it.*) You just live with this shit until you can't breathe no more. I swear to God. I was courtside for eight months and I was freer in jail than I was at home.
> *Asst. State's Attorney Rhonda Pearlman:* What are you looking for?
> *D:* I want it to go away.

P: I can't...
D: I want what Wallace wanted. I want to start over. That's what I want. I don't care where. Anywhere. I don't give a f***. I just want to go somewhere where I can breathe like regular folks. Get me that and I'll give you them.

D'Angelo has made up his mind to turn on his family. His attorney and the police arrange to keep him in a facility outside of Baltimore—precisely so his family will not have an easy time finding him. But the Barksdales' lawyer finds him and he must confront his mother, Brianna (Michael Hyatt). The conversation between them takes viewers further into the web of D'Angelo's predicament and that of the entire family.

D'Angelo Barksdale: How you all even find me?
Brianna Barksdale: Ain't no one going to keep a mother from her son.
D: (*Brianna takes a seat across the table from her son.*) You know, you're always talking family. Family is the heart, you say. Well, I'm family, ain't I? So, what about me for once? It ain't right.

D'Angelo Barksdale (Lawrence Gilliard, Jr.) ponders his fate in the interrogation room (*The Wire***, Home Box Office, 2002–2008).**

B: What's right? Huh? You like for him [*referring to Avon*] to step up and take the weight and let you walk? 'Cause he will. You know he will. But if he got to go away, that means you got to step up and fill his shoes. You ready for that?

D: You know I ain't. I ain't ready and I ain't never going to be ready for this game.

B: Dee, c'mon…

D: Look. They giving me a chance to walk away. To start over again someplace else.

B: And what you giving them? He messed up, okay? He knows it. Now if you want to get even with him, you can. But if you hurt him, you hurt this whole family. All of us. Me and Trina and the cousins and Donette [D'Angelo's wife], too. And your baby. Your own baby boy. This right here is part of the game. And without the game this whole family would be down in the terrace living off scraps. Shit, we probably wouldn't even be a family. Start over? Huh? How are you going to start over without your people? Without your own child, even? You ain't got family in this world, what the hell have you got?

With this appeal Brianna succeeds in roping D'Angelo back into the fold. He declines the plea bargain, refuses to testify against his family, and receives a sentence of 20 years while his uncle Avon escapes with only seven years. Viewers see a powerful reengagement of his inner conflict as his mother chooses to sacrifice her son for her brother. Brianna's action stems from a perverse loyalty to the only kind of inheritance she has known and for which she is willing to do whatever it takes to prop up a criminal enterprise against law enforcement. Her mixture of fierce family loyalty, sacrifice, and devotion to a dubious cause presents a portrait of disturbingly misaligned strengths and weaknesses.

Viewers begin to learn enough of the Barksdales' history to see an explanation for how the family game became a life of crime. But through D'Angelo's character development viewers also learn this explanation serves as weak justification for continuous reaffirmation of the family game. Viewers experience, along with D'Angelo, the real price of this game and know that it literally leads to dead ends. Although D'Angelo cannot find the will to testify against his family, he continues to struggle to find a way to avoid going down with what he knows is a slowly sinking ship.

The sense of gritty realism achieved in *The Wire*, when viewed from the point of view of the art of drama, raises another important question consistent with the "messenger" issue previously mentioned. If a dramatic production can rightly claim to be little more than a re-creation of real-life events, does it thereby gain immunity from criticism even when presenting incidents of extreme violence?

The answer relates to what was discussed in the introduction regarding outcomes inevitable to the process of reporting information. When reporting facts, it is not possible to report *all* the facts. And in the process of selecting the relevant facts, it is not possible to avoid constructing a context and conveying a point of view and a set of values through the particular choices made. Between narratives such as *Taxi Driver* and *The Wire*, which both claim to raise a mirror to reality, it is possible to see a difference of structure resulting in a difference in quality of drama and in potential effects on an audience.

The Wire facilitates multiple character identifications or connections, the lines of which become crossed and messy. Everyone is a victim in one way or another—victims of a system too far out of balance. And in a system out of balance, some victims are more victimized than others. The entire drama exposes the sense in which communities and bureaucracies live with the tension of constant negotiation of power and exploitation between individuals and groups. *The Wire* belongs firmly in the category of synagonal tragic drama and, to the extent the show can lay claim to realism, it also thereby exposes the complex nature of the problems in the culture and community of urban areas in the current era.

In shifting his career from journalist to dramatist, David Simon conceded the limitations of journalism to effect social change and decided to explore the potential of screen drama to draw attention to obdurate inner-city problems. But in doing so, he approached drama not as an entertainer and a seeker of fame and profits. In an interview via the HBO website, Simon said, "We are not selling hope, or audience gratification, or cheap victories with this show. *The Wire* is making an argument about what institutions—bureaucracies, criminal enterprises, the cultures of addiction, raw capitalism even—do to individuals. It is not designed purely as an entertainment. It is, I'm afraid, a somewhat angry show" (as cited in Mandel, 2013).

Interestingly, Simon uses the word "selling" in these comments. He claims *not* to be selling pure entertainment but offers only the clue ("a somewhat angry show") as indication of what he is selling. While he may be selling good measures of his own anger about the chronic failings of individuals and institutions, he places this anger in a dramatic structure which effectively avoids the selling of violence even as the show depicts violence. And while it may be possible that criminals and potential criminals may, through the show's realism, learn something about police strategies for defeating crime, these risks are outweighed by the many ways in which the show guides viewers to confront the destructive and violent consequences of narrowly conceived life choices and narrowly functioning bureaucracies.

The Killing
(2011–)

The Killing sets itself apart from other crime dramas in the believable and fascinating ways in which it undermines viewers' ready assumptions about the key characters, exposing progressively deeper layers of motivation. This excavation into character also increases the complexity of conflict, achieving uncommon synagonal development. There are no villains in this drama and as soon as a particular character and his or her actions appear to take on the mantle of villainy, further developments in the plot reveal sufficient elements of human virtue and vulnerability to force viewer reappraisal of that character. These shifts in perspective are achieved through scriptwriting so well done that, rather than feeling unfairly misled, viewers are constantly forced to squarely confront the shortcoming in their own tendency—the very human tendency—to misread behavior and to judge too quickly. For this lesson alone and the compelling ways in which it consistently achieves this effect, the show deserves awards for scripting and acting. Several cast members have received nominations for acting but only Michelle Forbes has won a Saturn Award for her second-season performance as Mitch Larsen.

The story for *The Killing* derives from a Danish television crime drama which first aired in 2007 and achieved great popularity in Europe. The show's success in Europe prompted Veena Sud—whose previous producing and writing credits include the CBS show *Cold Case* (2003–2010)—to pitch the show to networks in the United States. The show found production support from Fox TV and eventually aired on the AMC cable channel. At the end of season two, AMC reported it would not renew the show for a third season because its ratings had dropped from first-season levels. The show had, however, acquired a devoted following of fans who loudly protested the canceling of the show. Noting

Homicide Detective Sarah Linden (Mireille Enos) and Detective Stephen Holder (Joel Kinnaman) form a tense alliance to solve a murder (*The Killing*, AMC Network Entertainment, 2011–).

17. The Killing

the fan following, and understanding the quality of the writing and the cast for the show, AMC worked to find a way to continue. Finally, in January 2013, AMC, in conjunction with the Fox TV production company, announced that the show would come back for a third season of 12 episodes. So, as of this writing, the series continues production.

The Killing is unusual in featuring a strong female lead, Homicide Detective Sarah Linden (Mireille Enos), accompanied by a male subordinate partner, Detective Stephen Holder (Joel Kinnaman). The portrayed setting is Seattle, Washington, although the actual location for the series is in British Columbia. Consequently, the series has no problem achieving the noir mood it seeks with the consistent presence of overcast skies and a predominance of subdued colors and shades of gray. Enos has been criticized for her flat-affect portrayal of Linden, but her subdued emotions, sparse verbalizations, and stubborn intelligence work marvelously in tandem with the Seattle setting. It takes a while for viewers to catch on to her iron woman façade, but as each episode exposes layers of her personal life as a single mom in a difficult relationship with her son, and her professional life in her relationship with Holder, her integrity and compassionate spirit shine through the clouds.

Similarly, Holder, a new hire in the Homicide Department, projects little emotion and uses few words but, unlike Linden, has a dry sense of humor which he occasionally uses in attempts to break through Linden's fortified exterior. Their relationship begins on good footing as Linden prepares to leave the department to begin a new life in California and Holder enters as her replacement at the head of the Homicide Division. But Linden abruptly pulls back on her departure, at the request of her superior, to investigate the disappearance of a teenage girl, Rosie Larsen (Katie Findlay), under circumstances indicating possible foul play. Linden's return to the department stuns Holder, who suddenly finds himself as subordinate to a woman rather than lead detective. The case proves difficult to solve quickly and Holder encourages Linden to depart to California while assuring her that the Larsen girl is likely only a runaway. But Linden has an intuition about the case and, through persistent investigative effort, she discovers Rosie's body in the trunk of a car which has been pulled out of small, secluded lake. Now there is a murder and Linden shows no intention of leaving until the case is solved.

As news of the murder breaks, new tensions build in every direction

187

in the story. Linden and Holder settle into a tense and reluctant relationship as they recognize they will need to work as partners investigating the case. Linden and her son, Jack (Liam James), strain under the tensions imposed by the sudden decision to remain in Seattle without a place to live. Linden and her fiancé struggle as she postpones and eventually cancels plans for their wedding in California. The Larsen family begins to fall apart as each parent blames the other for the loss of their daughter and their other two children labor to comprehend it all. The campaign staff of mayoral candidate Darren Richmond (Billy Campbell) descends into a cloud of doubt and inner turmoil because the car in which Rosie's body was found belongs to his campaign. Tensions mount among Rosie's friends and her former boyfriend as pressure builds for them to provide information and recall the events leading up to when they last saw her.

With each new lead in the investigation new characters move into focus, creating new frictions and violent encounters. When one of Rosie's teachers at her high school, Bennet Ahmed (Brandon Jay McLaren), falls under suspicion for her murder, Rosie's father, Stan Larsen (Brent Sexton), and one of his employees, Belko Royce (Brendan Sexton), take him for a truck ride to the countryside, where they beat him nearly to death. Larsen later discovers that Ahmed could not have been the murderer. For his hot-headed actions, Larsen is arrested for attempted murder and placed in jail. This creates new stress between Stan and his wife, Mitch (Michelle Forbes), because she had been the one who goaded him into assaulting Ahmed.

Having learned nothing from the mistaken assault of Ahmed, Royce acts again on his own as mayoral candidate Richmond falls under suspicion when he refuses to account for his whereabouts on the evening of the murder. Royce attempts to assassinate Richmond with a handgun and succeeds in wounding him in the spine, paralyzing him below the waist, and thereby consigning him to a wheel chair for the rest of his life. Later in the series, suspicions fall on the mayor of Seattle and a member of his staff and also on the matriarch of an Indian tribe which operates a casino on reservation land. All of these suspects appear engaged in nefarious activities and yet each turns out to have had reasons for their suspicious actions other than covering up a murder. While these turns in the plot may be viewed as clever ploys for building suspense, they do align well with the experience of blindness when groping forward in an investigation. This process of detection, of attempting to read while not fatefully misreading persons and signs, provides an exaggerated heightening of what everyone encounters in negotiating daily life. Every reading of character is consequential and open to hidden potential for misreading.

Even when the murderer is finally revealed at the end of season two, the act itself turns out to be clouded and conflicted, the result of a tortured mix of motives and circumstances even Dostoyevsky would acknowledge as psychologically penetrating. The murder is another stunning and disturbing illustration of a desire to do good in which loyalty to an idealized chosen approach is so strong its success justifies any means and thereby subverts the good it would do. In one way or another, this is a hard insight forced on all key players in the drama. In Linden's case, especially, she must weigh her obsession with solving the case against the toll it takes on her son and fiancé. One cloud on her horizon lifts when the case is solved, but the cloud in her personal life remains. Other clouds from her past which have not been adequately confronted surface on the horizon at the conclusion of the second season.

Due to the ways in which the relational conflicts in *The Killing* repeatedly turn inward on individuals, opening or re-opening inner conflicts, this series may also be described as synagonal psychodrama, whereby viewers are led to see from many sides the inner conflicts playing out within the main characters as well as the relational conflicts. These conflicts are not necessarily resolved but are exposed sufficiently from opposing sides to leave viewers on the horns of tragic dramatic response—a measure of empathy for human failings and a measure of caution for the gesture of indifference the world often shows toward human aspirations. No instance of violence in the series can be experienced as unfolding in a way prompting any sense of justice done. While antagonal dramas are split in this regard, showing violence on victims followed by retributive violence, synagonal dramas depict violence in contexts revealing its deep injustice. Through its extended synagonal focus on the murder of Rosie Larsen, *The Killing* achieves, at least in its first two seasons, the heights of great drama while transporting viewers into the dark reality of the ruinous consequences and lasting injustices of deadly violence.

18

Hell on Wheels
(2011–)

The crime drama seems at times little more than a western updated to the 20th century—a man packing a gun either for or against the law. One reason the western has had some difficulty surviving into the 21st century centers on the fact that westerns must always have a "man" packing the gun. For many years this was also the case with crime dramas and action films. These films were a men's club just like priesthood. But as gender roles began to shift in the 1960s and '70s, women began breaking into the men's club and television shows eventually followed suit. As this trend progressed, television and feature-film westerns declined in popularity. Roles needed to be created for women on the same level as lead roles for men. Eventually this led to crime dramas in which women could be detectives and partner with men. And, as in the case of *The Killing*, a woman could be the lead detective in a male/female duo.

To place a drama in the setting of the Wild West of the late–19th century required, for purposes of historical accuracy, retreating backward to the creation of plots where women stood in the shadow of the men of action. This requirement meant westerns lost favor in the eyes of producers looking for material capable of appealing to a broader audience. The more active role of women in every type of occupation called for women to play roles in which they are significant participants in the action.

So when Joe and Tony Gayton, whose previous work includes the action film *Faster* (2010), had the idea of telling a story centered on the building of the transcontinental railroad, they faced the challenge of creating a western for the 21st century. They needed to place a woman among the lead roles for this action western and they came up with a very creative solution. The Union Pacific Railroad employs a surveyor,

Confederate Civil War veteran Cullen Bohannon (Anson Mount) and a refined English widow, Lily Bell (Dominique McElligott), work together to help build the transcontinental railroad (*Hell on Wheels*, AMC Network Entertainment, 2011–).

Robert Bell (Robert Moloney), to chart the course for laying track. He is accompanied by his wife, Lily (Dominique McElligott). In the second episode a Cheyenne kills Robert when he attacks the couple in a wooded area. Lily barely survives but manages to escape with Robert's scrolled maps, representing weeks of work, charting the course for hundreds of miles of track. Events thrust Lily into the position of a woman of action, called on to save the maps and return them to railroad management, headed by Thomas "Doc" Durant (Colm Meaney). In addition to this creative solution for placing a woman in a lead role, the Gayton Brothers also add a productive twist by making her a high society Britain. Lily becomes not only a woman on the frontier but a well-educated woman of refined sensibilities who definitely does not belong on the frontier and is ill prepared for everything it does and does not offer. Nevertheless, she has high spirit, pride, and tenacity and wants to personally see her husband's work carried out. The writers have a grand time showing an aristocratic Britain confronting the harsh realities of 1870s Nebraska and the assortment of ruffians populating the moving campsite—called Hell on Wheels—at the railroad's end of line.

Hell on Wheels, the end of rail camp, as the setup for a western, is truly an inspired choice. The possibilities for character development, conflict, and shifts in direction of plot prove endless. Two other characters, Confederate Civil War veteran, Cullen Bohannon (Anson Mount), and recently liberated slave, Elam Ferguson (Common), join Lily Bell and Thomas Durant to fill out the four lead roles. Bohannon drifts into the railroad operation in search of Union soldiers who killed his wife and young son. Seeing Bohannon's fearlessness and latent leadership, rail foreman Daniel Johnson (Ted Levine) hires him to supervise the black work crew. Bohannon occasionally clashes with Ferguson, who serves in a leadership role for the black track layers. The black crew competes with an Irish crew, creating ethnic tensions. Track-laying progress slows even further with the Plains Indians' intrusions into the railroad's plans. And, in case there should be any slow moments in this beehive of activity, head of railroad security, Thor Gundersen (Christopher Heyerdahl), adds a further ethnic twist as a dour Norwegian who deals calmly and violently with any challenge to his authority.

With such diversity in the cast, *Hell on Wheels* emerges as an American melting pot of characters. And in parallel fashion, it presents a melting pot of dramatic genres. With the unusual combination of storyline and characters, the writers directly or indirectly borrow from American 18th century captive dramas such as the Leatherstocking tales of James Fenimore Cooper, revenge sagas, romantic fiction, class and race conflicts, Indian and Civil War chronicles, immigrant histories, and frontier legends. All of these traditional American story influences tend toward melodramatic and antagonal dramatic structures.

To their credit, however, the writers consistently avoid easy options and choose to make the conflicts at the root of their stories messy. Nothing happens in quite the way that might be expected. For example, the revenge saga playing out with Bohannon and his search for those who murdered his family takes an unusual turn when his vigilante efforts lead him to kill a soldier who perfectly matches the identity of one of the guilty men. Bohannon then learns he was mistaken and the man he strangled to death was innocent—just as the victim had claimed before he died. The crushing guilt of his own crime, added to the weight he already carries in the tragedy with his family, leaves viewers on the edge of their seats about how or whether he will find a path forward with his life.

In a parallel story, vulnerable yet fiercely determined Lily Bell deadlocks in a power struggle with Durant over her role in managing the path laid out by her deceased husband for the railroad. Durant wants to detour from this path because he gets paid per mile of track laid, not per mile of track laid for the most efficient route. Nevertheless, Durante needs the surveyor's maps in order to learn the ideal locations for river crossings and to avoid geographic dead ends. He has no time for new surveys but he does have time to devote to a romantic interest in the attractive but aloof Lily. On his side lies the power of the coin and the ability to offer her comfortable lodging in his railcar palace. The conflict between these two proud, stubborn individuals also plays out in unexpected ways as each attempts to align the other to his or her advantage. Bohannon unintentionally fuels their conflict because Durant notices Lily keeps a roving eye on the foreman as she attempts to get to know him better. Durant's jealousy prevents him from noticing Bohannon is too bitter, enraged, and distracted by his past to chase Lily. Bohannon's isolation from others in the camp, including Lily, only makes her more curious about his past.

Tensions also run high between Bohannon and Ferguson. As a Confederate soldier and former slave owner, Bohannon immediately inflames Ferguson's contempt and raises suspicions about his motives for working on the railroad. For his part, Bohannon finds Ferguson's independent streak and arrogant attitude bordering on insubordination. But he understands loss and injustice and sees in the former slave something of his own rage. The two form an uneasy alliance and yet their tentative friendship constantly confronts challenges from shifting circumstances and cross-purposes. As a further complication in their relationship, both men are responsible for killings in the camp and each is the only one who knows the other's secret.

While every character in this series turns out to be in their own way a wild card, the most wild of the wild cards is the security chief, Gundersen, who is called "the Swede" by the camp population despite his being Norwegian. On one occasion Bohannon has the audacity to challenge his authority and from that point forward the Swede cannot do enough to make Bohannon's life miserable. When Foreman Johnson—suspected by Bohannon of knowing who killed his wife and son—is slain by Ferguson before Bohannon can get the information from him, the Swede is quick to hold Bohannon accountable for the murder. Thanks to the intervention of Durant, Bohannon escapes hanging and begins working for Durant as the new foreman. Now the Swede is even more outraged. Eventually, Durant fires him when his cruelty causes members of the camp to turn on him and punish him by walking him through the camp tarred and feathered. He internalizes his anger, which now blazes at blast furnace temperature.

With these developments, the Swede would appear to be the perfect candidate for the traditional villain. But the series' writers introduce an angle of complexity to his character when revealing his backstory as one of few survivors from the atrocity-ridden Confederate prisoner-of-war camp at Andersonville. This background information makes the Swede's contempt for Bohannon and the Confederacy more understandable. Everywhere the Swede turns, new injustices toward him multiply. The darkness surrounding his vision of life and of Bohannon casts a shadow into the future of the series. However, based on the unusual twists the series presents thus far, future confrontations between Bohannon and the Swede are not likely to proceed down predictable lines. Both men share fates as troubled victims and, therefore, one cannot play true villain to the other.

At this writing, *Hell on Wheels* has been approved for a third season. The series offers a fresh 21st century start for the western, which had gotten off to a rather bad start with television offerings such as *Deadwood* (2004–2006) and cinema offerings such as *Open Range* (2003). The latter recycles the western melodramatic clichés of ranch baron villains, excessive gun violence, intimidated townspeople, and tame supporting roles for women. The *Deadwood* series avoids clichés while attempting realism, deriving many of its characters from actual residents of the 1870s South Dakota mining town along with several story ideas from newspapers of the time. The narrow focus and muckraking aims of the writers, however, only succeed in conjuring the very worst from the ghosts of Deadwood's past—their petty politics, nasty vices, despicable killings, and foul language—all of which fails to add up to noteworthy drama.

Hell on Wheels similarly derives its setup from real events of the 1870s—the transcontinental railroad construction—but, aside from Thomas Durant, the writers create the characters and the basis for their interactions. Building their characters from scratch, they succeed admirably in organizing an ensemble of personalities, each with a unique set of strengths, weaknesses, and emerging backstories combining to create rounded and complex personalities. These personalities work in tandem with the synagonal visioning of conflict to frame the violence in this series in ways illuminating its intrinsic corrosiveness and the weight of its abiding consequences.

Summary and Conclusions

> It was the best of times, it was the worst of times, it was the age of wisdom, it was the age of foolishness, it was the epic of belief, it was the epic of incredulity, it was the season of light, it was the season of darkness, it was the spring of hope, it was the winter of despair, we had everything before us, we had nothing before us, we were all going direct to Heaven, we were all going direct the other way—in short, the period was ... like the present period.
> —Charles Dickens

Dickens's famous opening passage from *A Tale of Two Cities* has probably been cited every year since its year of publication, 1859, as an accurate description of each current period. To cite another well-worn phrase, the more things change the more they stay the same. And this may also be said of the current state of screen entertainment. Over the last month, I heard someone say the current time counts as the worst ever in the history of film and television, while another sees the current time as a Golden Age for the screen arts. It would be easy to suppose both opinions exaggerate the case and that the truth lies somewhere in the middle. But as Dickens suggests, history may have a way of excluding the middle while violating the law of contradiction. The more things change the more they stay the same, but, of course, they do not stay the same. When closely examined, every age has its paradoxical marriage of extremes warranting the label for the best and the worst of times. But the specific nature of the extremes and the particular forces giving rise to them constitute the unique feature of any given period.

Few offer a more compelling account of the current paradoxical cultural milieu than the French sociologist and philosopher Gilles Lipovetsky. According to Lipovetsky, in the last three hundred or so years western civilization has evolved through stages of the premodern, the modern, the postmodern, and now the hypermodern.

In Lipovetsky's account, the 18th century Enlightenment signaled a rebirth of classical rationalism and the thinking autonomous subject. Other innovators of the era laid the foundation for scientific methodology, adding a new and extraordinary level to the investigative powers of reason. Science of the 19th century inaugurated the Industrial Revolution, which in turn led to an unprecedented surge of commerce, dispersal of wealth, and the creation of a broad middle class. The spread of wealth and the creation of an extensive middle class enabled an increasing number of individuals to widen their choices and their horizons, empowering them with an autonomy previously realized only by a small aristocracy.

The Industrial Revolution set in motion a rapidly accelerating series of further changes. These changes occurred so quickly as to blur together in a whirl of overlapping transformations. Technological innovation culminated in highly sophisticated devices for information transmission and processing. Each set of innovations added new levels of capability and knowledge, initiating social and political changes that further empower individuals. These changes also led to legal protections for individuals based on the notion of human rights. This wave of transformations has, according to Lipovetsky, reached the proportion of a tsunami lifting some individuals to new heights while overwhelming and destroying others. Consequently, as recounted in the opening section of the chapter on *The Sopranos*, the current era presents a paradoxical blend of the best and the worst in individual coping and adapting behaviors. As Lipovetsky says, "Through its operations of technocratic normalization and the loosening of social bonds, the hypermodern age simultaneously manufactures order and disorder, subjective independence and dependence, moderation and excess" (2005: 33).

Any era will include persons of marginal stability and limited capacity for assuming personal responsibility for actions. But the current era presents an exceptional challenge. Stability of identity and character has long been a common staple of personal aspiration and a sign of success. The enormous increase in the freedom of choice presented for fashioning a personal identity would appear to be a great opportunity and an unquestionable good, but it also functions as a great challenge and a destabilizing source of confusion. As stultifying and limiting as tradition, ritual, and routine may appear to contemporary eyes, these inherited patterns served a positive function for many by providing ready-made identities and well-worn paths for finding a way through the thickets of life.

When familiar routines are removed or discredited and replaced by a bewildering assortment of untested alternatives, the potential for instability magnifies and spreads. For persons struggling with stability issues, exponential increase in stimuli and diversity in the cultural and social environment exacerbates instability, multiplies marginal cases, and amplifies the severity of coping failures. As a result, suicide rates rise alongside rates of psychological pathology. And although statistics show an increase of incidences of individual violence over the last several decades, the trend toward increasingly bizarre and alarmingly sizeable single perpetrator mass killings emerges as a prominent and growing public concern. Here, again, Lipovetsky notes the paradoxes:

> Hypermodern culture is characterized by the weakening of the regulative power of collective institutions and the corresponding way in which actors have become more autonomous *vis-à-vis* group imperatives, whether these come from family, religion, political parties or class cultures. Hence the individual appears more and more opened up and mobile, fluid and socially independent. But this volatility signifies much more a destabilization of the self than a triumphant affirmation of a subject endowed with self-mastery— witness the rising tide of psychosomatic symptoms and obsessive-compulsive behavior, depression, anxiety and suicide attempts, not to mention the growing sense of inadequacy and self-depreciation. The psychological vulnerability is less the result, as is too often claimed, of the extenuating weight of performance norms, or the intensification of the pressures exerted on people, and more a matter of the breakdown of the previous systems of defence and other frameworks that supported the individual [2005: 55–56].

Granting a measure of validity to this sweeping account of the current cultural condition, there would appear to be ample explanation for the kinds of violence plaguing hypermodern societies short of blaming violence on the entertainment industry. In this book, however, I have not attempted to portray the prevalence of violence in screen entertainment as the root cause of violence in society. Instead, I have argued that it must be understood as a contributing element—but a contributing element of considerable power which is all too readily underestimated in its ability to shape attitudes fostering a culture of aggression and violence.

Furthermore, I have not argued violent entertainment *in whatever form* contributes to institutionalizing a culture of violence. Instead, I have argued only that violence, presented in the context of varieties of highly antagonal dramatic structure, serves to promote and amplify the identities, attitudes, and behaviors consistent with a culture of violence.

The phrase "culture of violence" is usefully descriptive in this context but is also potentially misleading. Postmodern philosophers popularized the notion that every culture rests on a foundation of violence in which "violence" refers to the necessary oppression occurring in any society imposing and enforcing laws, constraints, and protection on its citizens. Additionally, "violence" occurs in any society institutionalizing the notion of land ownership, since one person is deprived of what another acquires. Similarly, the hyper-consumerism of hypermodern societies propagates further a kind of daily violence through the injustice or inequality of what one person has and another does not have. And though everyone may be said to have opportunity to acquire everything, levels of opportunity are never equal. This lack of proportion in opportunity and inheritance results in measures of what may also be labeled as yet another kind of inevitable violence.

But this kind of necessary organic violence is not part of what is here meant in the use of "culture of violence." Instead, "culture of violence" should be read as "culture of *unnecessary* violence." But it may well be asked, what violence, other than organic violence, is *necessary*? That said, defining instances where violence may be necessary presses the discussion into areas beyond the scope of this book. For current purposes the focus should remain on the unnecessary. Wherever extreme violence is aligned with a sense of justice and an impulse for hurrahs, the signs are in place for reading either an instance of unnecessary violence or an instance of unnecessary and inappropriate celebration.

The sense of justice and the impulse for hurrahs in the face of violence reflect the dysfunctional affirmation of violence lying at the root of a "culture of violence." A shift away from this kind of culture requires reorientation of the collective psyche. And no one, including myself, need assume such cultural retraining is called for only in the case of others. In whatever degree a culture of violence exists in the United States, everyone is immersed in it and influenced by it from an early age onward.

Like it or not, the hypermodern individual is freighted with a host of responsibilities consistent with a mass of stimuli, opportunities, and temptations unheard of in times past. And like it or not, a percentage of persons in every community will be overwhelmed by the challenges and unable to cope with the responsibility of constructing a functionally stable identity. And a considerable number of the challenges come from the ever-encircling and pervasive varieties of influence pumped through media.

Those who may occupy career positions in the business of mainstream entertainment also find themselves serving as gatekeepers for popular drama with accelerating responsibilities. And not to be overlooked, critics, reviewers, and commentators for screen entertainment are also important operatives in the entertainment industry. They exercise more influence than they may suspect and the responsibility they carry with that influence needs to be more keenly felt and widely understood. A colleague of Lipovetsky's, Sébastien Charles, summarizes the situation this way:

> This is perhaps the most astonishing fact: the society of mass consumption, emotional and individualistic as it is, allows an adaptable spirit of responsibility to coexist with a spirit of irresponsibility incapable of resisting either external temptations or internal compulsions. The fact is that the binary logic of our societies will continue to increase, and everyone will become more and more responsible for themselves. Never has a society allowed individual autonomy and freedom such far-reaching expression; never has its destiny been so linked to the behavior of those who comprise it [2005: 26].

As screen media increasingly dominate print media in the entertainment business, the film critic increasingly supercedes the literary critic. And with the greater potential for influence accompanying screen media and its immersive video and audio technology, the screen critic acquires responsibilities significantly exceeding those of literary critics of the past. Yet this growing responsibility heightens the concern that the media conglomerates through which critical commentaries on entertainment flow to the public are the same conglomerates generating that entertainment. The public would be better served if those doing the work of reviewing new entertainment received financial support from sources independent of the entertainment industry.

In this regard, late-media analyst George Gerbner (1994) proposed a possible solution. He suggested imposing a modest sales tax on theater tickets and cable television subscriptions for the purpose of raising funds to support independent publishing of reviews and commentaries relating to entertainment. However, government-subsidized consumer protection agencies have also proven to be easily co-opted by the industries being monitored. Alternatively, the internet serves as a growing source of independent commentary and has already opened the door for many individual commentators and bloggers who may, over time, generate public trust and a significant following. Non-profit organizations may also assume a larger role in media monitoring. CommonSenseMedia.org, for example, currently offers online independent reviews of movies, games, apps, websites, television programs, books, and music for ages between two and 18. However, even specialized monitoring sites such as this still require substantial consumer caution. Clearly more work needs to be done educating CommonSenseMedia.org's reviewers when, for example, consumers are left to wonder how much common sense plays a role in awarding a film such as *Killing Them Softly* (2012) four stars out of five and touting it as a "smart, cynical, bloody crime movie" (Anderson, 2012). It is more precisely a dim, sinister, and unnecessarily bloody crime movie. Regardless of the touted reliability of the source, there would appear to be ample reason to continue voicing the alarm: Buyer beware!

Nevertheless, motivating individual producers and consumers—not to mention members of Congress—toward taking more responsibility for the mythos of the culture of violence supported and created through particular violent media content currently remains difficult for a variety of reasons. Not the least of these reasons derives from the fact that producers in the entertainment industry see themselves as entirely in the business of selling products rather than making culture. Unfortunately, the products they sell constitute a huge and ever-expanding portion of culture itself.

The late cultural critic Neil Postman expressed another reason for the current difficulty in mounting campaigns for altering the status quo of content—a reason tracing back to communication media: "Everything from telegraphy and photography in the 19th century to the silicon chip in the twentieth has amplified the din of information, until matters have reached such proportions today that for the average person, information no longer has any relation to the solution of problems ... the tie between information and action has been severed" (1990). In another context,

Postman was even more blunt: "Information has become a form of garbage, not only incapable of answering the most fundamental human questions but barely useful in providing coherent direction to the solution of even mundane problems" (1992). Certainly, the information is available—for anyone able to corral it and absorb it—sufficient to justify the judgments presented in this book and to motivate the increased responsibility recommended in this conclusion. If the content in this book and others in the same vein can rise above the din, perhaps Americans can prove Postman wrong. On that note, please keep this book and its information separate from the garbage. Better yet, circulate it among friends in the entertainment industry who have children and therefore, hopefully, a strong investment in the future of community and the quality of the stories that will doubtless shape it.

Afterword

Good Drama and
the Aesthetics of Violence
Match Point *vs.* Crime and Punishment

Among the themes discussed in this book, one in particular calls for further attention. Chapter Ten raises the question of what counts as *great* drama and offers the partial answer that great drama requires the portrayal of great conflict. Great conflict occurs when forces pull in opposite directions as when "blood ties pull family members together and competing values pull them apart." But even conflict within a family, it was argued, can fail to be significant if it revolves solely around petty desires such as lust, greed, money, or power. This kind of struggle can be tense and raging as violence but not intense and engaging as conflict. It tends to devolve into spectacle.

One of the complaints raised herein against violent screen dramas derives from their failure to generate genuine conflict. The parties involved combat each other in violence with only the outcome to be decided, and, as in antagonal melodrama, even the outcome is essentially already decided. Only the precise course of action by which the villain will be vanquished remains in question. The distinction between genuine conflict and violent spectacle turns on the role of decision. If decision concerns only the choice of weapon and strategy, the issue is not itself in conflict. Conflict arises wherever there is significant indecision regarding what side to choose, what stance to take, in relation to whatever principle, value, or issue is at stake. This indecision may be portrayed primarily through the chief protagonist or it may transpire, through the artistry of the dramatist, primarily in the minds of the audience.

The philosophical basis for this understanding of conflict as indecision receives masterful treatment in the work of French philosopher

Jacques Derrida. For Derrida, the process of decision plays a defining role in the nature of conflict. Conflict can arise only when a decision is required. "If I know what I must do," Derrida explains, "I do not take a decision, I apply a knowledge, I unfold a program. For there to be a decision, I must not know what to do." Reaching a point of uncertainty initiates a weighing of alternatives followed by an act of decision. And every moment of genuine decision, according to Derrida, is an ethical moment. As Derrida notes, "The moment of decision, the ethical moment, if you will, is independent from knowledge. It is when I do not know the right rule that the ethical question arises" (cited in Raffoul, 2008: 285).

Derrida's view of the ethical would seem to run counter to the popular conception that the ethical comes into play through the construction of rules and laws. When those rules or laws are violated there is a breach of ethics. In many cases it would seem people know the rule or the law and simply choose to break it while hoping to avoid the consequences. In such cases a crisis of knowledge or lack of knowledge appears not to be at issue. And in most legal jurisdictions "ignorance of the law is no excuse" in cases of violation. So what is Derrida talking about when he asserts that the moment of decision, which is independent of knowledge, is the ethical moment? It would seem more reasonable to suppose that moments of lack of knowledge, moments calling for decision, are precisely those moments when "right" or "ethical" action is not clear. When there is lack of clarity about what the ethical choice may be, how can the person acting be held to an ethical standard?

By calling attention to the meaning of "decision" and to the "moment of decision" Derrida aims to draw out the difference between the automaton, such as a computer, and the human. If humans were to refer to a chart of rules and laws before every action and use this chart to make a decision in a particular instance, then this procedure would reduce the human to an automaton. And, as everyone knows, following a book of extensive rules for behavior will not even guarantee ethical behavior. Sometimes it is more ethical to lie than to tell the truth. Sometimes it is more ethical to break a law than to obey it. And if there are occasions when breaching rules and laws, when breaching the "ethical," is necessary in order to follow the ethical, then every moment of choice counts as a moment of decision. This is the case because if there are instances when breaching the rule or the law is the right thing to do, then every case must be weighed to some extent in order to assess whether it belongs to those cases in which violation may be the ethical course of action.

Whenever human behavior may be seen to belong to the category of the automaton, as in unconscious movements or involuntary reflexes, the behavior lies outside the ethical. And, similarly, whenever anyone attempts to justify an action by accounting for it solely on the basis of its correspondence to a rule or law, the ethical quality of the action may remain suspect. In this regard, Derrida's view of the ethical records the lessons learned from World War II.

The application of a knowledge or a program or a rule counts as something a machine could do as, for example, filling in the question mark in the following equation: $2 + 2 = ?$ No conflict arises between competing answers. But life in general and human relations in particular are rarely amenable to strict calculation. Reading situations and human behavior and character is often like trying to solve the mystery of a crime novel while having access to only a small part of the book. In real life, full context, adequate context, is often unavailable. Consequently, people are constantly confronted with the necessity for decision when responding to behaviors and situations.

However, the notion that human choices may always be reduced to moments of decision is a knife cutting two ways. Violating rules and laws, overruling authority, may be the right thing to do in some cases but may also be the most subversive and destructive thing to do in other cases. In such cases much depends on which justifications, which alternative set of rules and laws, may rightly substitute as higher authority. This, too, calls for decision, a moment of judgment in the weighing of competing values, some or all of which may have legitimate claims to make on human actors.

Returning again to the notion of conflict, human actors engage in genuine conflict when they are engaged in having to make a decision in the sense Derrida uses the term. Fictional portrayals of deadly violence do not rise to the level of conflict insofar as they do not adequately portray actions rooted in decision—which is to say, actions rooted in indecision or profound inner conflict. To the extent this conflict is not drawn out and thoroughly dramatized for a viewing audience, the drama fails to center on conflict and thereby becomes spectacle—the spectacle of violent actions playing themselves out like forces of nature. Spectacle in the place of conflict may, like fireworks, entertain but cannot substitute for the multi-faceted experience of good drama. And, as argued herein, violent spectacle in place of drama risks a great deal with respect to how it may be understood and interpreted by audiences.

Consider, for example, Woody Allen's film *Match Point* (2005). In an interview about the film, conducted by Eric Lax, Allen tells of an article he read that had been written by a Catholic priest. From the priest's point of view, *Match Point* sends a message of life lacking transcendent meaning whereby one action becomes as good as another. So if someone chooses murder and can get away with it, there is no reason not to do so. But Allen insists the film implies nothing of the sort: "What I'm really saying—and it's not hidden or esoteric, it's just clear as a bell—is that we have to accept that the universe is godless and life is meaningless, often a terrible and brutal experience with no hope, and that love relationships are very, very hard, and that we still need to find a way to not only cope but lead a decent and moral life" (Lax 2011: 123–124). Sensing the need to round out this explanation a little more, Allen continues:

> Now, there are plenty of people who choose to lead their lives in a completely self-centered, homicidal way. They feel, since nothing means anything and I can get away with murder, I'm going to. But one can also make the choice that you're alive and other people are alive and you're in a lifeboat with them and you've got to try and make it as decent as you can for yourself and everybody. And it would seem to me this is so much more moral and even more "Christian." If you acknowledge the awful truth of human existence and choose to be a decent human being in the face of it rather than lie to yourself that there's going to be some heavenly reward or some punishment, it seems to me more noble. If there is a reward or a punishment or a payoff somehow and you act well, then you're acting well not out of such noble motives, the same so-called Christian motives. It's like the suicide bombers who allegedly act out of noble religious or national motives when in fact their families get a financial payoff, revel in a heroic legacy—not to mention the promise of virgins for the perpetrators [Lax 2011: 124].

In light of this account of what the film is saying by none other than its creator, consider the story the film tells and ask whether this message is, as Allen says, "clear as a bell." For those who have not seen the film, here is a brief synopsis.

A young professional tennis player, Chris Wilton (Jonathan Rhys-Meyers), struggling with his finances, gains the attention of Chloe

Hewett (Emily Mortimer), the daughter of a wealthy businessman. Chloe loves Chris but Chris is passionate about Nola Rice (Scarlett Johansson), the fiancée of Chloe's brother, Tom (Matthew Goode). Chris and Nola have a sexual encounter but Nola refuses to continue the affair due to her engagement with Tom. Chris eventually weds Chloe and thereby marries into the wealthy family. But Chris then renews the affair with Nola when Tom breaks off the engagement, bowing to family pressure that Nola is not quite the right woman for the upper-class family. Nola then becomes pregnant by Chris and demands he leave Chloe. However, Chris has now become too accustomed to the high life to return to a life of relative poverty. He opts for money over passion and chooses to murder Nola to extricate himself from the dilemma. To confuse the police, he first murders Nola's elderly next-door neighbor, making it appear as a robbery of the neighbor that went wrong when Nola returned to her flat and discovered the robber in the hallway. To make the scenario convincing, Chris steals jewelry from the neighbor. He later tosses it all into the Thames. But Chris does not notice one ring hits the railing and slips back onto the walkway next to the river. Chris comes under suspicion for the murder when Detective Banner (James Nesbitt) discovers him to be the primary object of attention in Nola's diary—after Chris has denied any recent contact with Nola. Nevertheless, Banner eventually drops his pursuit of Chris when a local drug addict, suspected of previous violence, turns up dead with a ring in his pocket—the same ring that did not make it into the Thames.

Regardless of the merits or lack thereof of Allen's view of life and his intention of expressing this view in *Match Point*, the film is clearly not clear as bell in its message. Not only a Catholic priest might read the film in ways other than Allen intended. The clearest message that can be read from the film is that it is the story of one person among those people Allen describes as "people who choose to lead their lives in a completely self-centered, homicidal way." Just as Scorsese does in *Taxi Driver*, Allen offers absolutely nothing in *Match Point* to place the actions in a critical context. Any critical engagement with the content of the film is left entirely to the viewer. If the viewer chooses to take the content at face value, then the takeaway will coincide with the worst fears of the Catholic priest—namely, that life has no meaning other than what is given it and, therefore, crime pays if you can get away with it.

While there is certainly much to ponder in Allen's interpretation of life and the moral questions it raises, the current point at issue is less grand and centers on the question of what counts as good drama. And *Match Point* fails as good drama not because it features a person who sinks into moral depravity in his actions but because the film fails to present a compelling conflict. Although the featured protagonist, Chris Wilton, strains under the weight of the situation he has created for himself, he strains only with whether he has the audacity, cunning, and neurological fortitude to pull off what he knows he wants to do. He is not weighed down by indecision about what he wants to do. Consequently, he exhibits no profound internal conflict. Similarly, he encounters no external challenge to his thinking regarding his chosen course of action. No one suspects what he is about to do and, therefore, no one contests his plan. After he commits the murders, he becomes a suspect, but only the detectives on the case suspect him and they do so only briefly until they are convinced someone else committed the crimes. Since all opposition has either failed to materialize or been removed, Chris is never brought into conflict with himself or with others over his actions. The plot of the film is then reduced to the story of a man who creates a problem for himself, labors to find a solution, finds a self-serving and deplorable remedy, and proceeds on his way. Aside from the violence, the story would not be of much interest. Only the fact that Chris's problem has a violent solution makes the story exceptional. Violence, like sex, counts as exceptional because it has the power to attract attention in the manner of spectacle.

But Allen is correct to assert that *Match Point* does not aim at mere spectacle. He makes this point when speaking about how he portrays the violence cinematically.

> I don't want to see the murder.... I notice that's a theme of mine going all the way back, and it's not conscious. I always have my sex off camera, and I always have my real violence off camera. It's not that I can't do violence.... But for some reason, unconsciously I eschew it. In *Manhattan Murder Mystery* you never see the dead woman, she's behind something. In *Match Point* you don't see the shootings. The same in *Crimes and Misdemeanors*.... Someone else doing *Crimes and Misdemeanors* could have a brilliant murder scene. Alfred Hitchcock or Martin Scorsese—a guy knocks at the door holding flowers and she answers it and what ensues is a minute and a half of brilliant cinema. The only explanation I can give is that for me, because I'm more

writer than anything, all that stuff becomes material for me to make my points on, to talk about, to philosophize over. I'm not interested in the killing itself [Lax 2011: 133].

This passage confirms that Allen is not interested in the spectacle of action-thrillers or genre murder mysteries. In another context, Allen further explains his motives in the creation of *Match Point*: "There are two kinds of murder-mystery stories. There's the kind that's the airplane-read-type mystery story, and there's the type—I'm not making any comparison here—where the murder is used in a more significant way, like in *Macbeth* or *Crime and Punishment* or *The Brothers Karamozov*; there's murder but it's used philosophically and not as a whodunit. I was trying to give a little substance to the story [*Match Point*] so it wasn't just a genre piece" (Lax 2011: 24).

So, clearly, Allen intended to devise, in the case of *Match Point*, a film with some measure of philosophical significance. Returning again to the question of the message of the film, Allen makes another interesting point:

To me it's a damn shame that the universe doesn't have any God or meaning, and yet only when you can accept that can you then go on to lead ... a Christian life—that is, a decent, moral life. You can only lead it if you acknowledge what you're up against to begin with and shuck off all the fairy tales that lead you to make choices in life that you're making not really for moral reasons but for taking down a big score in the afterlife. So the film inspired a lot of talk in that area and I'm glad. I'm glad it wasn't regarded just as a suspense murder mystery, which, mind you, I'm not knocking.... But I had hoped to use *Match Point* to at least make one or two points that are my personal philosophy and I feel I was able to do that [Lax 2011: 125].

No one can fault Allen for making a film with a message, a film raising substantial moral and philosophical issues. But as Derrida has so often illustrated in the case of texts, any attempt to convey meaning "leaves us no choice but to mean (to say) something that is (already, always, also) other than what we mean (to say)" (1988, 62). Films, like texts, are exposed in the communal marketplace to different meanings, different exchange values. Allen cannot control what his film means or the messages it may convey. However, some formulations of meaning are more provocative than others and the extent of this provocative quality depends on the number of clues offered for deciphering the message. Clearly Allen intended to be provocative and, as he states, was glad the film "inspired a lot of talk" on important life questions. But the process of provoking questions ought to be distinguished from the process of conveying or intending a particular meaning. Allen explicitly states he regards the meaning and the message of the film to be clear as a bell. So his primary goal was not simply to be provocative. Instead, he uses a provocative plot line to underscore and draw attention to his philosophy of life and his view of morality. He sees *Match Point* in the entire context of his life and work in film and so, for him, the message of the film is obvious. But if viewed as a message in the form of an argument, Allen has left out the conclusion, the message, while presenting only the initial steps of the argument. Those familiar with his work and his opinions may be able to draw the appropriate conclusion, but those new to his work or inclined toward literalist interpretation may not draw the desired conclusion.

Based on what Allen says about *Match Point*, his remarks only make sense if the film is understood as a work of monumental irony. The film shows one thing: a man murders two people to preserve his marriage and his life of comfort and no one is the wiser. And Allen asks viewers to see something else: a man acts in a morally depraved manner and suffers no consequences—indeed, he benefits from his actions—which demonstrates that moral action, if it occurs at all, must occur outside the frame of God and rewards and punishments in an afterlife.

Allen's point is one that could arise in discussions about the film, but it most definitely is not a message necessarily contained in or readily deducible from anything in the film. The most readily discernable message in the film would seem to be that, with a good plan and a little luck, it is possible to use murder to advance a career. And the film seems to confirm that, on occasion, murder can be worth the risk. Nothing in the film requires a viewer to question this approach to life—other than to consider that it could produce a few harrowing moments of stress. The conclusion Allen would have viewers arrive at depends entirely on a sense of morality they must bring with them to the theater.

Again, it is easy to slip into the ethical and philosophical frame of reference and fault *Match Point* for its seemingly blithe depiction of moral depravity. But when evaluating film as a work of dramatic art, viewers should not lose sight of the crucial role of conflict in creating compelling drama. If characters as well as viewers are not drawn to a point of significant hesitation and indecision in the weighing of a thoroughly dramatized conflict, then the dramatist has not produced drama but, instead, a spectacle or an entertainment. These latter art forms are not to be condemned but ought to be understood for what they are and not confused with the work of good drama, as is so often done by critics, reviewers, and award committees.

Match Point counts as the kind of production described herein as reverse antagonal melodrama, featuring an anti-hero who undergoes an ordeal and experiences a kind of triumph. It bears a family resemblance to drama but lacks the conflict proper to drama. This lack of conflict places the anti-hero in a context in which character and actions confront no profound existential challenge, internally or externally, resulting in heightened potential—among viewers who may approach the production with a diminished sense of irony or inadequate contextualization—to understand the anti-hero as heroic. While the dramatist cannot be held accountable for all interpretations of his or her drama, it is possible to construct stories depicting extreme violence with greater care for reducing the potential for interpreting portrayals of violence as subtle, or not so subtle, advocacy of violence. This may be viewed as an ethical responsibility but it is also usefully viewed as an aesthetic priority. Engaging drama, drama presenting genuine conflict, will succeed, entertain, and inform on many more levels than mere entertainments.

Although Allen may be confused about the clarity with which his film imparts a particular message, he is, admirably, not confused about the stature of *Match Point*. He believes *Match Point* to be one of his best films but he concedes that it is not a great film. In fact, in his interview with Eric Lax, Allen concedes that none of his films are great films.

> I've said over the years that the only thing standing between me and greatness is me, I've been completely right about that. I've been given more opportunities than anybody. I've been given the money and freedom for thirty-five years now to make whatever I wanted. A musical? Okay. A detective story? Fine. A drama? Absolutely. Another drama even though the first one failed? Go ahead. Whatever you want. So there is no reason for me not to make great films.... I've had carte blanche for thirty-five years and I've never made a great film. It's just not in me to make a great film; I don't have the depth of vision to do it. I don't say to myself I'm going to make a great film and I'm going to be uncompromising. If necessary I'll work nights and go to the far ends of the earth. That's just not me. I'd like to make a great film provided it doesn't conflict with my dinner reservation [Lax 2011: 251].

Allen is probably right about the effort and commitment it takes to create great drama. But good drama with compelling conflict can be produced, as illustrated in the examples provided in several of the chapters herein, with perhaps only a little more effort and expense than it takes to produce really bad entertainment. But the chief requirement for creating good drama consists of an adequate understanding of the elements of genuine conflict.

As a further refinement of the distinctions between good drama and the aborted drama of mere spectacle, consider the structural differences between *Match Point* and a work Allen acknowledges contains similarities—Dostoyevsky's *Crime and Punishment*. In fact, at least two references to Dostoyevsky are made in *Match Point*, doubtless with the intention of calling to mind *Crime and Punishment*.

Crime and Punishment is the story of a young man, Rodion (Rodya) Raskolnikov, living in mid–19th century St. Petersburg, who has dropped out of law school due to his condition of grinding poverty. Fighting off hunger, depression, and alienation from everyone around him, he formulates a desperate plan to validate his belief in his own worth and potential greatness. After much deliberation and careful planning, he murders an old pawnbroker he perceives to be a wretched blight on the community in order to steal her money and jewelry. However, on murdering the old woman, he panics and hurriedly takes only a few of her valuables. While making his escape, he encounters the old woman's daughter and is forced to kill her as well. In the aftermath of these crimes he finds he is not quite the person he imagined himself to be before the crimes. Riven by inner conflict, he increasingly displays this conflict to the small circle of family and friends around him. The family includes his mother and sister who come to St. Petersburg to visit him and seek his advice on the betrothal of his sister. Friends who take an exceptional interest in him include Dmitri Razumihin and Sofya (Sonia) Marmeladov, a love interest and the prostitute daughter of an unemployed former government clerk killed in a carriage accident. In addition to the family and friends, a detective, Porfiry Petrovitch, investigating the two murders, finds his behavior suspicious and believes he is responsible. But the detective also senses how conflicted he his, understands there is a side of him worthy of appeal, and attempts to rehabilitate him by getting him to confess to the murders. The combination of the crumbling façade Raskolnikov presents to those around him and the increasing concern and scrutiny others, especially Sonia and Petrovitch, bring to bear on him eventually results in his confession. Sonia follows him to Siberia where he is imprisoned and continues aiding in his rehabilitation through her love for him and her steadfast belief in his value as a human being.

To avoid confusion at the outset, the first thing said about the differences between *Match Point* and *Crime and Punishment* must address the issue of morality. The primary difference between these two stories with respect to the subject of dramatic conflict need not be seen to center on the notion that one conveys a message of moral depravity and the other a message of moral redemption. For the purposes of dramatic conflict it makes no difference whether the chief protagonist undergoes moral redemption. Dostoyevsky considered other endings to his novel, including Raskolnikov's suicide and his ultimate rejection of appeals to overcome his criminal persona. These endings would not have obviated the power of dramatic conflict Dostoyevsky created because the conflict would have remained. Only the outcome would have changed. Arguably, Dostoyevsky chose the outcome he did due to its consistency with a major philosophical theme in his writing—belief in the potential of redemption through suffering. But less redemptive and morally uplifting endings would not have lessened the intensity of the dramatic conflict— the choices and emotions with which Raskolnikov struggled.

Despite the apparent differences in endings and in moral messages, *Match Point* and *Crime and Punishment* contain broad similarities of plot. In each the chief protagonist commits a dual murder, falls under suspicion for the crimes, undergoes interrogation by a detective investigating the case, has the support of family, but finally lands in a situation where only a confession will result in his being held accountable. However, in *Match Point* the chief protagonist, Chris, fails to manifest inner conflict in the manner of Raskolnikov and thereby succeeds in presenting a façade sufficiently free of mixed cues to avoid arousing suspicion among his family and friends. Only the detective has substantial suspicions. Before he can effectively act on them, however, and pursue the interrogation of Chris, a lucky break directs attention away from him and places it convincingly on a local drug addict found with the telltale ring on his dead body. Chris avoids accountability and punishment for his crimes and eventually escapes all suspicion. Allen deliberately constructs the character of Chris and the plot in order to make the point that life provides no guarantees that crime and depravity will be punished or that the scales of justice eventually balance. It is as if Allen is saying: Here are the facts of life. Make of this what you will.

In the language of tennis, Allen has struck a difficult serve. Viewers are in the position of having to react. But this requires sufficient skill and experience to return the ball. Allen provides no tips for how to do this and leaves viewers to their own devices—however much he may insist his film delivers a clear message of the need for human compassion and cooperation as a result of being in the same lifeboat. As a fan of Dostoyevsky, Allen imagines *Match Point* takes the message in *Crime and Punishment* a step further. However much it may be possible for privation and delusion to lead to crime for which the only atonement may be voluntary acceptance of punishment and suffering, it is perhaps more common and more likely, Allen suggests, for unbounded desire to lead to unnecessary crime and the potential for subsequent miscarriage of justice. By comparison, Allen's vision is much darker and he offers no solutions in the body of his film, though he believes viewers will draw the same admirable philosophical conclusion he does.

Dostoyevsky demonstratively had intentions different from Allen's in *Crime and Punishment* but he also understood that the dramatic potential of his story resided in the dramatization of profound conflict. And in order for his story to also be philosophically engaging he needed to dramatize as precisely as possible the nature of the conflicts experienced by Raskolnikov. Each character in the story serves as a source of external stimulation and provocation for Raskolnikov and someone with whom he must contend. Each character also represents a side of himself and his inner dialogue with himself. The conflicts brought to Raskolnikov are already prefigured in his own mind—and in some cases his imaginative construction of conflict exceeds its actual severity. This was the case when Raskolnikov imagined the police had summoned him to the station because they suspected him of the double murder when, in fact, they only wanted to speak to him about a debt he owed his landlady. As much as Raskolnikov desires to rise above human community and transcend its vulgarity, banality, and ugliness, he consistently finds himself drawn toward and irretrievably connected to people in ways he never suspected possible.

Raskolnikov may be a type of paranoid schizophrenic and of two minds about most everything he encounters, but he is not a sociopath. He may understand one thing rationally but he cannot stop himself from experiencing feelings contrary to his rational calculations. All of the characters in the story provoke unexpected feelings in Raskolnikov but Sonia and Detective Petrovitch succeed in burrowing the deepest into his psyche and raising a mirror to repressed dimensions of himself. Because these inner dimensions contradicted his rational mind he assumed they were inferior and symptoms of weakness. He learns from Sonia that the compassion he thought was weakness is actually strength, and he learns from Petrovitch that the rational side of himself need not always be a source of shame and betrayal.

In *Match Point* Allen has, as he has indicated, constructed a story in which, like *Crime and Punishment*, murder is used philosophically and not as a device in propelling a whodunit story. However, the subtlety of Dostoyevsky's storytelling and dramatization of philosophizing in *Crime and Punishment* illustrates the many different potential plot directions and lines of philosophical continuation possible from the origin point of the act of murder. The majority of Dostoyevsky's story shows what transpires after Raskolnikov commits the murders, whereas the majority of Allen's story transpires in setup prior to Chris's crimes. In Allen's story this is necessarily the case because the story is not about conflict within Chris. It is about getting away with murder, with the intention of confronting an audience with how they feel about that. Unfortunately, this choice of dramatization confronts viewers with violence but does not adequately confront them with philosophical conflict.

In *Match Point*, violence is the solution to conflict. In *Crime and Punishment* violence is the source of conflict. Moreover, the conflict between Chris and Nola never fully materializes as conflict for Chris because he does not hesitate about what he needs to do. He only hesitates about whether or not he can get away with it. In this sense, the conflict between Chris and Nola is not a conflict for Chris but a problem needing a solution. Chris's choice of deadly violence as the solution and his subsequent escape from punishment leaves viewers with many ways to go in drawing philosophical conclusions. If questioned after viewing the film, many will likely say they are troubled by Chris's actions and would never do anything similar themselves. But many may secretly say something like the following to themselves:

> You know what, if I were in Chris's shoes and thought there was a good chance I could get away with it, I would consider doing the same thing. After all, Nola had it coming. She was basically blackmailing Chris and attempting to coerce him into a decision he was not comfortable with. That is no basis for a relationship and for raising a child. Nola was overplaying her hand and she had it coming. As for the old lady neighbor, if you're going to commit murder, it's not going to be pretty. It's unfortunate she had to be collateral damage but she already had a long life and probably wouldn't live much longer anyway. No need to obsess with guilt about her. Who knows, she might have had cancer and Chris was doing her a favor.

Nothing in Allen's film prevents a viewer from wandering down the avenues of this kind of perverse rationalization of murder and supposing these dark avenues coincide with a defensible, if not admirable, philosophical position. These possibilities for interpretation are precisely what concerns the Catholic priest Allen mentioned in the interview.

From the dramatic as well as the philosophical perspective, the hard part does not consist of launching a difficult serve—portraying a dark and problematic side of life—but instead returning the service—answering the looming dramatic, philosophical, and moral question mark. A dramatist returning his or her own service may risk hitting it out of the court, may risk error and oversight and foolishness, but this risk pales next to the risk of portraying deadly violence in a context free of genuine conflict.

As many will have suspected by this point, genuine conflict cannot emerge in drama or in life apart from its emergence in the inner life of particular persons. In this sense, every drama is psychodrama. The two forms can only be distinguished by way of the emphasis the dramatist places on overt action—an emphasis natural to theater and cinema as visual arts. In this regard, Dostoyevsky has a slight advantage as a writer when portraying the inner life, the inner dialogue, the inner conflict of a character. Allen tells of a conversation he once had with playwright Paddy Chayefsky in which the latter remarked: "When a movie is failing or a play is failing, cut out the wisdom" (2011: 123). Furthering this point, Allen adds the insight of friend and colleague Marshall Brickman: "The message of the film can't be in the dialogue" (2011: 123). These are good words of advice, but the solution in the visual arts for portraying inner conflict and different perspectives and philosophical views at work inside a character comes by adding other characters who reflect or enact what a main character may be thinking or saying.

Despite working in a textual medium, Dostoyevsky was a master of this technique and *Crime and Punishment* is the exemplary masterpiece. The conundrum of his own identity with which Raskolnikov wrestles emerges and transforms through the voices of the characters he encounters. Each character speaks the voice of an "other" within himself. And, if in life or drama, the voice of another does not take on the weight and value of an inner voice, then that person or character has not come alive in the drama of a given person or character. It would be misleading to think of this internalization as the voice of "conscience" because, in the active inner life of any person, there are likely to be many competing voices.

Near the end of *Match Point* Chris meets the ghosts of Nola and her neighbor and hears their voices. The scene is powerful in the way in which it shows how Chris rationalizes their murders and closes off their voices.

Nola: Chris.
Chris: Nola? (*He slowly turns toward her.*) It wasn't easy. But when the time came I could pull the trigger. You never know who your neighbors are until there's a crisis. You can learn to push the guilt under the rug and go on. You have to. Otherwise it overwhelms you.
Neighbor: (*Emerging from Chris's left.*) And what about me? What about the next-door neighbor? I had no involvement in this awful affair. Is there no problem about me having to die? An innocent bystander?
Chris: The innocent are sometimes slain to make way for a grander scheme. You were collateral damage.
Neighbor: So was your own child.
Chris: Sophocles said to never have been born may be the greatest boon of all.
Nola: Prepare to pay the price, Chris. Your actions were clumsy, full of holes, almost like someone begging to be found out.
Chris: It would be fitting if I were apprehended and punished. At least there would be some small sign of justice, some small measure of hope for the possibility of meaning.

When asked what he believes will become of Chris and how he will live out his life, Allen responded in this way:

I think he's in a situation he's not delighted with. He's married to a woman he's not passionate about. He's a son-in-law who likes the easy life he's married into but is claustrophobic working in the office. His wife is already saying to him that she wants another child. He has no thoughts about the crime. He's got what he wanted and he's paid the price for that. It's a shame that that's what he wanted. I can see down the line that he won't be content in that marriage and maybe he'll be on such good financial footing that he'll leave her [Lax 2011: 125–126].

If this is what Allen imagines for Chris's future then it becomes clear that a sequel would similarly not offer much in the way of dramatized philosophical challenge to wanton and self-serving violence in human community. But many lines of continuation are possible and it could be wished that a sequel would take another direction. In fact, if another direction were taken the result might not be a sequel so much as act three of a three-act drama in which conflict, as in *Crime and Punishment*, emerges and becomes central.

In this projected act three for Chris Wilton the voices of the other characters remain external and do not even speak in relation to the topic consuming his inner life. The paucity of internalized characters and voices creates a condition whereby the voices of the other persons in his life, his wife and extended family, are essentially dead to him. Wilton's inner life wilts and dries up as he allows too few voices, too few substantial characters, into his inner drama. Others cannot speak to him because they no longer know him. He has closed off a significant part of himself to others and cannot allow that part to speak. To do so would result in the collapse of the identity façade he has labored, through murder and lies, to create. These voices must remain silent. Otherwise he will be forced to return to square one in his life.

But the life he has made for himself turns out to be a slow death because he remains essentially cut off from community, just as he must remain cut off from a part of himself. The entire thesis of this line of continuation in imagining the life of Chris beyond *Match Point* turns on the truth—to the extent it may be truth—of the notion that when the inner conversation of voices dies or is significantly truncated and closed off, then so, also, the external conversation and connection with other persons wilts and dies. The inner conflict taking shape in Chris will then resemble the conflict dramatized in Tony Soprano. The conflict begins with anxiety and restless unhappiness and evolves toward greater attempts at repression as he fails to give full voice to the most potent characters capable of populating his inner drama. To the extent repression continues, his life may seem to remain free of conflict but not free of violence—the extraordinary violence he has succeeded in doing to himself. And this conflict can be dramatized through his interactions—or lack thereof—with others. Match point, indeed.

Bibliography

Aleaziz, Hamed. 2011. "Interrogating the Creators of *Homeland*." www.mother jones.com, http://www.motherjones.com/media/2011/10/homeland-season-2-claire-danes-howard-gordon-alex-gansa, November 4.

Amira, Dan, and Stefan Becket. 2013. "82 Things That Dzhokhar Tsarnaev Tweeted About." www.nymag.com, http://nymag.com/daily/intelligencer/2013/04/dzhokhar-tsarnaev-twitter-tweets-boston-suspect.html, April 19.

Anderson, Jeffery M. 2012. "Review of *Killing Them Softly*." www.common sensemedia.org, http://www.commonsensemedia.org/movie-reviews/killing-them-softly, November 27.

Andrews, Nigel. 2012. "Review of *The Book of Eli*." www.ft.com, January 15.

Aristotle. 1984. "Poetics." In *The Complete Works of Aristotle*. Jonathan Barnes, ed. Princeton: Princeton University Press.

Bailey, Andrew. 1972. "A Clockwork Utopia: Semi-Scrutable Stanley Kubrick Discusses His New Film." *Rolling Stone*, no. 100, January 20, 20–22.

Baumeister, Roy F., and Brad J. Bushman. 2003. "Emotions and Aggressiveness." In *The International Handbook of Violence Research, Volume 1*. Norwell, MA: Kluwer.

Benedetti, Paul, and Nancy DeHart, eds. 1997. *Forward Through the Rearview Mirror*. Cambridge: MIT Press.

Bok, Sissela. 1998. *Mayhem: Violence as Public Entertainment*. New York: Addison Wesley.

Brainz.org. 2013. "15 Films That Inspired Real Life Crimes." www.brainz.org, http://brainz.org/15-films-inspired-real-life-crimes/, February 8.

Buncombe, Andrew. 2007. "US Military Tells Jack Bauer: Cut Out the Torture Scenes … or Else!" www.independent.co.uk, http://www.independent.co.uk/news/world/americas/us-military-tells-jack-bauer-cut-out-the-torture-scenes—or-else–436143.html, February 13.

Burke, Kenneth. 1937/1984. *Attitudes Toward History*. 3rd ed. Berkeley: University of California Press.

_____. 1966. *Language as Symbolic Action*. Berkeley: University of California Press.

Campbell, Joseph. 1949/1973. *The Hero with a Thousand Faces*. Princeton: Princeton University Press.

Caputi, Jane. 1999. "Small Ceremonies: Ritual in *Forrest Gump*, *Natural Born Killers*, *Seven*, and *Follow Me Home*." In *Mythologies of Violence in Postmodern Media*. Christopher Sharrett, ed. Detroit: Wayne State University Press.

Charles, Sébastien. 2005. "Paradoxical Individualism: An Introduction to the Thought of Gilles Lipovetsky." In Gilles Lipovetsky, *Hypermodern Times*. Andrew Brown, trans. Malden, MA: Polity.

Clark, C. 2012. "Children's and Young People's Reading Today." *Findings from* the *2011 National Literacy Trust's Annual Survey*. London: National Literacy Trust.

Claustro, Lisa. 2007. "Show Exec Makes Sure Viewers Won't Take After *Dexter*." www.buddytv.com, http://www.buddytv.com/articles/dexter/show-exec-makes-sure-viewers-w-12689.aspx, October 17.

Coleman, Loren. 2004. *The Copycat Effect: How the Media and Popular Culture Trigger the Mayhem in Tomorrow's Headlines*. New York: Paraview.

Cornish, Audie. 2012. "Tarantino on 'Django,' Violence, and Catharsis." www.npr.org, http://m.npr.org/news/Arts+%26+Life/168193823, December 28.

Covert, Colin. 2010. "The Bad, Bad, Book of Eli." www.startribune.com, http://www.startribune.com/entertainment/movies/81526697.html?refer=y, January 14.

Criminal Justice Degree Guide (CJDG). 2012. "8 Horror Films that Inspired Real-Life Crimes." www.criminaljusticedegreesguide.com, http://www.criminaljusticedegreesguide.com/features/8-horror-movies-that-inspired-real-life-crimes.html, December 24.

Dargis, Manohla. 2005. "Underneath the Mask of a Heroine." www.nytimes.com, http://movies.nytimes.com/2005/12/09/movies/09geis.html?_r=0, December 9.

_____. 2010. "Review of *The Book of Eli*." www.nytimes.com, http://movies.nytimes.com/movie/399516/The-Book-of-Eli/overview, January 15.

Denby, David. 2012. "Risky Business." www.newyorker.com, http://www.newyorker.com/arts/critics/cinema/2012/09/24/120924crci_cinema_denby, September 24.

Derrida, Jacques. 1988. *Limited Inc.* Samuel Weber, trans. Gerald Graff, ed. Evanston: Northwestern University Press.

Desilet, Gregory. 2006. *Our Faith in Evil: Melodrama and the Effects of Entertainment Violence*. Jefferson, NC: McFarland.

Desilet, Gregory, and Edward C. Appel. 2011. "Choosing a Rhetoric of the Enemy: Kenneth Burke's Comic Frame, Warrantable Outrage, and the Problem of Scapegoating." *Rhetoric Society Quarterly*, 41, no. 4.

Dewolf Smith, Nancy. 2006. "Review of *Dexter*." www.wsj.com, http://online.wsj.com/article/SB115949032468577451.html?mod=2_1168_1, September 29.

_____. 2013. "Review of *The Following*." www.wsj.com, http://online.wsj.com/article/SB10001424127887323468604578247452025976978.html, January 17.

Dillon, Nancy. 2012. "Spike Lee Boycotts Quentin Tarantino's *Django Unchained*: Slavery Was Not a Spaghetti Western." www.nydailynews.com, http://www.nydailynews.com/entertainment/tv-movies/spike-lee-outraged-django-unchained-article-1.1226762#commentpostform, December 26.

Ebert, Roger. 2005. "Review of Memoirs of a Geisha." www.suntimes.com, http://rogerebert.suntimes.com/apps/pbcs.dll/article?AID=/20051215/REVIEWS/51213001, December 10.

_____. 2013. "Faster, Quentin! Thrill! Thrill! www.suntimes.com, http://blogs.suntimes.com/ebert/2013/01/django_unchained.html, January 7.

Foster, Jodie. 2011. Video Interview. www.afi.com.

Fowles, John. 1965. *The Magus*. New York: Dell.

French, Philip. 1977. *Westerns: Aspects of a Movie Genre*. New York: Oxford University Press.

Friedman, Lester D. 1999. *Arthur Penn's Bonnie and Clyde*. Cambridge, MA: Cambridge University Press.

Gerbner, George. 1994. "Reclaiming Our Cultural Mythology: Television's Global Marketing Strategy Creates a

Damaging and Alienated Window on the World." *The Ecology of Justice*, 38 (Spring). Available at www.context. org, http://www.context.org/iclib/ic38/ gerbner/.

_____. 2002. *Against the Mainstream: The Selected Works of George Gerbner*. Michael Morgan, ed. New York: Peter Lang.

Gerbner, George, and Nancy Signorielli. 1988. *Violence and Terror in the Mass Media*. Westport, CT: Greenwood.

Gillespie, Eleanor Ringel. 2005. "*Memoirs of a Geisha*: Big Budget Soap Opera." www.accessatlana.com, http://www. accessatlanta.com/s/entertainment/m ovies/content/shared/movies/revie ws/M/memoirsofageisha/ajc.html/, December 9.

Golden, Arthur. 1997. *Memoirs of a Geisha*. New York: Alfred A. Knopf.

Gross, Terry. 2013. "Quentin Tarantino, 'Unchained' and Unruly." www.npr. org, http://www.npr.org/2013/01/02/ 168200139/quentin-tarantino-un chained-and-unruly, January 2.

Heilbron, Alexandra. 2009. "*Dexter* Fan Kills Little Brother." www.tribute.ca, http://www.tribute.ca/news/index. php/dexter-fan-kills-little-brother/ 2009/12/11/#.UV3BpDfH2So, December 11.

Heilman, Robert Bechtold. 1968. *Tragedy and Melodama: Versions of Experience*. Seattle: University of Washington.

Hill, Logan. 2007. "In Neil Jordan's New Movie, Jodie Foster Plays a WNYC-ish Radio Host Turned Vigilante." www. nymag.com, http://nymag.com/guid es/fallpreview/2007/movies/36626/, August 24.

Hiscock, John. 2007. "Quentin Tarantino: I'm Proud of My Flop." www.tele graph.co.uk, http://www.telegraph.co. uk/culture/film/starsandstories/36647 42/Quentin-Tarantino-Im-proud-of- my-flop.html, April 27.

Hornaday, Ann. 2012. "A Slave's Insur- rection, Captured by Tarantino." www.

washingtonpost.com, http://www.wa shingtonpost.com/gog/movies/djan go-unchained,1209972/critic-review. html, December 25.

Horsley, Jake. 1999a. *The Blood Poets: A Cinema of Savagery 1958–1999; Volume 1: American Chaos, From* Touch of Evil *to* The Terminator. Lanham, MD: Scarecrow, 1999a.

_____. 1999b. *The Blood Poets: A Cinema of Savagery 1958–1999; Volume 2: Millennial Blues, From* Apocalypse Now *to* The Matrix. Lanham, MD: Scarecrow.

Howell, Peter. 2010. "Shutter Island: Horror in All the Wrong Places." www. thestar.com, http://www.thestar.com/ entertainment/movies/2010/02/19/shut ter_island_horror_in_all_the_wrong_ places.html, February 14.

Huesmann, L.R. 1988. "An Information Processing Model for the Development of Aggression." *Aggressive Behavior*, 14, 13–24.

Huesmann, L.R., and Laurie S. Miller. 1994. "Long-term Effects of Repeated Exposure to Media Violence in Childhood." In *Aggressive Behavior: Current Perspectives*. L.R. Huesmann, ed. New York: Plenum.

Jones, Gerard. 2002. *Killing Monsters: Why Children Need Fantasy, Super Heroes, and Make-Believe Violence*. New York: Basic Books.

Karagiannis, Nathalie, and Peter Wagner. 2005. "Towards a Theory of Synagonism." *The Journal of Political Philosophy* 13, no. 3, 235–262.

King, Mike. 2009. *The American Cinema of Excess: Extremes of the National Mind on Film*. Jefferson, NC: McFarland, 2009.

Kirsh, Steven J. 2006. *Children, Adolescents, and Media Violence: A Critical Look at the Research*. Thousand Oaks, CA: Sage.

LaSalle, Mick. 2010. "Review: *The Book of Eli*." www.sfgate.com, http://www. sfgate.com/movies/article/Review-

The-Book-of-Eli-3275765.php, January 15.

_____. 2010. "No Escape from *Shutter Island*." www.sfgate.com, http://www.sfgate.com/movies/article/Review-No-escape-from-Shutter-Island-3199472.php, February 19.

_____. 2013. "*Django Unchained* Review: Sweet Revenge." www.sfgate.com, http://www.sfgate.com/movies/article/Django-Unchained-review-Sweet-revenge-4143929.php, December 24.

Lax, Eric. 2011. *Conversations with Woody Allen: His Films, the Movies, and Moviemaking, Updated and Expanded*. New York: Alfred A. Knopf.

Lehane, Dennis. 2003. *Shutter Island*. New York: HarperCollins.

Lipovetsky, Gilles. 2005. *Hypermodern Times*. Andrew Brown, trans. Malden, MA: Polity.

Lippman, Mike. 2004. "Know Thyself, Asshole: Tony Soprano as an Aristotelian Tragic Hero." In *The Sopranos and Philosophy: I Kill Therefore I Am*. Richard Greene and Peter Vernezze, eds. Chicago: Open Court.

Maerz, Melissa. 2013. "9 Hot New Shows: The Following." www.ew.com, http://www.ew.com/ew/article/0,,20661352,00.html, January 4.

Marsay, Peter. 2010. "Review of *Shutter Island*." www.e-n.org.uk, http://www.e-n.org.uk/5044-Shutter-Island.htm, February 15.

McLuhan, Marshall. 1962. *The Gutenberg Galaxy*. Toronto: University of Toronto Press.

_____. 1964. *Understanding Media: The Extensions of Man*. New York: McGraw-Hill.

McLuhan, Marshall, and Quentin Fiore. 1967. *The Medium Is the Massage: An Inventory of Effects*. New York: Bantam.

_____, and _____. 1968. *War and Peace in the Global Village*. New York: Bantam.

Mandel, Nora Lee. 2013. "Mandel Maven's Nest on *The Wire*: The Best Novel on Television." www.mavensnest.net, http://mavensnest.net/Wire.html, January 12.

Meyers, Peter Alexander. 2013. "What to Look for When Gun Control Fails: America's Cinematic Culture." www.huffingtonpost.com, http://www.huffingtonpost.com/peter-alexander-meyers/gun-control-fail-cinematic-culture_b_3036183.html, April 8.

Morgenstern, Joe. 2012. "Tarantino, Blessedly 'Unchained.'" www.wsj.com, http://online.wsj.com/article/SB10001424127887323984704578205371996961476.html, December 27.

Pinkerton, Nick. 2010. "Scorsese's Head-Trip *Shutter Island*." www.villagevoice.com, http://www.villagevoice.com/2010-02-16/film/scorsese-s-head-trip-shutter-island/full/, February 16.

Postman, Neil. 1985. *Amusing Ourselves to Death: Public Discourse in the Age of Show Business*. New York: Viking Penguin.

_____. 1990. "Informing Ourselves to Death." Speech given to German Informatics Society, 11 Oct 1990, Stuttgart, Germany. Available at www.eff.org, http://w2.eff.org/Net_culture/Criticisms/informing_ourselves_to_death.paper, October 11.

_____. 1992. *Technopoly: The Surrender of Culture to Technology*. New York: Alfred A. Knopf. Synopsis available at www.hartman.us, http://www.hartman.us/todd/BookReviews/0679745408-Technopoly.html.

Pow, Helen. 2012. "He Wanted to Be a Mortician: Friends Describe Chilling CSI Student, 17, Arrested for Murdering and Dismembering Jessica Ridgeway." www.dailymail.co.uk, http://www.dailymail.co.uk/news/article-2222567/Jessica-Ridgeway-murder-17-year-old-CSI-student-arrested-murdering-dismembering-Jessica-Ridgeway-MOTHER-turned-in.html, October 24.

Raffoul, Francois. 2008. "Derrida and the Ethics of the Im-possible." *Research in Phenomenology* 38, 270–290.

Rafter, Nicole. 2000. *Shots in the Mirror: Crime Films and Society*. New York: Oxford University Press.

Ramsland, Katherine. 2005. *The Human Predator: A Historical Chronicle of Serial Murder and Forensic Investigation*. New York: Berkley.

_____. 2013. "Movies Made Me Kill." Trutv.com, www.trutv.com/library/crime/criminal_mind/psychology/movies_made_me_kill/1_index.html, February 2.

Reiner, Andrew. 2011. "Batman: Arkham City." www.gameinformer.com, http://www.gameinformer.com/games/batman_arkham_city/b/ps3/archive/2011/10/14/the-best-licensed-video-game-ever-made.aspx, October 14.

Schager, Nick. 2010. "Review of *The Book of Eli*." www.slantmagazine.com, http://www.slantmagazine.com/film/review/the-book-of-eli/4635, January 14.

Sepinwall, Alan. 2011. "How TV Reflected 9/11." www.hitfix.com, http://www.hitfix.com/blogs/whats-alan-watching/posts/how-tv-reflected–9–11, September 9.

Shermer, Michael. 2004. *The Science of Good and Evil: Why People Cheat, Gossip, Care, Share, and Follow the Golden Rule*. New York: Times Books (Henry Holt).

Silverman, Natalie. 2011. "Breaking Bad May End Next Season." www.hollywood.com, http://www.hollywood.com/news/tv/7814570/breaking-bad-may-end-next-season, July 7.

Slotkin, Richard. 1973. *Regeneration Through Violence: The Mythology of the American Frontier, 1600–1860*. Hanover, NH: Wesleyan University Press.

_____. 1985. *The Fatal Environment: The Myth of the Frontier in the Age of Industrialization, 1800–1890*. New York: Atheneum.

_____. 1992. *Gunfighter Nation: The Myth of the Frontier in Twentieth-Century America*. New York: Atheneum.

Smith, Craig R. 2009. *John Macksoud's Other Illusions: Othe Inquiries Toward a Rhetorical Theory*. Pittsburgh: Duquesne University Press.

Stephens, Daniel. 2012. "10 Films to Have Driven People to Murder." www.top10films.co.uk. http://www.top10films.co.uk/archives/7618, December 18.

Stevens, Dana. 2010. "I'm Surrounded by Crazy People." www.slate.com, http://www.slate.com/articles/arts/movies/2010/02/im_surrounded_by_crazy_people.html, February 18.

Stoehr, Kevin L. 2004. "'It's All a Big Nothing': The Nihilistic Vision of The Sopranos." In *The Sopranos and Philosophy: I Kill Therefore I Am*. Richard Greene and Peter Vernezze, eds. Chicago: Open Court.

_____. 2006. *Nihilism in Film and Television: A Critical Overview from Citizen Kane to The Sopranos*. Jefferson, NC: McFarland.

Trend, David. 2007. *The Myth of Media Violence: A Critical Introduction*. Malden, MA: Blackwell.

Twitchell, James B. 1989. *Preposterous Violence: Fables of Aggression in Modern Culture*. New York: Oxford University Press.

The Vancouver Sun. 2008. "Alleged Copycat Killing Is Nightmare Come True for *Dexter* Producer." www.canada.com, http://www.canada.com/vancouversun/news/story.html?id=43336322–4a85–4d22-a55d-9d96d7f658f1, November 10.

Van der Post, Laurens. 1983. *Merry Christmas, Mr. Lawrence*. New York: Quill. (Originally published by William Morrow in 1963 as *The Seed and the Sower*.)

Warren, Scott. 2010. "I Go to the Cinema to See Blood and Gore, Says Tarantino as He Defends Violent Movies in British Academy Film Speech." www.dailymail.co.uk, http://www.dailymail.

co.uk/tvshowbiz/article–1242783/ Quentin-Tarantino-pays-tribute-power-violence-British-Academy-Film-speech.html, January 13.

White, Armond. 2010. "Review of *The Book of Eli*." www.nypress.com, http://www.nypress.com/article–20803-the-book-of-eli.html, January 13.

Williams, Joe. 2012. "*Django Unchained* Is Tarantino Unleashed." *St. Louis Post-Dispatch*, http://www.stltoday.com/entertainment/movies/reviews/django-unchained-is-tarantino-unleashed/article_bdaa223c-d891–5b24-a19c-f7063625ea51.html, December 24.

Woerner, Meredith. 2010. "Is *The Book of Eli* a Christian Movie? We Ask the Hughes Bros." www.io9.com, http://io9.com/5447710/is-book-of-eli-a-christian-movie-we-ask-the-hughes-bros, January 14.

Yacowar, Maurice. 2007. *The Sopranos on the Couch: The Ultimate Guide.* New York: Continuum International.

Yeats, William Butler. 1962. *Selected Poems and Two Plays of William Butler Yeats.* M.L. Rosenthall, ed. New York: Macmillan.

Zacharek, Stephanie. 2010. "*The Book of Eli*: Read It and Weep." www.salon.com, http://www.salon.com/2010/01/15/book_of_eli/, January 14.

Index

Numbers in *bold* italics indicate pages with photographs.